Ra

Ralph

J. Gounod Campbell

The Pentland Press Limited
Edinburgh • Cambridge • Durham

© J. Gounod Campbell 1994

First published in 1994 by
The Pentland Press Ltd.
1 Hutton Close
South Church
Bishop Auckland
Durham

All rights reserved.
Unauthorised duplication
contravenes existing laws.

ISBN 1 85821 123 9

Typeset by CBS, Felixstowe, Suffolk
Printed and bound by Antony Rowe Ltd., Chippenham

To the lass with the laughing eyes . . . Irene.

CONTENTS

Once Upon A Time . . . Ralph McCaa	1
My Stage Debut	9
The Pantomime	17
Smart Alex	27
A Bicycle Built For Who?	33
The Balloon	39
Punishment I Couldn't Refuse	43
The Shows	55
George Lane	61
A Nelephant	65
Disenchantment	69
Baker's Dozen	75
Robinson Crusoe	83
Stung	89
Sticky Largesse	97
Oedipus Rex	105
Secondary Education	113
Work - Initiation	119
The Coal Heavers	125
Sarah And Betty Blue Dress	133
Big Mike	145
Eenie Meenie Yes Or No	153
The Gutbucketful	161
The Big Fight	171
All the Comforts of Home	184
The Interview	185
Another Interview	195
Oedipus Wreaks	205

Oedipus Wrecks	219
I'm In The Army Now	227
The Depot	235
Scrub, You So And So	245
Ep Ite Ep Ite Ah Haut	255
Soccer	265
Where Goeth Thou?	271
Old Friends	281
Aldershot	291
Inverness	301
Auld Reekie	313
Amour! Amour!	319
Grave Memorabilia	329

ONCE UPON A TIME... RALPH McCAA

Kelty. Never heard of it, eh? That's all right. I wouldn't have heard of it either, had I not been born there. It happened in Mayfield house, Kelty, Fifeshire, Scotland. Hovering and active in their respective roles were my father, Dr. Simpson the family doctor, Elsie Bell who had been the family midwife for hundreds of years, and of course, my mother. Dr. Simpson was very efficient. He specialized in delivering babies and sending people to bed with two aspirins. As he grew older, he delivered fewer babies and sent more people to bed with two aspirins than Miss MacTavish's drama group. Both my parents were extraordinarily calm but Elsie, who had brought my mother into the world, was griping as she had done for as far back as anyone could remember. It was an easy delivery and although born with a limited vocabulary, I showed no dearth of volume. Fierce as the competition was, I outbellowed Elsie by seventy-seven decibels.

It was at the moment when the competition was at its most unrestrained that Dad called gruffly, 'For Heaven's sake stop griping.' By coincidence, I stopped screaming. If I had been born with any knowledge of English at all I would have told Elsie to shut up. After all, this was the most important day in my life. It was MY day. Elsie outdistanced me. Glaring at Dad, she yelled, 'Poor little mite. You should be ashamed of yourself. Crying at birth is natural.' Again, though this is pure hypothesis, if I had been endowed with an education at birth, I would, perhaps, have appreciated Elsie's heroic support while deploring her reference to me as an insect. Dad merely sighed.

'Is he all there, Doc?' Dad enquired.

'Everything intact and in its proper place, Jake.'

'What's he look like? A fireman or an engine driver?'

'More likely a scholar of some sort - a writer maybe. Understands English already. Notice how he stopped griping the moment you yelled?'

'You know damn well it wasn't him I yelled at,' Dad grinned. 'It was...ELSIE...DO - YOU - MIND?' Elsie quit her hullabaloo, which gave me an incentive to further practice, so I screamed again while Dad looked on with undisguised appreciation.

It was on my eighteenth birthday that I was told of this.

'Oh yes, I remember it all so clearly,' I said.

'How do you know it was Elsie and not you I yelled at?' Dad grinned.

'I was there, remember?'

Dad favoured me with one of his pursed-lips grins which meant, without words, 'Smartass'. What he said was, 'Eat your cake, son.'

I reminded him that someone had gone to the guillotine for a similar remark.

'I don't hold you or the Doc any grudge, but you are on very thin ice,' Dad answered.

At the appropriate time I was christened 'Ralph'. It was inevitable that at some time, somewhere, someone would tack on 'ie'. Some people didn't know how to pronounce Ralph. Some said Ralf, some Rafe. However, there were more Ralfs than Rafes and I let it go. But Ralfie was a bit too much, and when I was old enough to resent being an 'ie', it was discouraged effectively, though sometimes painfully, when an apology didn't follow. In some cases blood was shed and the path of satisfaction strewn with the wounded and crying. Occasionally I was one of them. Another sore point was my hair. It was ginger, like Granta's moustache, and poker-straight. It would never brush back but hung stubbornly over my brow in two wings, parting naturally in the centre. I began to hate boys with thick black curly hair which I now know was quite unfair. Little did I realize that it was my hair that would be responsible for the most exciting activity of my later life.

Miss MacTavish, our English teacher, who, someone told me, had never been more than two miles from her home (which has nothing at all to do with what I am about to say, and which is of no importance whatever and should never have been mentioned) collared me in the lobby between the Headmaster's office and the boys' washroom, where some of us lingered when we practised smoking cigarette butts. She eyed me with greedy success.

'Caught,' I thought.

She was smiling. She was not a smiley person. In fact she had been even less smiley than usual. She was a disciplinarian where teaching was concerned. At seven and a half years of age, I thought she was more like a dragon, not physically of course, because she was slim (we called it skinny then) and she was always dressed neatly in black.

She looked at me so hard and long that I felt like making a run for it. I could almost feel the leather strap bouncing off the palm of my hand. Miss MacTavish never used the strap herself. With her it was even worse. She gave us extra homework. I was beginning to feel really uncomfortable when her smile widened and her mouth opened, showing her dentures. I thought of Davy Crockett who grinned a bear to death and I backed away.

'Ralphie?'

There it was again: 'Ralphie'. She was still smiling, so I took a chance.

'My name isn't Ralphie. It's Ralph.'

'I'm sorry, Ralph. I shall remember that,' she said. Her smile widened even more and she inclined her head to one side - you know, like a dog who knows you have a tidbit for him and it is just a matter of time before he gets it. Miss MacTavish came straight to the point, which saved me from lying about the cigarette caper.

'Ralph, how would you like to be an actor?'

I was dazed and I think it showed. I could hear the audience applaud and stamp their feet as I took a bow.

'Well, Ralph?' - Miss MacTavish's voice brought me back to earth.

'I — I don't know,' I stammered.

'Do you mean you would like to give the matter some consideration, or do you mean that your tongue has been immobilized by doubt?'

She couldn't help it. She always talked funny. I was still mulling the

question when she slapped me out of it with a frozen, 'Ralph!'
'Yes, Miss MacTavish?'
'Ralph... when you answered 'Yes, Miss MacTavish,' did you mean, 'Yes, I would like to be an actor,' or did you mean, 'Continue, Miss MacTavish?'

This was exciting. Was I destined to become another Charlie Chaplin or a Chester Conklin? I knew that Miss MacTavish was involved importantly in play productions, probably just Shakespeare and stuff like that, but it was a start.

'Ralph. Where are you?'

I leapt out of my reverie. If you think a seven year-old is without guile, you're wrong. I had the advantage. I felt it in my marrow.

'You need me in one of your plays?'I asked, trying to conceal the tremor in my voice.

Without hesitation – 'Ralph, you are made for the part.'

'When do you need me?'

'Seven-thirty prompt, this evening.'

'I'll get a haircut and stick it down with soap.'

She made a choking sound in the back of her throat and her face twitched into an expression of fixed alarm. 'NO, NO,' she yelled, which was even more startling than being caught smoking. 'Just come as you are. Promise me?'

'Sure, Miss MacTavish, if that's what you want.'

'That is precisely what I want.'

'Thank you, Miss MacTavish.'

Oh, boy! Unable to control my excitement, I ran.

'Oh, Ralph.'

I stopped. 'Yes Ma'am?'

'Do you know where to come?'

'Yes... I mean no.' I felt foolish, dashing off and not knowing where to go.

'The Old United Church Hall. Do you know where it is?'

'Yes. I'll be there. Seven-thirty.'

'Prompt.'

One Upon A Time...

Mustering my fledgling dignity, I walked away with what I considered nonchalance. It wasn't until I was sure that I couldn't be seen by Miss MacTavish that I ran. I wasn't going anywhere except back to the classroom, so I soon slowed down to a walk. Although I had never been in a play, my parents had seen several of the productions in which Miss MacTavish had been involved. On their arrival home from a play, if I was still awake in bed, I could hear them discuss how marvellous or how rotten the male lead had been. I gathered the male lead had a great deal to do with the success or failure of a play. Maybe it was too late to ask. Without realizing it, I had come to a stop and wondered if I should retrace my steps in the hope that Miss MacTavish would still be there. I wheeled around to see her regarding me quizzically. I came right out with it.

'Miss MacTavish... Is it the male lead?'

She pursed her lips and sucked in air between her teeth. She took so long to answer that I was sure she was lying when she said, 'No Ralph. It is - not - the male lead.'

My heart was pounding between exaltation and self-doubt. How many boys of my age get the chance to start at the top? Would I be able for it? Would the audience be too critical? Would Mum and Dad take me apart as they had done sometimes with other male leads?

'Ralph.' Miss MacTavish's voice pierced me like a rapier. 'Seven-thirty, sharp.'

She strode off before I even had a chance to thank her. When school was out, I ran all the way home. Should I keep it a secret or should I blurt it right out. When I got home, Mum and Dad were unusually excited. How could they have known? Had somebody overheard and rushed home to tell them first? Mum was the first to break the silence.

'Ralph, we have a surprise for you.' Suddenly, from one of the bedrooms, Dorothy appeared. 'Da da da daah, da daah,' she yelled musically. Then she sprang at me like a tiger and, lifting me off my feet, she planted a long, sticky kiss on my lips. Gee, she was pretty, and it gave me incomprehensible pleasure to be kissed by Dorothy with such fervour. I thought she would never put me down and as I dangled there it seemed to me that she had enjoyed it as much as I did. She smiled at me and said, 'My, how you've ... (I kissed her right back on her ruby lips) ... grown!' she gasped, dropping me with an unexpected thud. Dorothy Meikleson was an old friend of the family. She was from Edinburgh and she was an actress. Petite, blonde and girl-shaped, Dorothy was a member of a pantomime company that went on tour, staying only one or two nights at any theatre. I wouldn't have missed the pantomime for all the pandas in China. So, this was the surprise. Boy, did I have a surprise for them - especially Dorothy. We were both in the same business now. Dorothy was more experienced, of course. She had been in the business for some years. Everybody was talking at once, and I couldn't really hear anything clearly. Dorothy grabbed me again but didn't kiss me. She just squeezed. It was up to me, I thought. If what I heard was true, everybody in Hollywood kissed everybody else, married or not. This wasn't Hollywood, of course. So what? I kissed her again, square on the lips. Mum was laughing, at my boldness I supposed. Dad looked uncomfortable. 'Better drop him, Dorothy,' Dad said. 'Looks like he's running a temperature.' Dorothy was not very big, but gee willikins, she was strong. And warm. As I pointed out back there, I was seven; seven and a few months, so I have no hesitation in saying that I was not a sex fiend. That came later. What I mean is - accusations came later. My feelings towards Dorothy were more than the feelings of a boy for his teddy bear, nevertheless I had no thought of anything relating to sex. I didn't even know about it. After she released me and I had regained my breath, I asked, 'When is the pantomime on?'

'Tooonight - tonight,' Dad said with obvious glee.

'Beauty and the Beast,' Dorothy gurgled.

'Dorothy is playing Beauty,' Mum cried, laughing.

As if I didn't know. She could hardly be the Beast.

I suddenly remembered I was to be at rehearsal - 7.30 sharp.

'We kept it as a surprise,' Dad said. Observing my worried look, he asked, 'It IS a surprise, isn't it? I mean it is a pleasant surprise?'

My pit was in the heart of my stomach. I was confused and crushed.

One Upon A Time...

Shall I tell them about my great opportunity, or will I say nothing, go to the pantomime and throw my career out the window? None knew of the turmoil that raged within me. Would anyone care? Dad broke the silence.

'Is something wrong? I suggest you have a bath, take an hour or so to rest, then put on your Sunday clothes. We're going to The Gardens for fish and chips before the show.'

This was a situation which I wouldn't wish on my worst enemy, not even Alex A. Noel. The pantomime or my career? I plumped for my career. In a faint voice I said, 'I can't go!'

The announcement was met with stony silence. I looked around at the dumbfounded faces. Dad was livid, possibly because he had bought and paid for the tickets. Mum burst into tears, and Dorothy, as though mortally stricken, collapsed into Dad's armchair, which had a broken spring and went 'proing' when it was sat in. Dad was the first to recover and he demanded to know what good reason I had for making such a ridiculous statement, then, without taking another breath, said he didn't want to hear it. What should have been a moment of triumph was, with the utterance of a few words, changed into a sink of hatred and suspicion.

'This will be the last time I will include you in a visit to the pantomime,' Dad declared angrily. Dorothy rushed to my defence.

'Don't say that, Jake,' she cried jumping out of the chair, which again went 'proing'. Everybody, except me (I was too unhappy), looked at the chair with utter loathing. Dorothy said, ever so quietly, 'Jake, I know exactly how he feels. I remember my first rehearsal. Nothing - NOTHING would have kept me from it.' I rejoiced within. Good old Dorothy. Were we not creatures of the same clay? Were we not cast from the same mould? Players - Performers - Lesbians. Of course I know. But at that age, I had never heard of the word, which would never have been used when I was included in the conversation.

I was engulfed in a gigantic wave of affection for Dorothy. SHE understood. She had suffered the same agonizing experience as myself. I gazed at her, knowing that she felt the depth of my affection. Her soft,

Ralph

brown eyes told me everything. The future was clear. 'When I am old enough we'll form a team. We'll be married, and we'll tour the continent, performing in the great theatres in all the capital cities in Europe. I bet you a year's pocket money she feels the same about me. How could I have been so blind until now?' These were only some of the thoughts that raced like the Flying Scotsman through my mind in the sobering silence which followed Dorothy's declaration of support.

'All right, you can go.' It was Dad who spoke.

I wasn't sure where I was supposed to go, but I went anyway, but not before stealing another glance at Dorothy's impish face. I remember thinking that her expression belied the intensity of her thoughts. After an appropriate dramatic pause, I made my exit in silence, dragging my feet like two great clubs. I had to admit it to myself, I felt like a heel missing the pantomime, but Dorothy understood.

I couldn't go to rehearsal in Uncle George's hand-me-downs, which had been shortened in the legs but were quite baggy in the buttocks, so when it was time to go to the Old United Church Hall, I sneaked into my new trousers, which gave me a more sophisticated look. My new trousers were for Sunday School and Church service only, so I had to change on the sly. Darn it, with more notice I could have asked Miss MacTavish to change rehearsal night. Darn it, anyway!

MY STAGE DEBUT

The Old United Church Hall, referred to by members of the Harlequin Players as OUCH, was made available to the Harlequins some years ago when a new and slightly larger Hall was built to accommodate bodies of the congregation whose activities, if more generously upholstered, were destined to be even more fruitful and multiply.

The new Hall was built for the comfort of members who spent long hours at bingo, whist drives, also such lucrative industries as bazaars, which included a white elephant table, bake sales, afternoon teas where a 'by' person would pour. The NEW was now untrammelled by the Harlequins who inherited the OUCH. The OUCH was now a poor relation. The Harlequins inherited also the benches, which were not only meagre in number, but were wobbly and generously endowed with gaping cracks.

I arrived at OUCH at 6.45 p.m., only to find the Hall locked and in darkness. Miss MacTavish had said 7.30 prompt. Perhaps I was too prompt. For about twenty minutes no one came, no one even passed by, and I was stricken with a horrifying doubt as to whether it was tonight or tomorrow night I had been asked to appear. No, she said 'tonight' - or was it... I heard footsteps. It was so lonely and so cold sitting on the stone steps that I had started to snivel. Frankly, it wouldn't have mattered if the owner of the footsteps had been Jack the Ripper. Out of the darkness a beefy man appeared.

'You all right, son?' he asked, looking down at me.
'I have a bit of a cold,' I lied.
'You should be home in bed. A hot bath and bed is what you need.'
He had a kind face for such a huge man, I thought.

'Miss MacTavish told me to be here at 7.30 prompt,' I said. 'Did she mean tonight or tomorrow night?'

'I see. It's tonight, kid. But you're early.'

He fumbled a key in the door. 'Better come inside with that cold. Sit on that bench over there. I'm going to light the heater.'

He must be the caretaker, I thought. I sat where he told me and watched as hordes of people arrived in ones, twos and threes during the next half hour. They began to change into costumes so beautiful I could hardly believe my eyes. The men wore tunics with ruffles and frills, embroidery and ribbons and – Oooo! it was marvellous. I recognized the Paisley pattern on some of them. The ladies' costumes were even more wonderful; more extravagant. They wore wide, flowing skirts and scads of lace and stuff up top. Some of them weren't too careful who saw them change into their costumes. Twice I caught a glimpse of knickers, and once a bare behind. I pretended not to look, but I had been told not to look and I wanted to know why. Miss MacTavish was about the last to arrive. She looked sternly at any who came in after her and grunted, 'You're late.' They simply said 'Sorry' as if they didn't mean it and started to change. Miss MacT. waved an imperious hand at me and said, 'Follow me.' Her voice didn't seem as flinty as it was in class, but it had the authority of one in charge.

I followed her as she marched through the others, who were striding and flouncing about muttering to themselves. The beefy caretaker with the kind face was hardly recognizable. He looked even beefier in his heavy robes, and he wore a solid gold crown studded with pure diamonds, rubies, sapphires and emeralds. He wandered into a corner all by himself, and was glaring and griping at nothing I could see. He scowled at me as I passed and looked as if he was about to try scoring a goal from the fifty-yard line with me as the ball. I don't remember anyone in pantomime looking as horrible.

'Ralph?'

'Oh, coming Miss MacTavish.' I followed her into the room packed with rows of costumes and furs and gauntlets and spears and hats and – Oh, God! Where did they get all these things?

My Stage Debut

'I'll get you an outfit,' she said. I felt six feet tall.

Without scratching her head even once, she snatched a mud-coloured tunic which could have used an ironing, and tossed it to me.

'Now, let's see,' she mumbled. 'Here it is.' She grabbed a pair of drab looking stockings to which a chunk had been added at the waist, transforming them into a sort of soggy-looking leotard. Next, she found a hat that resembled a soft spittoon. 'Take these,' she said, thrusting them into my arms. Then she found a limp lump with a belt attached.

'A sporran?'

'No,' she answered. 'It's a pouch where you keep your...' her voice trailed off.

'Where I keep what?' I asked tremulously.

'Anything. A jawharp, an ocarina, a bagel, a drumstick. Anything.'

'I'm a musician?'

She rubbed her forehead with the tips of her fingers, then she said, 'No. Just put on these things, then bring this goblet and tankard into the Hall, and I'll tell you what to do.' Then she disappeared, vamoosed, took off like a rabbit. I thought she could have spent more time with me. I had many questions on my mind. And I couldn't be expected to know everything about theatre at my first rehearsal. I also thought, with all these costumes hanging there doing nothing, she could have given me something more exciting. I wasn't going to be temperamental, that would come later, and naturally, after I had established myself with the public. I started to dress. There was a scabby-looking mirror nailed to one of the walls. Glancing fearfully at the weird apparition reflected in the mirror, I felt I had been paralyzed. The stockings sagged in unpatterned creases around my legs, and I looked like I had messed myself. Maybe the tunic will cover it, I thought. It didn't. It was too short and too big. Maybe the belt would pull in the slack. It couldn't. The holes in the belt stopped about seven inches wider than my girth.

I entered the hall, confident that Miss MacTavish would rush me back into the costume room and supply me with a more elegant rig. She hardly looked at it.

'Now,' she said, 'you take the goblet and tankard – I'll tell you when –

and you walk over to the throne. Then, you fill the tankard from the goblet and hold it out to the King.'

'It's empty,' I said.

'This is a dress rehearsal. It will be full for the performance.'

'What'll be in it?'

She looked bewildered, I thought. She took so long to answer that I could see she had never thought of that.

'I don't know,' she hissed. 'Lemonade, root beer, anything. Just do as I ask.'

'Should I fill it with water for now?'

'No, Ralph. The King has the unwavering notion that water is exclusively for washing in.'

This didn't surprise me. He looked the type. I hoped they knew what they were doing.

'All right, let's try it,' she called in a commanding voice. 'The King is sitting on the throne. You approach the King and...'

'He's walking about in that corner, muttering,' I said, pointing.

'Pretend, Ralph,' she ordered.

'It's not going to be easy with nobody there,' I said shakily.

'Harold,' she shouted at the top of her voice, which startled everybody. The King stopped mumbling and walking and looked over at us.

'Harold, do you mind sitting on the throne for a moment? And Gwen, please? The King, who had looked so pleasant when I was sitting on the steps outside, had certainly changed, for now he looked as rotten as they come. He sat on the throne, his nose palpitating in a sneer. Gwen, who was almost as pretty as Dorothy, stood before him, her head bowed in utter misery.

'Harold – will you take it from 'Therefore my dear,' said Miss MacTavish.

'Okydoke,' said the King, then he emitted a huge yawn and settled down on the throne like a large sack of potatoes. Some king! He'd never make it in the pantomime. What was he going to do with Gwen? Boil her in oil? Miss MacTavish nodded and Harold snarled, 'Therefore, my dear...'

My Stage Debut

Miss MacTavish gave me a shove. It was unexpected, and I tripped over my feet. The tankard, the goblet and the tray on which they were placed skittered along the floor towards the throne. Everybody stopped muttering and moving about. It was weird. I got up and felt my nose. There was no blood.

'Well, pick 'em up,' Miss MacTavish rasped. The tankard had landed at Gwen's feet. She gave it a stiff kick in my direction which, at the time, seemed very unladylike. Retrieving the pieces, I returned to the wings beside Miss MacTavish.

'Are you ready?' she inquired.

I nodded. She pointed at the King.

KING: 'Therefore my dear,' (I rushed in) 'you will be confined' (I poured) 'to your private chambers until' (I held out the tankard) 'such time as you are disposed to consent to our marriage.'

So that was it. The King sank back into the oversize throne. With his flab he needed it.

I glanced at the others. Their attention seemed to be riveted on me. My arm, extended to its full length, was getting tired.

King: 'Desmond!' A smart-looking young man rushed forward and bowed. 'Escort the Lady Gwen to her chambers.' (Another sneer). 'And lock the door.' The King sank even lower into the throne.

'The brute,' I muttered under my breath as the Lady Gwen was led away, weeping bitterly. So far, there hadn't been a laugh in the whole thing. If I could only get the chance to play the King, I would stuff Beefy into my lousy outfit, then I would take Gwen's dainty hand in mine, raise it gently to my lips and with a resounding kiss that everyone could hear...

'RALPH!' It was Miss MacT's icy voice. 'You are dribbling the wine all over the floor.'

My arm had dropped almost to my thigh. I glanced at the King who was eyeing me with sheer hatred. He withdrew his arm, which had been waiting for the goblet.

'Sorry,' I said to Miss MacT. 'My arm got tired. Could I hand him the one with the handle?'

She said, more emphatically than was necessary I thought, 'No! You will have a goblet. That is what one drinks from. You will also have a flagon...'

'A flag? On the goblet?'

'A flagon. A chalice.'

I wasn't given a chance to ask what that was. The King, with a nod from Miss MacT., gave the Lady Gwen the shove off once more and again sank back on to the throne, sneering and screwing up his face. I thought he had forgotten all about the goblet, so I said, 'Pssst.' Everybody laughed, even the King. Everybody, that is, except Miss MacT. I was a hit, but maybe I should have played it bigger for Miss MacTavish. She wiggled a finger for me to come over to her. In the pantomime I would have taken a swallow myself, then hiccoughed. Her expression had softened but her voice was chilling.

'It's all my fault, Ralph,' she said. 'I should have explained to you that you are a lackey, a scullion, a sorry knave.'

It sounded very important, so I tried to look regal and at the same time sorry.

'Ah, not quite,' she said. 'Stand over near the throne and observe.' She relieved me of the tankard, goblet and tray, then she went through the motions of pouring, then proffering it to Beefy. She didn't get a solitary laugh.

'Take ten, then we'll take it from the top,' she announced.

The men released their stomach muscles, and some of the women joined some of the men in a smoke.

I sat on a bench while one or two of the cast started mumbling to themselves again. His Majesty, who didn't look so mean now, sat down beside me with a bump.

'OUCH! OH! OH! OH!' The crack in the bench had closed on my bum. The King rose and I was released.

'Sorry, kid. We all get it once,' he grinned. 'You know about the cat who sat on a hot stove, don't you kid?'

I didn't, but I never sat there again. If I had been sitting three inches further back in those baggy things I was wearing, it would have been the closest I have ever come to being a eunuch.

The lovely Lady Gwen was warming her rump at the stove. She didn't look a bit sad. 'I got it too, last week. I have a bruise to prove it. Look,' she said, throwing her long dress over her shoulders and sticking her bott close to my face. Fortunately, she was wearing those long white knickers that reach below the knees. She stood up and grinned. Then she winked at me and said, 'Did you see it?'

'No,' I said without hesitation.

'That's show biz, son. Sometimes you see it, sometimes you don't.'

Miss MacTavish sent me home early. She said my mother had asked her not to keep me too late.

THE PANTOMIME

Did I miss the Pantomime? No. When I got home from rehearsal, Mum and Dad were listening to the gramophone. First the miserable rehearsal, now this. My thoughts were so preoccupied with what I had been through that it didn't occur to me that my parents ought to be at the Pantomime. The record was Finlandia - you know, Jean Sibelius. Even at that age, I knew every note of it because it was played a lot in our house. Dad wouldn't have what he called 'rubbish' polluting the air around him. He had quite a large collection of recordings, all classical music, symphonic, choral, solo instrument, opera and... well he had everything, everything except the good stuff like 'Yes, we have no bananas,' 'I wouldn't leave my little wooden hut for you-oo,' and 'How much is that little doggie in the window?' The only place I could hear that kind of music was at the pierrots who performed in a bandshell at Lundin Links beach. Anyway, I blame Dad for the fact that my taste for music changed so much that I have acquired, over the years, many of the records he possessed plus many which were not available when I was very young.

'How did the rehearsal go?' asked Mum. I told her as briefly as I knew how. 'Sit down then. I'm going to make a pot of tea.'

'I'll stand.' 'You'll stand,' Mum mimicked. 'All right, what's the matter? You walked in kind o' funny. Did someone boot you out?'

That was more than I could bear. Bursting into tears, I ran into the bedroom. Mum followed and sat on the bed beside me. 'I didn't mean that,' she said, 'I was only joking. Now, tell me what's wrong.'

I told her about the crack in the bench and how the King had dumped his overweight carcase next to me. I got the immediate sympathy I expected and the tears vanished. That was one of my earliest realizations that words were stronger than wounds.

'Drop your pants.'

'Oh, no! It's not that bad. It's only...'

'Drop your pants.' I obeyed. How can a seven year-old cope with this sort of thing, short of running away from home?

'You'll have a sore bott for a few days but it's nothing serious. Now, come into the living room. Dad has something to say to you.'

The record had finished and Dad turned off the gramophone. He didn't look at all angry. Suddenly I remembered Dorothy and the Pantomime.

'Where's... shouldn't you be at the Pantomime?' I shouted.

'We didn't go,' Dad said.

I was stricken with remorse at having been the cause of their missing the show. And what would Dorothy think? She probably hated me. She might even leave the stage and become a recluse, shutting herself away from all contact with people. Of course she could have cats. Cats are good companions for people who shun contact with all humanity. Dad's voice came to me like the voice of some spirit, faraway and...

'Ralph, are you listening to what I'm saying? We didn't go tonight because, through Dorothy's influence, we managed to get tickets for tomorrow.'

'Tomorrow?'

'That's what I said. It's a sell-out for both nights. The seats are in the gods, but at least we can all go together.'

I was gripped in the clutches of remorse. Everybody had taken it so well. And I - I had thought only of myself and my future.

'The gods? Aren't they hard benches up there?' I asked.

'It was the best we could do under the circumstances,' said Dad.

'Why didn't you tell me sooner,' I griped. 'I would have asked Miss MacTavish to postpone the rehearsal until tomorrow night.'

'That's very thoughtful of you, Ralph. I'm sure everyone would have been happy to oblige you.'

'Well, I don't know about everyone. I'm not sure if the King did that

deliberately or not,' I answered.
'Did what, son?'
Oh God! Did I have to go through all that again?
Mum cut in quickly. 'Later, Dad. The kettle's boiling.'
Dad understood. 'Oh,' he said. 'Well, sit down and have some tea... Or stand if you want to. There's a chair over there... or there's lots of room to stand... if you prefer to stand.'
I was sure he was making it as easy as possible for me.
'You will be sitting on the hard benches in the gods, anyway.'
I stood by the fire munching a biscuit with a cup of tea in my hand.
'Another cup, Ralph?'
'No thanks, Mum. I think I'll go to bed.'
Mum was really marvellous. Putting Dad off like that. Saving me all the embarrassment of having to explain what had happened. He wouldn't remember a thing about it tomorrow. 'Goodnight, Dad!'
'Goodnight, Son.'
'Goodnight, Mum.'
'Goodnight, Ralph. If you lie on your side, you won't feel so uncomfortable.'
Oh geeze! Why did she have to say that? I rushed out before she could say more. That's the trouble with parents. They keep reminding kids about things like this. I knew Mum was concerned and meant well, but geeeeze! I didn't get to sleep for some time because of my sore bum, but I was happy. I wouldn't miss the Pantomime after all.
The theatre was a work of art. Everywhere you looked, there were cherubs, monsters and demons, some of them not too careful about how little they wore. The orchestra stalls and the balcony were equipped with padded seats. The gods had only long wooden boards without backs. Sometimes the twit behind you liked to keep time to the music with one leg, which meant that with every downbeat you got the toe of a shoe in your kidney. Although it was dark, I could always pinpoint the victims of the foot-swinging addicts. We could hear, 'Hey, pinhead, quit your bally dancin'. 'You kick me once more 'n' A'll break your —— neck.'

Ralph

That sort of thing.

Mum was always ready before anyone else. She was outside when she called out in a loud voice, 'Don't forget your cushion.' See what I mean?

We went to the Savoy for supper. Dorothy insisted it was her treat, so instead of going to Toni's Fish and Chip Gardens, we went to the Savoy, a posh restaurant where, Dorothy said, some of her friends ate. The Savoy wasn't anything like Toni's. However, I am not going to say anything about Toni's - except that it was our favourite restaurant when we could afford it, which was about four times a year. The Gardens were nicely arranged. The first thing that struck you was the name on the outside: Toni's Fish & Chip Gardens. You couldn't miss it. As you entered the front door, two great palms leaned over towards the centre, giving the entrance a lovely tropical atmosphere. Inside was just as tastefully set with red, blue and yellow chequered tablecloths and vases of everlasting flowers on every table. 'No Smoking' signs were prominent but unnecessary, because everybody stubbed their cigarettes in the soil of the palm trees. 'No Dogs Allowed' was another good sign, but it didn't apply to us. Also, there were partitions between the tables to prevent people staring at you. The sawdust on the floor was always clean and fresh, with a nice smell of cedar, not strong enough to obstruct the tantalizing aroma of fish and chips. Another good point: the flypapers were always hung high enough not to get in your hair, and the tablecloths were brushed clear of chips and crumbs after every customer. The decor, too, was interesting enough to read while you were waiting. You could read about everything that was going on in town, and pick up a few bargains from the notices pinned on the wall. The Gardens must have been the envy of every restaurant in town. Besides fish and chips, they served black and mealy puddings. Drunks were not tolerated and were ejected, but fast, by two of Toni's brothers. What more could you ask for? But I don't want to say anything about the Gardens.

The Savoy was nothing like this. It was too dark - to save on the electricity bill, I suppose. The music was so quiet, I had to strain to hear it. Small tables were scattered about the room in the most haphazard

The Pantomime

manner, and everybody could see what you were eating if they peered hard enough. The tablecloths were – I suppose – white, but they looked grey in the poor light. They also had menus, unnecessary at the Gardens, where the prices were on the wall where you could see them. If you wanted vinegar at Toni's, all you had to do was reach. At the Savoy you had to ask for it. As we inspected the menus, a shifty looking waiter hovered over us, scribbling down everything we said. At the Gardens, the waitresses didn't need a pencil and pad. They had memories like elephants. 'Two fish and chips.' 'One fish and no chips.' 'One fish with double helping of chips.' 'One black pudding with chips.' It didn't matter what you ordered, they never got it wrong. They could even take orders from two tables, all speaking at the same time, and never make a mistake. But I don't want to say anything about the Gardens in case you think I was prejudiced. It is enough to say that when I left the Savoy I was still hungry. We finished eating an hour and a half before curtain time. Dorothy explained that getting into her costume and makeup took some time, and we should get going. Besides, the seats in the gods were not reserved, as were the upholstered ones, so we went straight to the theatre. Instead of going in by the front entrance where all the lights and stuffed shirts were, we entered by a small door, similar to our kitchen door, where we had to start climbing. There were no lights on the staircase, but ushers with flashlamps were stationed on each landing. As the customers trudged up the stairs, the ushers waved their flashlights, urging them to 'get the lead out.'

To my surprise, the first three rows were already occupied, so we were obliged to sit in the fourth row. We spread out as much as possible, trying not to make it too obvious. It didn't work this time. About fifteen minutes before 'curtain', a man of about twenty-five years of age dithered past the people between us and the aisle, mumbling, 'Do you mind? Do you mind?' Obviously some did mind, for there were grumblings like 'Come on, get on with it,' and 'Get off my toes, you creep.' We had to cram closer together as he wriggled himself into the space available between me and a woman with a large abdomen. Her tummy was even bigger than Mr. Noel's, Alex's father. Dad told me that

Mr. Noel drank a gallon of beer every day. She looked like a five-gallon-a-day woman. I didn't know then that she was with child. The man who had squeezed himself into the space we had made for him lit a cigarette. He didn't strike the match on the sole of his shoe; he didn't strike it on the bench, or on the seat of his pants. Oh, no! Stretching his arm aloft so that everybody could see and admire him, he scratched the match on his thumb nail. Neat. He held the cigarette close to his lap, and the smoke made a beeline for my nose. Not so neat. I wished he would fall into the orchestra stalls. If we had been in the front row, I would have been happy to help him over the railing.

The fire curtain had fifty or so advertisements on it. They were painted in bright colours and had a black border. I got Dad to play 'guessing' with me. 'Guessing' was a great way to pass away the time. Taking turns, we gave the other players the initials of the proprietor, or the store, or their wares. When somebody guessed what the initials meant, then he or she would get a turn. Oh, those were the good old days. They don't make curtains like that any more. I had a really good one when the lights blinked. The babble of voices subsided, then the curtain began to roll up. As the feet of the actors became visible, there was complete silence. Maybe something jammed, maybe the ropes slipped through someone's hands, anyhow the curtain dropped with a thud. Most of the audience in the gods whistled and stamped their feet. A few of them yelled, 'Fire that idiot!' 'Send him home!' 'Try sleeping alone!' Things like that. Again the curtain rolled up slowly, like an upside-down avalanche, and the yakking stopped. Everybody applauded. The music got louder and louder, then they started cavorting like anything. It was marvellous. I tried to catch a glimpse of Dorothy but she wasn't there. 'I don't see her,' I murmured, nudging Mum. She gave me a stern look. 'Sht. This is the Core de Bally. Dorothy is one of the leading characters.' The music changed to something dreamy and they danced off stage. The father came in first, whining about losing some ships at sea. Leaning over, I said, 'I don't see.....' 'Sssht,' warned Mum. Next came the two gristly sisters. Real dogs. One of them did a pratfall, and the other one, turning to look behind her, fell over her and knocked

The Pantomime

over the father who was going to help them up. All three of them lay squirming on their backs, their arms and legs waving about like dogs trying to mangle their fleas. This brought down the house, as they say. It wouldn't have brought down *their* house, you can bet on that. It was made of rocks with giant pillars here and there made of solid marble. It seemed odd, though, that whacking great trees with branches and no leaves, as well as rose bushes, should be growing right out of the floor. The father and the two gristly sisters, that is Dorothy's sisters, the father's daughters, sorted themselves out and I gave no more thought to the indoor trees, because Dorothy appeared.

Of course, Dorothy didn't come in like the two gristly sisters – like navvies. She tripped in daintily, like a fairy without a wand. She kissed her father, then patted her sisters compassionately on the cheeks. Even from the gods, we could see the pity for them on her face. Boy, she could give the Lady Gwen a few tips on acting. The father told his daughters how he must go away and look for his lost ships. His horse must have been listening because it trotted in right on time. The music played a waltz and everybody on stage stopped to watch as the horse did a comic dance. The audience clapped in appreciation, the horse bowed and then stepped to one side while Father came down to centre stage and looked sadly at the audience. He promised to bring back anything his daughters wanted. The gristly twins, who looked more like policemen than two female women, wanted jewels and fine clothes. Beauty wanted only a rose, and the horse nodded approvingly. Why she wanted the old man to bring back a rose, I'll never know. The place was cluttered with roses. Father kissed the two gristlies, wiping his mouth on his sleeve after each kiss, but when he kissed Dorothy – Beauty – it lasted a long time. He seemed to be enjoying it more than he should have. I felt a twinge of jealousy. Anyway, he jumped on his horse, which sagged in the middle and, looking at the audience for sympathy or something, took off on his journey. The audience went wild, especially when the horse groaned when he mounted it. The horse came back with Father, whose feet were now touching the floor, and they bowed. The horse wiggled his rear end at us, then they departed. The audience clapped and stamped their feet. After some wrangling, the three sisters disappeared. The orchestra came in with some eerie music, the lights faded on the marble, the rose bushes glowed into full bloom, and Father appeared, dragging behind him the weariest horse you are likely to see anywhere. They were both played out, and they looked it. Father said he was lost. The man sitting directly behind me shouted, 'Get lost.' Father lamented that he would probably die in the forest, and the horse sat down, resting it's head on one of its front elbows. Very dramatic. Father talked a lot about his three lovely daughters. He rambled on about not being able to bring them what they asked for.

'You know *you're* askin' for it,' somebody shouted.

Raising his head which he had dropped on to his chest, he declaimed, 'They ask for so little.' Half the audience yelled 'Awwww!'

He rambled on about this being the end of a miserable life – with two daughters like them, who wouldn't be rambling – and the horse, who was rolling about in agony, was all that saved the situation.

'If I die, I die,' wailed Father.

'It's okay by me,' yelled the man behind me.

Some people laughed. Some shouted 'Shaddup' and 'Pipe down.'

Father sagged to his knees and was about to expire when he noticed the rose bush, blazing like a Christmas tree beside him. Hesitantly, he plucked a rose and sniffed it. Suddenly, from behind the biggest tree, the Beast appeared. Somebody in the gods yelled, 'Look at the head on that.' There was such an uproar with people laughing and shouting things like, 'Take it away,' and 'Kill it, kill it!' that we couldn't hear what was being said for a few minutes.

The Beast accused Father of stealing his roses. Father explained that it was for Beauty, but he was lost, etc, etc. The horse listened intently during all this unnecessary talking. Only when Father promised to send Beauty back to marry the Beast was he allowed to go.

'But I am lost,' groaned Father.

'You are not lost,' boomed the Beast.

The guy behind me again: 'It's me that's lost!' And he started to weep. Again, there was pandemonium in the gods, and a lot of flak from

The Pantomime

below. The man who started it was removed by two brawny ushers. The actors waited until this was all done and order restored.

'The horse knows the way home,' said the Beast. There followed the most dazzling piece of choreography. The horse nodded in agreement and motioned to Father to jump on. Father mounted him. The Beast vanished behind the tree. Father rode off. The three sisters rushed in. The rose bushes faded and the marble was bathed in light again. The horse cantered in, bright and fresh as one of Ovenstone's meat pies. 'So you see,' cried Father, 'all you have to do is marry the Beast.' Beauty wasn't too keen. Would you be? When Father explained that if Beauty didn't go he would die, Beauty quickly changed her mind and, after more needless talk, she found herself in the Beast's garden. The Beast appeared as before and stood admiring Beauty, then he said, 'You have come,' which was pretty obvious. Even Simpson's wirehaired terrier would have seen that for himself, and he didn't know how to roll over when he was told. And another thing. The Beast had a pretty sissy voice for a thing with a head the size of a wheelbarrow, but I got accustomed to it. He was ugly as a run-over porcupine. How he had the gall to ask Beauty to marry him was beyond me. I don't want to go over the whole story, but eventually Beauty agreed to marry him and he was suddenly swallowed up in a great cloud of smoke. When it had cleared away, he had changed from a Beast with a sissy voice to a handsome prince with a sissy voice. It was great stuff and the applause was deafening, especially when they clutched each other and kissed. Eat your heart out, Miss MacTavish.

The Core de Bally appeared from the gloom, and the lighting, which had dimmed, came up again, and everybody was happy including the audience. The dancers took a bow, then the sisters - the gristly ones - and Father came out alone and took a bow. Dorothy, the Prince and the Horse took a bow and that was it.

Dorothy changed quickly and insisted we go for coffee to the Savoy. She was soon joined by others, and introduced us to them.

'My sisters,' she said. Two men.

'The Horse.' Two more men.

'The Prince.' A tall, good-looking woman.
'And Father.' A man only half the age he was in the pantomime.
I didn't like the sisters. They were always trying to hold Dorothy's hands. That's show biz, I suppose.

SMART ALEX

On Sunday morning, the day after the Pantomime, I was cleaning out the pigeon house when I saw Alex A. Noel coming. So he's back again. 'Where are you going?' I had asked him when he went. 'Edinburgh.' 'Why?' 'To broaden my horizons,' he answered. Now, after six months – broadening his horizons – here he was, back again to pester me with his stories and theories. Dad said he was a brilliant young man. Granta said he was an egghead. Alex was fifteen when I was six and a half. He didn't look any older than he had six months ago when he told me that the Queen went to the bathroom the same as everybody else. It was the same Alex Noel who had told me about a year before that at Christmas fathers with children stuck on a long white beard and other stuff, and that babies were not found under a bush next to the big lilac tree behind our house on Argyle Lane, which was widened to accommodate growing traffic which was becoming a problem according to people who couldn't afford to cars. I didn't really like Alex. A knowall, if ever I met one. How he ever got around to some of the things he talked about is a mystery to me.

'Hello, Ralph.'
'Hello.'
'Did you enjoy the pantomime?'
'Of course.'
'What was it about?'
'Why didn't you go and see it? Then you would know,' I answered. 'Just got home last night. Can I help you?'
'No thanks. I'm nearly finished.' I could have said, 'If you can ever get your hands out of your pockets, maybe.' Alex was tall and athletic

looking, maybe, a little heavy for his age. His hands were always in his trouser pockets and he seemed to be searching for something on the ground most of the time, like he had lost a threepenny bit. I locked up the pigeon house and turned to Alex, who had sat down on the low stone dyke surrounding the yard. This is going to shake him, I thought. He wants to know about the pantomime.

'I've got connections,' I said.

'Connections?'

'Yeah. Connections.'

'It is always good to have connections,' he said with his superior air. I knew he was desperate to hear about the pantomime, but he was playing cat-and-mouse with me. All right – two can play at that game. I'll just feed him a little bit to draw him out.

'It was Beauty and the Beast. Dorothy Meikleham was Beauty and in my opinion she stole the show. The horse was good too, but Dorothy is a personal friend of mine and I know her quite well.'

'I'm sorry I missed it,' he said. I had him where I wanted him.

'Do you want to know more?'

'Of course,' he replied, hiding his excitement.

I told him the story, leaving out the parts that didn't matter. Then I told him about going to the Savoy and meeting the Beast, who was not really a Beast but a woman dressed as a Beast who was a Prince disguised as a Beast.

Then he changed the subject the same as he always did. He asked me, 'Did you know that the romantic male lead is always a woman, and the nasty aunt or the ugly sister is always a man in pantomime?'

'There weren't any nasty aunts in this pantomime,' I told him.

'You see,' he continued, as if he hadn't heard me, 'women have nicer legs than men, generally. Who wants to see a man with stringy legs in tights, playing the romantic male lead?'

Do you see what I am getting at? Mr. Knowall Knowall. I thought of the time, six months ago, when he had said, 'Ralph, how on earth could everyone in the country find babies under one stupid lilac tree?'

'A bush,' I had said.

'Or bush.'

The shocker, though, was the bit about the Queen. 'What about the Princesses?' I asked.

'The same.'

'You watch your mouth,' I shouted.

'Sit down, Ralph.'

'You ordering me?' I sneered.

'No. But I'm going to sit and you may as well be comfortable.'

Alex sat just where he was. I didn't want to sit beside him, so I sat on the small crate which I kept handy beside the door of the pigeon house.

'So... I'm sitting.'

'Something bothering you, Ralph?'

'You bother me,' I answered. 'Where do you get all this junk you keep telling me?'

'I read a lot.'

'Why do you always pick on me?'

'Because you are a good listener. And because you ask questions.'

'I haven't asked you one single question all the time I've been sitting here. Have I? Besides, you don't think I believe everything you tell me, do you?'

He shrugged. 'Apart from me, what's bugging you?'

'What business is it of yours?'

'Sometimes it is helpful to tell somebody what is bothering you.'

'All right,' I said, 'if you must know, it's what you said about the Queen.'

'Touchy, aren't you? Are you expecting the Queen to dinner or something?'

'No. I am not expecting the Queen to dinner or something...but,'

'But what, Ralph?'

'Everything's going to hell. Everything I believed in down the drain,' I shouted. This was the first time I had said 'hell', but he asked for it.

'You're right,' he said. 'Things are not too good, but maybe the election this year will bring better times.'

'It's not that!' I shouted at the top of my voice.

'What is it then? The Queen?'

'Don't pretend you don't know. It's that, and the bit about the long white beards, then the stuff about babies.'

Unruffled, he said, 'You've got to know sometime.'

'Look, Mister Smart Alex,' I said, and I was really angry. 'I'm not saying I believe you and I'm not saying I don't, but... but suppose I lived on a desert island, I wouldn't have to listen to all this.'

'True,' he said, nodding his head pretending agreement.

'Nobody would tell me things like that, would they?'

'There wouldn't be anybody to ask, would there?' he replied.

'I didn't ask.'

'But you listened.'

'But I DIDN'T ask.'

'You don't have to listen now if you don't want to.'

He had me there. I wanted to jump up and walk away, but he was like a snake with a bird. I hated him but he fascinated me.

'Suppose,' he said, '... Suppose you were visiting a friend of your Mum and Dad, and suppose the wife of that friend had just had a brand new baby...' He hesitated. Maybe to see if I was paying attention.

'Go on,' I said, waiting to catch him out, 'I'm listening.'

He continued: 'And you said, "That's funny, Mrs Smith found one under the very same bush this morning," wouldn't you feel stupid?'

'Who's Mrs. Smith?'

'Pretend, Ralph. Pretend you know a Mrs. Smith, and that her baby had arrived that very same morning. Wouldn't you?'

'Wouldn't I what?' I hated his attitude. He spoke with such deliberation, slow, and with long intervals between some words.

'Wouldn't you... feel... stupid?'

He put too much weight on the word 'stupid'.

'Do you know something, Alex? I don't like you.'

'I know, Ralph. But aren't you glad I told you.'

'That I'm stupid,' I snarled.

'I didn't say you were stupid. I just wanted you to know the truth.'

'I know the truth,' I answered, staring him out.

'And what is the truth?'
'Don't you know?' I replied.
'Yes, but do you?'
'Questions, questions!' I blared. 'Of course I know the truth. The Doctor brings them in his black bag.'

Alex blinked. He really annoyed me. It was a long time before he spoke.

'I have to go now, Ralph, but I would like to have another chat with you when I get back. There is something you ought to know.' He rose and stuffed his hands even deeper into his pockets.

That had been six months ago, when he had gone off to Edinburgh, 'to broaden his horizons.'

A BICYCLE BUILT FOR WHO?

'This is not the best of times and it's gonna get worse.' Everybody was saying it - the grown ups that is. Dad had been laid off. I didn't quite understand why he was so unhappy about it, because he was able to stay at home and make things for people who wore their Sunday clothes all the time. Dad could make or fix anything. He could make electric clocks, build wireless sets that worked with crystals and cats whiskers. None of the cats I knew seemed the worse for it. He also made beautiful pictures of boats with sails, animals and scenes with forests, on his fretsaw, inlaid and polished, which he sold to some of the neighbours and sometimes to a variety store on the High Street. And we had gone to the pantomime, so what was bad about that? It was about three days before Christmas, and like most kids of my age, and younger, I hollered up the chimney for Santa Claus to bring me a bike for Christmas. Between what smart Alex said and remarks by some of the older kids I knew at school, I think I knew. You know what I mean. Even so, I didn't want to take any chances, so I hollered up the lum. Mum said that Santa was overstocked with boots and socks and winter combinations, and that I should not be disappointed if, instead of a bike, he left the things she had mentioned. We always had a tree with lights, and in the morning we rushed to the tree and opened our parcels of socks and combies. Usually though, there were other goodies like a toy gun or a puzzle, and always an apple, an orange and some nuts. This year I was old enough for a bike. My heart was set on it.

'How are the pigeons, Ralph?' It was smart Alex Knowall again. I needed him about as much as I needed a thick ear. It was Sunday, the day I always cleaned out the pigeon house. Why wouldn't he leave me alone?'

'Are you worried about them?' I asked very politely.

'No. I just asked how they are.'

'That so?' This'll floor him, I thought. 'I'm getting a bike for Christmas.' He peered at me through his... did I tell you he wore spectacles with thick lenses? ... Well, he did. He peered at me through his specs, his hands in his pockets as usual, then scratched his head. And that is one of the few times I have seen him without both hands in his trouser pockets.

'A bicycle, eh?' He never lifted a finger to help in any way. Just talk, talk, talk. Peering at me like that, he reminded me of a dead fish.

'Bicycles are very expensive,' he said.

'What's that got to do with it?'

'This is not the best of times. Why don't you wait until next year?'

'It's too late,' I said smugly. I didn't mention that I hollered up the lum. He would have started to ask a lot of questions, trying to make me sound like a blithering idiot.

He just mumbled, 'Hmm, I see,' and walked away.

Good riddance, I thought.

The next day, I came in to find Dad inspecting an old bike. It was a scabby-looking thing with hardly any paint left on it and the front wheel missing. The chain was covered with dirt and rust and... well, it was just a mess. I wondered if somebody had found it in the dump and brought it in for repair. There was a knock on the door. I opened it to find Alex standing there with a bicycle wheel in his hand.

'Hello, Ralph. Is your Dad in?'

'Soooo... that's who it was for! Dad recognised his voice and came to the door. 'Come in Alex.' Alex stayed outside.

'I brought the wheel. I hope it works all right.'

'Good chap. It's perfect,' Dad answered, taking the wheel from Alex. 'Can I...?' Dad reached towards his hip pocket.

'Thank you, no. I'm just glad I remembered where it was,' Alex said, raising his hands like the Pope blessing the people.

'Sure you won't come in?' Dad asked him.

A Bicycle Built For Who?

'Thanks all the same, but I have to catch up on my reading.'

Big deal! Catch up on his reading! Probably wanting to catch up on his stories, I thought. I hadn't forgotten his lies about the Queen. When he was gone, I asked Dad, 'Who's the old wreck for?' He didn't answer. Instead, he shoved a bundle of sandpaper in my hands. 'There, get rid of all that rust and old paint, then we can work on it from there.'

I must have looked sick. I don't believe I hated anyone as much as I hated Mr. Knowall Noel.

'Are you all right, son?' asked Dad.

'Fine.'

'Then get busy. It'll take about two days to clean it up.'

I thought about suicide but not for long. Besides, I didn't know how and I didn't know anybody who did. Instead, I worked on the old crock for about two hours. Then, before it got dark, I went for a walk in Spinkie Den. It was so beautiful, so quiet. Birds, frogs, ants and sometimes a hedgehog frolicked or sang or crawled among the trees and grasses. In the burn, under the rustic bridge, tiddlers rushed for safety when my shadow touched the water. I supposed that besides angels and harps, heaven was something like this.

It got me thinking about the Church and how – I hesitate to tell about it – how I was tempted by the devil. Before Dad was laid off work, Mum always put sixpence in the plate. However, when we had to tighten our belts, Mum could only afford a threepenny bit, sometimes only a penny. It was placed on the plate very quietly and, to some extent, surreptitiously. There were still some who put in a halfcrown which dropped with a clatter on any other coins already on the plate. I could always guess how many halfcrowns were dropped and, in some cases, from what height – without even looking. Two weeks previously I had suggested to Mum that she gave me the penny for the plate. It wouldn't be too difficult to swap it for one of the halfcrowns. She was shocked and promised me a good hiding if I ever mentioned such a thing again. Dad said that whilst it was very enterprising, it was dishonest. 'Also,' he said, 'You might get caught.' My conscience bothered me for a few seconds and I never mentioned it again. Dad was more specific. After the service, he put the fear of retribution in me by saying that I could be sent away to a Correction Home and have a criminal limp for the rest of my life. The idea of a limp scared the hell out of me. If only the world were full of birds and animals instead of people, how beautiful it would be. I spent the next day and a half sanding and scraping dirt off the old bike. Maybe it was a punishment, a judgement. Alex Noel. That scabby bike. On Christmas Eve I went to bed early, but I lay awake for hours.

This was the first and the only time I was sneaky about it, but I rose quietly and crept into the living room to see if I could find what was under the tree. There it was! God! God! It was beautiful. Even in the dim light there was no mistaking it for the bike that was such a mess a few days ago. The bike that I had spent so many hours on, sanding and griping. Dad had given it a new coat of paint. The chain glistened with oil in the lights of the tree. I couldn't hold back the tears. What Alex A. Noel said about Santa Claus was right then, but I didn't think about that till later. I rushed back to bed and lay there snivelling with happiness until I fell asleep.

Next morning, after the hugging and kissing was over, I couldn't get out fast enough to show off my lovely bike and to gloat at those who had gloated earlier. Now, I was the gloater and they were the gloatees. There were a few boys and a few girls around. And there was Effie. Who is Effie? Effie was a real tomboy. She was just over six feet tall and in her last year in higher grade. Effie played with the boys at 'kick the can' and 'tig, you're het.' She didn't play with the other girls as far as I could see. I was one of the younger boys who played 'kick the can', and I suffered in that I couldn't run as fast as the older boys, and when I got the can, which was our football, I was often bowled aside by the bigger boys. Effie was pretty good at protecting me. Often, when I was about to be roughed, Effie was there. She would give the bigger chap the shoulder, sending him into a nose dive. She could have done a good commercial for iodine. She would then veer off, letting me get a good kick at the can. There were no teams. It was every man for himself. There was no goalkeeper. This phenomenon was sustained by the instinct for self-preservation.

A Bicycle Built For Who?

Effie was the one who taught us how to ride a bike. We didn't all have bikes, but when one of us was lucky enough to become the proud owner of a bike, Effie was there to get us started. Effie was so thoughtful that, even after a boy had become proficient enough to manage on his own, she would continue to help him along with patience and comradely affection. When I emerged from the house on Christmas morning with my bike, the world looked beautiful. It never occurred to me that I couldn't just leap on the vehicle and sail off to boy-heaven. Stepping on the pedal, I pushed myself off and threw my leg over the saddle with complete confidence. Before my right foot reached the other pedal, I was lying in a heap underneath my bike, rubbing my right leg and shoulder. I was in pain. Maybe I was dying. I couldn't get up. Two strong hands removed the bike and lifted me up by the armpits.

'Are you all right?' It was Effie.

'I think so,' I answered, rubbing my leg. 'Maybe the bike is too big, or the seat is too high or something.'

I couldn't see the difference, not really.

'I'll hold the bike and walk alongside you,' she commanded. When I say 'commanded', I don't mean in 'military'. She didn't have to raise her voice; there was a quality in her tone that made you follow her instructions. I believe Effie could have masterminded a crime syndicate right here on Argyle Street, and we would have followed her without any compunction.

'Okay, Effie, but don't let go. Okay?' I said.

'I won't,' she answered. 'Get on. Up and over.'

Once more I threw my leg over the saddle and reached for the pedal.

'You've got your hand caught under me,' I said.

'That's the best way, Ralph. You just concentrate on keeping your balance.' I started to giggle. Effie's fingers started to wiggle. Mum happened to come out just then. Effie pulled her hand from under me and she gripped the back of the saddle.

'How is he coming along?' Mum called.

'Just fine, but he's gonna need a lotta practice,' Effie replied, shaking her head hopelessly. Mum wagged a finger at me.

'Now, you do exactly what she tells you,' she cautioned me. Effie grinned at me and said, 'Maybe you've had enough practice for one day. One thing though - I have my own secret method of teaching you, so you won't give away my secret method, will you?'

'No. Of course not.'

'Promise?'

'I promise.'

Effie gave me two more lessons, then she said, 'I believe you can manage on your own now, Ralph.' She started me off then let go. I managed to stay on just fine, a little wobbly but I didn't fall off.

'Will I need any more lessons?'

'No, Ralph. You'll be all right on your own, now.' I think it was a little disappointing, but she was right. Besides, Alex Noel's younger brother needed lessons. I noticed Effie was using her secret method on him too.

THE BALLOON

Uncle Louis is the most terrible liar who ever lived. He isn't my real uncle. In fact I don't know if he is anybody's uncle. You all know of Louis Forte Hammervaagen? That's not his real name. He even made that up. His real name is only Tom Smith, without any y or e in it. Simply Tom Smith. Maybe he even made that up. He liked the kids to call him Uncle Louis.

Along with some other kids, I used to sit for hours listening to Uncle Louis' lies, taking it all in as he waited for a fish to bite. Brother – was he glib! He'd put a pitch-man to shame. But give him his due, he had a certain modesty. By that I mean he was never noisy, but oh, so persuasive, so smooth, so ... 'plausible', I think, is the word I'm looking for. We used to sit there with TV eyes, soaking it up, eating it, wallowing in it.

Take, for instance, his lies about the steel balloon. I feel my face burning when I think of it. Ye gods, what a line! He had us believe that this character, Professor Oddaplomb (the name should have tipped me off that there was something screwy. I thought it was French), the greatest scientist who ever lived, had built a stainless steel balloon which was to take him into the stratosphere and beyond. It was nothing like the ordinary, everyday stuff which Jules Verne and H.G. Wells used to write about. The professor, Uncle Louis told us, had subsplit the atom. He had devised a means of imprisoning the explosion of the split atom, then re-exploding it clean out of existence. Then, from nothing, he created a material so light that it was as light as nothing.

Now, I'm not going to pretend that I was not excited. All of us were, and many a licking I got for coming in late for meals. And many a hot palm I had too for not knowing my homework the next day at school. This stuff was opium. Chuck Robinson – he was my special chum at that time – asked more questions than anyone else. It was quite a while before I plucked up enough courage to ask questions. Says Chuck, 'Why did the professor call his balloon a steel balloon when it was made of nothing and how was he able to get hold of the stuff to see what he was doing in the first place and where did he keep it and didn't the neighbours object?' If you think these sort of questions scuttled Uncle Louis, you're wrong. He would smile. A gentle, slow, benign-eyed, bland, child-like, lop-sided smile, and would hear us out. Then he would say – looking us straight in the eye, mind you – 'I was just coming to that'. As the questions increased in number, the story increased in incredibility. Professor Oddaplomb had been granted special permission by the government to build his balloon. There were no neighbours because, you see, it was all very secret. Top secret. For this reason, Uncle Louis was able to withhold knowledge of how the Professor was able to 'handle' nothing. Yes, a good many other answers were so encased in the plaster cast of 'Official Secrecy' that we started being careful not to overstep the line of loyalty to our country in our eagerness for power. Yes! Power it was to be in possession of such revolutionary and devastating knowledge as that of Professor..... Oooooh! Could that man lie! A balloon a mile in diameter. Thickness of shell – forty feet. Method of propulsion? – *Top Secret*. Inside furnishing? There was everything in it that money could buy and a lot that money couldn't buy as well. There were buildings, roads, bicycle paths, cinemas with toilets upside and down. There were swim pools and boats, no girls or schools, and everything else you wanted including free ice cream. 'Just like heaven,' said Chuck, drooling. That was the only time I ever saw Uncle Louis look uncertain. That, and the time Chuck asked him if there were cigarettes aboard the ship. Thinking back on it, I don't recall getting a direct answer to that question. By the time we got through outfitting the balloon, we had a kind of modern scientist's Noah's Ark, only bigger. It had two of everything we needed, ten of everything we wanted, and none of anything we considered useless or sissy. She was a great ship, the greatest of her kind. In fact she was the only one of her kind. Well, came the day when we had had just about all we could take of this old earth. Then Uncle Louis (just when we were all keyed up to take off) pulled a fast one on us. He said that the balloon had been up there for the past twenty years. It had been equipped for twenty years' travel and now the time was up. The world was in a ferment. Nobody could make contact with the balloon, presidents, prime ministers, dictators and kings, were all thundering insult and abuse at each other, accusing every foreign country of interfering with the professor's efforts to make contact with the earth. Billions of pounds had to be spent to build equipment designed especially to locate the missing ship. Then a new line of thought emerged. The professor HAD managed to make it back to earth, but the spacecraft had missed Leven and was being held captive by some foreign power, a country hostile to Scotland. 'I'll bet that'll be the Orkneys,' shouted Chuck. 'You dodo,' yelled Jock Murdoch, 'I have an auntie and two cousins in the Orkneys. They wouldn't do anything like that.'

I suppose both of them were overwrought and had developed frayed nerves in the crisis which had developed so suddenly. Still, Chuck didn't have to haul off and belt Jock one on the nose. When Jock saw the blood trickling down his jersey, he handed Chuck a solid one right in the eye. The left eye. You should have seen the colour of it the next day. These were the only two blows in the fight. Uncle Louis was holding them apart with his two strong arms and when they had cooled off a bit he let them go and sat down again. 'You know,' he said, 'that's just how wars start. People get het up over nothing at all. They start calling each other names and the next thing you know, they're at each other's throats before anyone can stop them sometimes. And the awful thing about it is, as like as not it's all over nothing at all. Just like this story. A whole slew of words without a splash of truth in them.'

Uncle Louis had reeled in his line as he spoke and casually he recast it. Chuck and I looked at each other for a moment in silence. We could hardly believe our ears.

'Do you mean to say, Uncle Louis, that none of this is true? There's no balloon? And no Professor Oddaplomb? And no swimming pool or anything?' He looked at me steadily for a few seconds as if he were trying to make some great decision. Then he lowered his eyes and turned back to the water without a word. I was too unhappy to think of anything to say. Then I said, 'I don't believe there's such a thing exists as human nature. Come on, Chuck.'

We walked off in silence and it was probably twenty minutes before either of us spoke. It felt as if there had been a death in the family.

'What a terrible liar he is,' said Chuck.

'Yeah,' I answered.

The following day something drew us towards the scene of the disaster. There was Uncle Louis with three new kids, talking away to them as if nothing had happened the day before. They sat there, wide-eyed, gaping, just as we had been doing before them.

'Should we go over and warn them?'

Chuck must have taken it pretty hard. 'No,' he said, 'let them find out the hard way, like us.'

That was twelve years ago. What made me think of it all of a sudden? Right there, on a shelf in the book store, amongst the other soft covers: THE BALLOON by Louis Forte Hammervaagen. I reached for it. On the back cover was a picture of Uncle Louis, smiling like a cat who had just finished a saucerful of milk, maybe a little older. I turned it over. Sure enough, *The Balloon*. But in smaller print: 'And other fabrications'. I looked inside the cover. Two shillings. That's a lot of dough for a soft cover. I had to have one though. I felt I had to know what happened to the professor. Maybe I missed something.

Funny, too, how much more you really have to have something when you've got to pay for it.

PUNISHMENT I COULDN'T REFUSE

It came to me as a revelation; not a theological divulgence, but by the simple act of looking. For the first time, I noticed it in print. Right across the top of the Bulletin Board were the words 'Baptist Church' preceded by the name of the street. I already knew the name of the street; I lived only two blocks away. But I hadn't noticed that it was a Baptist. There was a lot of other information there, including, prominently, the name of the minister. I had always thought I was a Protestant, and all the time I was a Baptist.

There were two great religions, I had thought, Protestant and Catholic. I said to Granta one day when we were sitting on the breakwater near the Shorehead, 'Am I a Baptist?'

Granta said, 'If you feel you are a Baptist, then you are a Baptist.'

'Oh. I always thought I wasn't a Catholic.'

'What did you think you were?'

'A Protestant.'

'Then, that's what you are.'

'I'm glad I'm not a Catholic,' I said.

'Why?'

'Because people around here would shout things at me.'

'What sort of things?'

I told him how we shouted at young Mike Flanagan who had just arrived and was a Catholic, and how some of the boys wouldn't play with him.

'What do you shout at him?' Granta asked.

'Well, you know...'

'No... I don't know.'

'Well, things like:
"Holy Father, I killed a cat.
That's bad my boy, you'll suffer for that.
But Father, it was a Protestant cat.
Good boy, you'll go to heaven for that".'

Granta sat in silence for a few moments, then asked, 'How do you know it was a Protestant cat?'

'I don't know. He wouldn't kill a Catholic cat.... Would he?'

Granta peered at me with half-closed eyes. Sometimes, when he looked at me like that, he reminded me of Alex Noel. But I could never dislike Granta. Never. Never, never.

'You have a cat?'

'Yes. Whiskers.'

'Is Whiskers a Catholic or a Protestant?'

What a question. 'I don't know.'

Granta leaned over like a conspirator and whispered, 'Maybe he's a Catholic.'

'I don't care what he is. He's just a cat with long white whiskers,' I blurted.

'Has...what is his name...Mike Flanagan ever tried to kill him?'

'No.'

'Ah! That proves he is a Catholic. Now, your pigeons - are they Protestant or Catholic?'

I was beginning to feel sick. 'They're probably Baptists,' I answered. I knew I was on shaky ground. I knew Granta was going to trap me, but how? I was wishing I hadn't said that, because Granta folded his arms across his stomach and squirted a spit into the sand. This was the sign that he was about to 'strike'.

'Maybe you'll have to get rid of the pigeons - or the cat.'

I knew he was waiting to see what I would say to that, so I said nothing.

'Which is it? Pigeon pie or cat stew?'

I looked up at him, and his eyes were all crinkled in a big smile.

I started to laugh, then Granta's face straightened up; his smile vanished. He pointed a finger at me and said, 'Now listen, boy, and listen carefully. You may not understand what I am about to tell you at the moment, but you'll remember, and you'll understand later. There was a priest,' he said, 'and a Protestant minister. They were good friends. One day, the Protestant church caught fire and burned to the ground. It wasn't really a bad thing.'

'It wasn't?' I responded, confused.

'No, it wasn't. It was a rickety old tin can anyway. Just after the fire the minister and the priest were sitting in the local having a pint of bitter.'

'Then they found out that the Catholic priest did it?' I cried. Granta continued as if I hadn't spoken. 'Some people – Protestants, the narrow-minded and the bigoted, said the priest did it. The minister told everybody it couldn't have been the priest because he was with him in his study during and after the fire.'

'I thought you said they were in the pub?'

'That's not important. Pay attention.'

'He lied,' I shouted.

'That is what is called a white lie. It didn't hurt anybody.'

'Yes, but...'

'Now, the question was – are you listening?'

'Yes.'

'Should they renovate the old church, or should they build a new one with brick walls?'

'I thought you said it was burned to the ground?'

'I exaggerated. The congregation decided to build a brand new church, saving anything that wasn't too damaged. A lot of people gave large donations as well as the small ones. Are you listening?'

'Yes.'

'One day the priest and the minister were having a chat in his study, and the minister said, "Joe?"'

'Joe?'

'Joe Flaherty. That was the name of the priest. "Joe," he said, "it would be nice if you gave a donation, like all good Christians, to build our new church." Father Flaherty rapped his fingers on the counter – I mean on the desk like this. You try it.'

I rapped my fingers like Granta on the log on which we were sitting.

'You've got it. Sometimes it helps you to think better.'

'How come it helps you to think better?'

'Sometimes it prevents you from saying the wrong thing, gives you more time to think. "Well now," says the priest, that was after he stopped rapping, "I can't give you a donation to build a Protestant church, but I'll be happy to give you one to help demolish the old one."

'That was very nice of him,' I said.

'Yes, it was,' Granta agreed. 'And the next time you see young Mike, I would like you to apologise to him for shouting that stupid rhyme.'

I apologised and we became good friends. It wasn't long before all the other boys were playing with him too.

I was very fond of Granta. My grandfather was never called anything else but Granta. His grandchildren, his children, when they became grown-ups, his wife Maggie and his neighbours' children all called, or referred to him as Granta. I always sat next to him in church. He was a good Christian, for he was able to doze off without snoring during the sermon. It was my job, however, to wake him up because he could keel over if I didn't catch him in time.

I liked Sunday for two reasons. First, there was no school on Sunday. Second, Granta took me for long walks on Sunday after church service. Granny was custodian of the pan drops, sometimes called Scotch mints. Granny always sat at the end of the pew next to the aisle. There may have been no reason for her position. On the other hand, there was no way anyone in our group could vanish without her knowledge, and I'd have bet my favourite dabbie nobody could disappear with it. Our seating positions were routine and permanent. First came Granta, next to him myself, then Uncle Andy, who was three years older than me, my mother, Uncle Henry, then Granny. Dad went only once. He wouldn't go again because, he said, 'The organist hit two sour notes in one of the hymns.'

Another family, the Crabtrees, entered the pew from the other aisle.

They glared at us if we took up too much room. The pan drops were available when any of us developed a cough. We were the coughiest family in church, and Granta was the champ. He was hardly seated when his throat began to bother him. Granny would then pass a pan drop to Henry, who passed it to Mum, who passed it to Uncle Andy, who passed it to me, and I slipped it to Granta. This was always accompanied with nudges, because we had to be sure the preacher didn't know. Sometimes the pan drop wouldn't reach Granta and he would have to cough louder, which made the Crabtrees glare at us. It wasn't long before I learned to cough almost as often as Granta, but I always let him go first. One day Granny forgot to bring the pan drops and we were all coughing like mad. We had to wait until the choir was letting it rip and the Reverend Alistair MacAndrew was hiding down in the pulpit studying his notes before word could be passed along that Granny had botched the pan drop routine. Our throats seemed to get better after that.

The Rev. MacAndrew was a man of about fifty. I noticed two things about him: he was bald and he was very serious. I didn't expect him to burst into laughter at any time, but he never smiled. In fact he always seemed to be angry about something. Maybe it was because he was bald, maybe not. Alex's old man was practically bald and laughed all the time. At least once during every sermon, the Rev's eyes would blaze, and he would tell us, in no uncertain terms, how rotten we all were. He didn't use the word 'rotten' but he might as well have done, because he certainly made me feel rotten and I'll tell you why. There was a young woman in the choir who had the face of an angel, like the ones you see in paintings. She was the most desirable creature I had ever seen, except Dorothy, of course. When the Reverend glared right at me, I felt wicked and guilty, because I imagined all sorts of things, like meeting her on the beach near the salmon nets at Lundin Links and walking for miles holding hands and talking, just walking and talking and holding hands. After a few hours, she would peel off, slipping her dainty hand from mine, and she would go home to her husband. Yes, that was why I felt so guilty. She had a husband. She was most desirable when she was singing the Hallelujah Chorus, especially when it came to the last 'loooo'. One Sunday, when I was concentrating on her last 'loooo', Granta keeled over. Fortunately, he keeled to the right, against me. If he had gone to the left, he would have landed in the lap of Mrs. Crabtree. I was always afraid it would happen to me for these reasons: I might get caught dropping off during the sermon and the Reverend would have had me 'cast down' when I died, and thirdly, if I was sucking a pan drop, it might fall out of my mouth and roll down towards the pulpit. This would bring disgrace to everybody in the family, especially Mum.

The floor of the church was made of hardwood and it had a rake, that is a slope, from the entrance downward to the pulpit. It happened one day. Not to me, but to Granta. He fell asleep, the pan drop hit the floor and bounced. It sounded like the crack of a billiard ball making a cannon off the red. Some of the customers stared at us. The Reverend was a master of the dramatic pause - for those of you who don't know what this means, a dramatic pause is when an actor forgets his lines and has to be cued by somebody in the wings.

There were a lot of dramatic pauses in Miss MacTavish's Group. It didn't take the Reverend long to get a grip on the situation. Spreading his arms like a cemetery angel, he shouted, 'And I say unto you...' I didn't hear what he had to say because I was listening to the pan drop rolling towards him. It was hypnotic. It was strangely musical as it rolled, coming almost to a stop where it encountered an indentation formed by a hundred years of foot shuffling. Twice it curled round the lips of one of them, like a golf ball on a putting green. Escaping both times, it struck out unerringly for the pulpit and the Reverend Alistair MacAndrew. I didn't know what to expect. At the least, flames would devour Granta and he would disappear like a pinch of magnesium powder, like the stuff we bought at Tam Shepherd's magic shop on Queen Street in Glasgow when we went on one of the Saturday railway excursions. Nothing at all happened. After clearing his throat, the Rev. carried on as usual. I noticed, though, he was looking straight at Granta during the rest of the sermon.

It was many weeks before I plucked up enough courage to slip a pan drop on the floor, keeping my toe on it until the right dramatic pause. I did it only twice. The second time I tried the pan drop caper, Granta leaned over toward me and whispered, 'I saw that!' I was stricken with fear. Not fear that he would tell, but if he saw it, who else besides him? If Granny knew, I was in trouble. She had no sense of humour. She liked to say, 'Little boys should be seen and not heard,' but she made fried mince better than anybody on earth. She cooked it over an open fire in a heavy cast iron frying pan, and it smelled delicious. Unlike coffee, it tasted as good as it smelled. When she wasn't telling me the 'little boys should be seen' stuff, she seemed always to be cooking mince. Sometimes I wondered what would happen to Granta if she got sick and went into hospital. She didn't seem to have many friends, unlike Granta who had more friends than anybody I knew. Granta was tall and slim and bred airedales and Scottish terriers, and a walrus moustache which covered his lower lip. He had calloused hands and crows feet and he lifted his moustache with his left forefinger when he drank anything so that he wouldn't get it all sticky.

Granta was a baker by trade and when he was not working or wandering in the countryside with me, he liked to work outside with the dogs. He built his own kennels and he was always happy. Oh, yes... when we got outside, Granny said, 'Come here boy.' Her tone told me everything. I was shaken. She always came right to the point, and this time was no exception. 'You dropped that pan drop deliberately, didn't you?' I was even more shaken when Granta – before I had time to deny it, said, 'Don't lie, Ralph.' To Granny, he said, 'I saw it, too. With my own eyes, I saw it. A sinful act. A deliberate act of impiety.' He gave me a stern look, then whispered something in Granny's ear. 'You're right,' she said, and turning to me she barked, 'Next Sunday you will not be allowed to come with us to church service.' Granta pulled her aside and whispered, but I overheard what he said.

'That's not enough. He should be punished for at least two weeks. That'll teach him a lesson and give him time to think over his wickedness.' Granny nodded in agreement, and turned to me. I looked as penitent as I could, and Granta, who was now standing behind Granny, grinned.

Ralph

When Granny finished delivering the sentence, Granta winked at me.

The following Sunday, Granta suddenly had trouble with his back. He suggested that a nice, quiet walk on the beach would be more beneficial than sitting upright in a hard pew. Reluctantly, Granny agreed. We found a comfortable log to sit on and Granta's back improved considerably. 'There's no use being dismal, even if I am in pain. Is there Ralph?' We threw sticks in the water for Nell, then went for a stroll on the golf links behind the sandbanks. We found several golf balls, one of which was still rolling. It was actually on the beach, however. 'Therefore,' Granta said, 'it was as good as lost.' We helped the golfer find it, and when he asked what we owed him, Granta said, 'Oh, give the boy a penny.' When the golfer had gone, Granta said, 'Now, look Ralph, never pick up a ball until it has stopped rolling.' I was flabbergasted. 'But I didn't,' I mumbled. 'It was you who picked it up.' He looked me straight in the eye. 'Ralph,' he said, 'you ask a lotta questions and that's healthy, but you have to learn when to keep your mouth shut.'

As we were already on the beach, we stayed there, Granta strolling along quietly while I cavorted with Nell. I chased her, then she chased me. We had a great time. We passed the bothy where the fishermen stored and repaired their nets, then we went out on to the hard, wet sand, rippled with the tide marks and dotted with whelk-encrusted boulders. Here we came across a log at the water's edge. We sat down but Nell was nudging me, urging me to throw a stick in the sea for her to retrieve. I found just the right piece and threw it in for her. She brought it back immediately and put it in my hands. Nell was still a puppy and I borrowed her any time I asked. Granta threw a stick, but no amount of urging would make her swim out for it. 'Tell her to fetch it,' said Granta. 'Fetch it, Nell!' She immediately dashed in the water and placed the stick in my hands. 'Mm, hm,' Granta mumbled. 'You know, that little bugger likes you more than she likes me.' I was worried. Maybe I wouldn't get her when I wanted her for one of my excursions into the woods alone. I looked at Granta, who was studying Nell, his lips pursed into a large pout. His walrus moustache pointed at Nell accusingly.

'Ralph,' he said and waited.

Fearfully, and somewhat timidly, I answered, 'Yes...Granta?'
'How would you like to have Nell - for yourself, I mean?'
'...FOR MYSELF? TO KEEP?' I shouted. 'AN AIREDALE? - TO KEEP?'
'That's right. To keep.'
I threw my arms around him and hugged him so tight he said, 'Take it easy. I don't want that mad dog to attack me.'
Oh Nell, Nell! Oh! Mum said, 'No dogs, one cat.' She said 'I have enough to do looking after my pigeons.' I could feel tears welling up in my eyes.
'Don't worry, I'll fix it,' said Granta, a bit too smugly I thought.
'Are you sure?'
'Leave it to me.'
'Oh Nell, c'mere.' Nell dashed over to me and I hugged her until she yelped to get away. Granta had lit his pipe and looked a picture of contentment.
Without looking round he said, 'Stop whimpering. I said I'd fix it, didn't I?'
We started for home, Nell trotting lazily by my side, looking up at me for instructions every few steps. That afternoon Granta 'fixed it'. Mum was no match for the charm and endurance of her father. 'How is your back?' Granny inquired when we got home.
'Much better, Maggie. Much better thanks,' he answered.
'Good. You'll be able for church next Sunday.'
'I think that is possible. If my leg is better.'
'Your leg?'
'The pain seems to be travelling. It should be all right in a couple of weeks.'
'I didn't see you limping.'
'Of course you didn't,' Granta answered with a straight face, 'you know what the neighbours are like.'
Granny gave me a searching look.
'Here Granta, lean on me,' I said, offering him my shoulder. I was learning fast.

'Thanks, boy. I have to make up some more pills. Help me to the shed.'

'Are you sure you are up to it?' He looked at me, well, funny like, then raised his eyes to the sky. I don't mind telling you, I was a little scared myself. It was still the Sabbath.

There were still about a dozen pills strung out in a necklace on the window of the workshed. 'Can I have one?' I asked.

'Are you constipated?'

'No.'

'Any headaches?'

'No.'

'Heartburn?'

'No.'

'A severe cold?'

'No.'

'Have you got *any* ailment?'

'I don't think so.'

'Then you don't need one. They're good only for what ails you.'

He filled the basin with bran, then put in a few squirts and dollops from various bottles and jars.

'What's in them, Granta?'

'Bran, treacle, cascara, cod liver oil, malt and a dash of caster oil,' he said, popping one into his mouth and swallowing it whole. 'Good for my leg,' he announced. I'm glad I didn't get one.

He mixed the whole mess with his hands, then rolled a hefty pinch of the concoction in the palms of his hands. The pills were about twice the size of moth balls. They were then placed on a shelf to dry. Alex Noel and his father happened to pass by. 'Hi, Harry,' Pete called as he passed. Alex kept on walking. He probably didn't know his father had stopped because, as usual, his hands were in his trouser pockets and he was still looking for that threepenny bit.

'Come on in, Pete,' Granta shouted.

Pete sauntered in. 'What are you up to, Harry?'

'Making some more pills, Pete. Do you need some?'

'I was hoping you'd ask,' said Pete, popping a hard one into his mouth. How anyone got that down his throat without suffocating is beyond my comprehension.

'One a week and your hair'll be as glossy as my airedales. Here, put these in your pocket,' said Granta, giving him three more. Pete pocketed the pills, then he ran his hands over his bald scalp as though he had a magnificent head of hair.

'I'd better catch up with Alex. See you soon. And thanks for the pills.'

And he was gone. 'I hate that fellow,' I said.

'Pete Knowles?' Granta answered, looking surprised.

'No, Alex.'

'Why?'

'For what he said about the Queen.'

I told Granta. 'He's lying, isn't he?'

Granta looked worried and after he had wiped his hands he rubbed his chin. This was another of his tricks when he was not ready to agree, so I pressed my point.

'Well... isn't he?'

'Spread these pills out on the shelf to dry,' he said.

I started to place the pills out to dry, then Granta spoke.

'Did you ever hear about the fat cat who wouldn't squat?'

'No.'

'Well...this man had a fat cat who ate everything he could get his paws on. Couldn't get enough...but he never went to the bathroom.'

'Never?'

'Never. And he got fatter...and fatter...and fatter...until one day, it BURST!'

I jumped back. 'Phew,' I gasped.

'They found pieces of him from the salmon bothy to the Bawbee Brig.'

'That was awful.'

'What a mess! And the stink was enough to blind you.'

'Maybe...maybe he should have had some of your pills,' I suggested.

'Watch what you're doing,' said Granta. 'Leave a good space between the rows.'

I didn't know whether to believe the story about the fat cat, but it certainly got me thinking. Of course Granta wasn't like 'Uncle' Louis.

THE SHOWS

That's what we called them in Leven: The Shows. In Kirkcaldy, the Links Market. Elsewhere, I don't know. The Fair probably. At the age of eight and nine, The Shows was one of my favourite haunts. It stretched, or so it seemed, for miles along the promenade. In the centre of the magic there was an elaborate merry-go-round with the most magnificent steeds imaginable. They were wild-eyed thoroughbreds, beasts with angry tails and gaping jaws, fearsome to behold, but watchful, each one ready to defend its rider from the many other dancing, prancing, malevolent firebrands raging up and down in a majestic circle. Oh, what wonderful days those were! Often I have watched with pounding excitement, wishing I too had the price of a ride on them – any one of them. Further along, there was the swing boat, huge and inelegant, ploughing its screaming and squealing cargo through the air. It was tuppence on the boat. This particular day I polished the two pennies in my trouser pocket and turned my back on it. I could have six balls for a try at the coconuts, three a penny, but that was too easy for me. The barker wasn't too happy to see me, and there is a limit to even an eight year-old's appetite for coconuts. There were wooden ducks and clay pipes to be demolished with a .202 rifle or B.B's. There was crown and anchor, darts and numerous other means of extracting money from the gullible flow of humanity that wandered aimlessly throughout the glittering arena. Then there were the side-shows where, for a small sum, we could gawk at the fat lady fumbling with her thirty-six inch garter, the bearded lady who looked suspiciously like a young man, and the dwarf. His name was Tom Thumb. Granta, between drags on his pipe, declared him a fraud.

'The real Tom Thumb,' he said, 'died about a hundred years ago.'

Who was I to believe – the barker or Granta? Granta, of course! He didn't tell fibs like 'Uncle' Louis. There was a man who lived in a large basket with snakes, and the skinny man who ate worms. Maybe he had been fasting. He didn't seem to like it very much but managed a sickly smile when the customers applauded. The worms were dead and looked more liked dyed spaghetti than wrigglies, unless they were tapeworms. I could hardly face spaghetti for some weeks. The stallion with the bright red saddle was something else. Threepence a ride, and I had only tuppence. In a flash it came to me. I could roll my two pennies. Maybe the first one would land on a penny. If it missed, maybe the second one would land on a threepenny bit. I ran like a maniac to the stall. It was crowded. I noticed that there were more pennies than threepenny bits. Also, there were more threepenny bits than sixpenny bits, AND, there were less shillings than anything else. I noticed, too, the shillings were very near the edge of the table. Shrewd observation told me that the pennies customers rolled down the grooved piece of wood always went far beyond the shillings. When necessary, which was constantly, the eagle-eyed owner warned customers to start their roll between the two marks on the runway. How could anybody beat this handicap? Granta – he would know. I walked away, slight depressed. Granta, that evening, listened with rapt attention. Then he lit his pipe.

'There's no guarantee you'll land on a shilling, or for that matter, anything at all.' I recall heaving a gigantic sigh of resignation then sitting beside him. 'But,' he continued, 'and don't keep interrupting.'

'I didn't say.....' Then I clammed up.

'But, with practice you have, mebbe, an even chance.'

'Practice?'

'Do you know what backspin is?'

'No. Well, yes, and no.'

'Fetch me a strip o' wood from that pile over there.'

'How about this?' I asked, producing a strip from the pile.

'That's fine. In the shed there, you'll see a hacksaw. And bring some small nails,' he called as I ran. 'And a hammer,' he shouted. I brought what he needed. When he had it nailed together, he said, 'Now, we'll

The Shows

have tae go inside,' and he motioned me with a finger to follow. Placing the contraption on the tablecloth, with two books under one end, he asked, 'Is that about right? Now watch.' With a finger under the grooved runway and his thumb above and slightly behind the penny, he pressed. The coin raced off and fell off the further edge of the table. 'Ralph, go intae the left-hand drawer o' the chest o' drawers in the back room, and you'll find a small tube o' rubber glue under ma masonic apron.'

As I rushed off to get it he called, 'It's right beside the solder and flux in that small cardboard box.' When I returned with the tube of glue, he smeared a little on the ball of his right thumb and held it up to dry. 'Now Ralph,' he grinned, sticking his pipe in his mouth with his left hand, 'strike a match and hold it over ma pipe.' Surely this was some secret known only to one or two people in the whole world. Was the trick to blow tobacco smoke on the penny as he pressed it? After a strong drag of tobacco, he blew smoke on the treated thumb. So...that's it, I thought. Smoke on the glue on the thumb! Gosh, Granta knows all sorts of tricks.

'Here, Ralph, blow on this,' he ordered, holding his thumb up near my lips.

'Do I...?'

'Do you what?'

'Do I have to take a mouthful of smoke? It'll make me sick.'

'Just blow on it 'til it's dry, boy. Never mind the smoke.' I blew.

'Right, now.'

With that remark, Granta placed his thumb on the penny and pressed again. The copper seemed to stagger down the groove, then, after a moment of trying to make its mind up, it fell flat on its tail. His eyes twinkled as he reached into his trousers pocket for some change. He dotted a few pennies on the tablecloth and a shilling just a few inches from the run. He tried again. Missed, but close.

'Here, Ralph, you try.' After applying the glue to my thumb, I had nine or ten shots, then I landed on the shilling. Holding my breath, I wheeled around to face Granta. He had dozed off. I took the pipe

Ralph

gently from his hand and put it in an ash tray on the sideboard. Collecting the money quietly from the table, together with the coin track, I headed for home. I practised for a good hour. By then I was getting one in every six or seven tries. Rushing back, I found Granta in his workshed. Excitedly, I told him that we could both become wealthy in days.

'Hold on there, boy. Do you think for a minute you'll be allowed to continue playing if you're winning? Besides, you don't have any money, do you?'

'No, Granta, but we'll form a partnership.'

'What kind of a partnership do you have in mind, Ralph?'

'Well, if you supply the money, I can win. I know it!'

'Tell you what I'll do,' said Granta, 'I'll give you a shilling. You will play all of them. If you win, you play them again until...'

'But it'll go on forever,' I griped.

'Damn the fears,' said Granta. 'They'll stop ye if ye win ower much.'

I gave him his shilling back and he counted out some pennies to make a round dozen. After school the next day, I dashed down to the Shows, eager to waste no time in becoming a millionaire. My thumb was prepared, my confidence unshakable, my demeanour calm, impassive. With appropriate dignity I shouldered my way to the table, ignoring the coarse remarks of some of the customers. This place was just right. Two shillings gleamed invitingly only about fourteen inches apart. I placed a penny in the groove and pressed. Missed, by gum! Another penny. Missed again! Don't panic, I thought. The third and fourth penny missed. I could feel the perspiration on my neck. I had to stop and concentrate.

'You gonna play or not?' growled a gruff voice behind me. I placed another penny, number five, and pressed. The lousy thing circled leisurely around a shilling then, for no intelligent reason, reversed its balance and fell away from its victim. Centrifugal force Granta said it was when I described it to him the following afternoon. I didn't know at that time what it meant and I didn't ask. I set the sixth penny and pressed. It rolled past the shilling on my left, then did a sort of back-flip to land neatly on about two thirds of the shilling. 'Nice going, kid,' somebody muttered, 'play your luck.' The croupier, or whatever he was, handed me the shilling and my penny. 'I would like pennies,' I said in a squeaky voice. He gave twelve pennies for the shilling and walked away. The gruff voice said again, 'If you're gonna play, play.' I said, 'He hasn't put the shilling back.' 'Yeah,' growled Gruffy, 'Hey man, you left a blank space. You gotta put a bob down there.' The croupier glared at him and snarled, 'If you don't like it, go around the other side.' Gruffy pushed me aside and yelled, 'Look Mister, you replace that bob or I'll wring your bloody neck!' The croupier became uglier. 'Don't threaten me or I'll call a policeman.' 'You're too late, you creep, because that's just what I'm gonna do myself, RIGHT NOW!' Gruff brushed his way out and I never saw him again. When I turned back to the table, the shilling was there. I rolled again and it landed neatly on the bob. The croupier was red-faced. 'How old are you, kid?' 'Eight,' I replied. 'Here's your shilling. Now beat it, you're under age.' He turned to go. 'What about my penny?' He threw a penny in front of me which I picked up and left, but not before I had a ride on the charger with the bright red saddle.

I told Granta the whole story and gave him back the shilling he lent me. 'You did all right, Ralph,' he said. 'Did we agree on a partnership?' 'Well, we didn't actually shake on it,' I answered. 'Uh-huh. Well, our partnership is dissolved. No questions. And you stay clear of that stall from now on, do you hear?'

'Yeah, I hear.'

GEORGE LANE

I hated him. George Lane, I mean. Of course, I didn't hate him as much as I hated homework; it was just ordinary hate. George was in Miss MacTavish's play. He was another sorry knave, but he came in late because he didn't have any lines and he was probably jealous. The drama critic with the local newspaper mentioned me personally by name. He said I was the sorriest knave he had ever seen. George didn't even get a mention. About two months after the play, I had a fight with George that made my flesh crawl. It couldn't be called a fight really, because.. well, here is how it happened. Actually, it was a happy incident. How, then, did it make my flesh crawl? You may remember that I couldn't bear being called Ralphie. That's all right when you are a baby, but I was close on eight, almost an adult, and it was time to quit the baby talk. At that age, I was becoming aware of things like drowning, watching out for traffic, and infection – especially infection. I could die by putting unfamiliar objects in my mouth. So when George Lane found a mouth organ, which he couldn't play and which I could, he said, 'Play something.'
'Where did you get it?' I asked.
'I found it,' he answered.
'Uh-huh,' I replied, explaining to him how he could die a horrible death by putting strange mouth organs in his mouth.
'You're chicken!' he shouted, and made the most horrible noises on the mouth organ. He had no ear for music. I told him to quit, but he shouted a vulgar five-letter word and continued sucking and blowing on the instrument. Can anyone blame me for hating him?
Another time, he found a balloon in the ally behind Effie's father's toolshed facing the wash-house and he blew it up. His mother, who was

hanging out her washing at the time, warmed one of his ears and told him he was dirty and disgusting. I happened to be there and I agreed, mentioning the incident of the mouth organ. Mrs Lane warmed his other ear and that was when George accused me of being a snitch. I meant it for his own good. Besides, how was I to know she would belt his other ear? George didn't see it that way and started calling me Ralphie. The way he said it sounded more like Ralpheee. This made me mad. George could run like a hare and after chasing him for half a block I gave up. I didn't want to catch up with him anyway. It could start a fight. It was best just to remain sworn enemies. That way we could hate each other without any bad feelings. The only thing I liked him for, during the period of our mutual hatred, was when we collected nine cats which we shoved through Mrs. Henderson's scullery window. There were five of us in it and George managed to collect three cats, an awesome figure if you think about it deeply. He deserved our admiration. But he persisted in calling me Ralpheee. Then I would chase him again for half a block, then I would give up. Oh, yes..about the fight. One day, he came right up to me and said, 'Hello, Ralpheeee.' He didn't run. Instead, he stuck out his chin. 'What's the matter, Ralpheee? Scared?'

I didn't know what to make of it. 'How come you're not running as usual?' I asked.

'Lost your nerve, eh? You're scared to punch me on the jaw, right there,' he sneered, pointing to his jaw. 'Chicken!'

'That's twice you have called me chicken, George,' I shouted, clenching my fists, 'You're asking for trouble.'

He grinned and stuck out his jaw even further. His face looked twisted. It looked queer.

'Do you know what you are Ralpheee? You're a sorry knave.'

It didn't sound as good as when I read it in the paper. Pulling my right arm back behind my shoulder, I brought my arm round in a beautiful, but deadly arc. My fist landed solidly on his protruding jaw. He sat down in a heap. Blood and green stuff tricked down his chin.

'OH GOD!' I screamed. This was the first time I had hit anybody, and I thought I had busted his brain. That's when my flesh began to crawl. All my hatred disappeared. The blood didn't matter. Blood flowed when you had a tooth yanked out by the dentist, or when you fell and bashed your nose on the ground. It was the green stuff. I looked at George, horror stricken. He lifted his head and he was grinning like Mrs. Ogilvie's cat.

'Thanks, Ralph. Thank you very much.'

He's gone mad, I thought. Maybe if I could stop the leak there would still be some hope for him. He was still smiling.

'You busted my gumboil. The dentist couldn't see me for a couple of days and I couldn't stand the pain.'

'You used me!' I yelled, all my hatred coming back again.

'I had to. What else could I do?'

'You scared the hell out of me,' I screamed. 'Of all the dirty tricks.'

'Don't get so worked up about it. I'll never call you Ralphee again.'

'You won't?'

'Never again. Cross my heart and hope to die if ever I should tell a lie.'

All my hatred disappeared. This time for good. George and I became very good pals, but that green stuff - ugh. Only once did I have doubts about George, but not for long. It was when a fellow, about sixteen years old I'd say, cornered us near home one day.

'All right, kids,' he said. 'How much money do you have on you?'

'What's it to do with you?' I answered.

'How'd you like me to beat you up?' he growled. His voice had broken. George made a run for it and escaped but I was cornered. I thought George should have stayed. Maybe between us, we could have given him a fight. George lived just around the corner from where we were. Maybe he was going for help. This was a pretty big chap.

'What are you waiting for?' he snarled.

'Nothing. I haven't got any money.'

'Empty your pockets.'

'Why?'

'Because I'm telling you to.'

'I told you, I don't have any money.'

'Let's find out. Empty your pockets. Look, I haven't got all day to waste. Move.'

'I can't move with you standing in front of me.'

'Don't get smart with me, kid. Turn out your pockets.'

'If you let me pass, I'll get some money. I have some at home.'

'I'm not stupid, you little twerp, and I'm getting tired of your yakking. Now turn 'em out and be quick about it or I'll beat you up and do it for you.' I could see George tiptoeing back. He had a frying pan in his hands, one of those solid iron ones like Granny's. I was staring past the thug, not at George, but at the frying pan which he was holding high above his head. He was about to bring it down on the back of the mugger's head. He noticed that I was staring past and above him, and sensing something was going on behind him, wheeled about. At that precise moment, the frying pan was in full flight, and it connected, not with his napper, but with his mug. He fell, no, not so much like a log as an oversized inner tube that had suddenly lost its air. Blood gushed from his nose.

'Geepers, you've killed him,' I screamed.

'He asked for it,' said George calmly, 'I just hope the pan hasn't twisted.'

'You're crazy,' I shouted. 'This is no joke.'

'I'm not joking. This is my mother's favourite pan.'

'What are we going to do about him?'

'The same again, if he starts anything.'

We stood waiting for him to recover enough to get up. It took about a minute. He shook his head and struggled to his feet, cursing and wiping his nose with his sleeve. George raised the pan above his head again, at the same time doing a sort of dance as though he was mashing grapes. One look at this weird apparition wielding a frying pan and jerking like a marionette was enough for the mugger and he got off his mark like a whippet.

A NELEPHANT

I couldn't resist collecting animals. It was little short of a passion with me. I had a cat, Whiskers, a dog, Nell, pigeons and a bantam cock that followed me about all over the place.

When I saw an elephant at a menagerie, it seemed to me that no backyard would be complete without an elephant.

'Where would you keep an elephant?' Dad inquired. Instead of just telling me outright that it was impracticable, he asked a lot of questions. At the time it seemed a roundabout way to say 'no'.

'Outside.' I answered.

'Of course. In the pigeon house?'

'No. But I could tie it up to the pigeon house.'

'I see. And the second day you have it – after it has smashed the pigeon house into kindling?'

'I didn't mean I wanted it right away.'

'You would like to think about it for a day or two?'

'Ah – yes.'

'I think that's very wise,' said Dad. 'Meantime, concentrate on the cat, the dog, the bantam, the parrot and the pigeons.'

Andy Rintoul had a mouse. It was white and it had red eyes.

'What's it's name, Andy?'

'Pinkie.'

'Do you always keep him in that small cage?'

'No. Sometimes I keep him in my pocket.'

'Does he bite?'

'No.' Andy took him out of the cage and put him on my shoulder. I put my hand up to him and he immediately crawled on to it and

disappeared up my sleeve.
'Where'd you get him?'
'Edinburgh.' Andy disappeared into the bathroom.
'Whereabouts in Edinburgh?'
'The pet shop.'
'What pet shop?'
'On the steps.'
'What steps?'
'From the station.'
'Waverley Steps?'
'No.'
'The other steps?'
'Yeah.'
'To Cockburn Street?'
'Yeah.'
'Whereabouts on the other steps?'
'On the way up.'
'How far up? Near the top, or the bottom? Halfway?'
'Maybe halfway... I think.'
'Does he have any more?'
'Not many. They were going fast.'
'How much are they?'
'You thinking of getting one?'
'I would rather have a nelephant.'
At this point, Andy flushed the toilet and threw the door open. Pinkie, who had appeared on my jacket collar having explored the inside of my sleeve, took fright and leapt to the floor. He vanished towards the toilet. Andy was unconcerned.
'Sorry. You shouldn't have pulled the plug.'
'He took off to the bedroom.'
'Yeah...well...that's O.K. I think you made the right decision.'
'What decision's that Andy?'
'To get a nelephant.'
'You got to feed a nelephant.'

'You gotta feed a mouse.'
'He's pretty big, though.'
'A mouse?'
'An elephant.'
'Of course you couldn't lose him - not under the bed anyways.'
'That's right, Andy. Not under the bed. I have to go.'
'How much did they cost?'
'Geese, I don't remember exactly. Hey, you'll be the only fella with a nelephant.'
'That's for sure. Well I gotta go Andy. See you.'

Andy was still talking when I left. I don't know what he was saying exactly. Something about selling fertilizer to the neighbours. When I got home I started to collect some things to make a box big enough to hold a mouse. The main thing I needed was a piece of chicken wire. Before I had managed to get it all together, we went on another excursion to Edinburgh. I had saved up two shillings and fourpence during the past three months.

When we left the train at Waverley Station I said to Dad, 'Could we go up the other steps for a change?'

'Why not, if your mother feels up to it?'

'Fine with me, if you have enough money to buy whatever it is you happen to want so desperately.'

I raced up the steps and about halfway up I saw it and dived in. There they were. About a dozen of them, pretty little white things cowering in a palpitating ball in a corner of the cage.

'How much are they, Mister?'
'Ninepence each,' he said.
'Does that include the cage?'
'No. But I have small cage at one and fourpence.'
'Oh.'
'That would be...two and a penny? It's a little too much?'
'You can have both for two shillings...or...I can put him in a paper bag with airholes for him to breathe. You can make him a cage when you get home.'

Ralph

Dad had followed me inside, and he was standing behind me. He said, 'What about Whiskers? Cats and mice are not the best of playmates.'

'Oh, Whiskers won't bother him once she gets used to him,' I replied. 'And I have enough money to pay for him. I'll make a cage so that he won't get lost under the bed or anything. Okay, Dad?'

Dad nodded. 'Okay, Mum?'

'If you think you know what you are doing...okay.'

I bought one and called him Whitey.

Whiskers ate him.

DISENCHANTMENT

It was on Sunday morning, the day after the excursion to Edinburgh, the day after Whiskers ate Whitey, that I was in the pigeon house when I saw Granta coming towards the house. He wasn't dressed for church service. I was all ready, dressed and hair combed. Mum had inspected my ears to check if they were clean and had given me the O.K. I rushed down to meet him but he reached the door before I could catch up with him. Granta knocked and walked in.

'Where's Ralph?' he inquired, peering around the room.

'I'm here, Granta,' I said from behind him.

'Ooo. Where did you come from?'

'I was in the pigeon house.'

'In these clothes, boy? You deserve a good...' Dad appeared from another room. To Dad, he asked, 'Can Ralph come with me for a walk?'

'Do you want to go, Ralph?' Dad needn't have asked. He knew my answer.

'Oh, yes, yes, but ah...' 'But ah,' Dad said, pretending to be angry, 'you shouldn't have been in that dirty pigeon house with your good clothes on. Go and change.' When I was changing into Uncle George's hand-me-downs, I thought of my angel; my Hallelujah angel. Remember? I was deeply in love with her although I didn't really know what love is. It was an unrequited love, and not likely to be anything else. For one thing, we had never spoken, but that was the least obstacle. The real obstruction was our ages. I was about seven, she was getting on, probably three times my age. She was beautiful and delicate and, I'm sure, gentle. I could imagine her shooing flies off her food instead of swatting them with a newspaper like Mr. Munro, who smelt like a brewery most of the

Ralph

time. Heaven, I thought, would be lucky to get her.

'What's keeping you, boy?' It was Granta's voice.

'Coming,' I yelled, rushing into the living room with my boots in my hand.

Mum asked, as she always asked, 'Did you fold your Sunday clothes?'

'Well ah...' 'Then get back in there and do so right away.'

I got back in time to hear Granta tell Dad that he was going to the Bing, and from there into the woods. The coal Bing was next to the golf links, opposite the salmon bothy just beyond Lundin Links.

Being where it is, the Bing was neatly located some miles from the nearest church, though I don't believe it was originally planned. The surface of the Bing was cunningly concealed by whins, which screened the activities of small groups of miners who prayed for a winning hand at pontoon, sometimes called black jack. There were lookouts who could smell a policeman a mile away and give ample warning to the gamblers, who would scatter in ones and twos. It would have astonished today's naturalists – or any other day's for that matter – how many bird watchers and rugged Sunday strollers with blackheads in their pores roamed casually among the whins when the alarm sounded. Those Sabbath pursuits were good for everybody except their families. Non-participating fellow creatures were not welcome. Indeed, it could even be dangerous to venture into this area unrecognised. Granta and I were always allowed to pass without any trouble. Granta knew many of them and as he passed he would greet some of them with such remarks as: 'Go easy, Jimmy', 'You winning today Rab?', 'How are the wife and kids Dusty?', 'Is your airedale better now Frankie?' Some of them would say, 'You coming in, Harry?', 'Hey, Harry, lend me five bob. I'll pay ye back six on Friday.' Things like that. Granta never sat in with them and he never gave them any money. He was always greeted as a friend, however. When we were out of their hearing, about halfway past the neep field, he stopped in his stride one day. 'Ralph?' he said.

'Yes, Granta.'

'Did ye notice anything about them...in particular?'

'They're very friendly.'

'The ones I spoke to were friendly.'
I thought about it for a moment, then I remembered something.
'You don't always speak to the same men.'
'You missed something boy. What else?'
I shrugged. I didn't know what he was getting at.
'I always speak only to the men who are winning.'
Granta peered at me, his eyes all crinkled up into a smile, but his mouth wasn't smiling. Clearly I was supposed to say something.
'How do you know...who's winning, Granta?'
'There are two things to look for, and both of them are staring you in the face. The ones who are winning have a pile of money in front of them.'
'And?'
'And they have a smile on their face.'
'They all seemed to be smiling,' I said.
'The winners were smiling and the losers were grinning. And their grins were - for the most part - about as artificial as a plastic grape.'
'Are they unhappy?'
'Aye, but no' as unhappy as they'll be when they go home skinned.'
I said, 'I don't think I'll play at cards when I start working.'
'Well, let's go a bit further, eh? Do ye feel up tae it?'
'Sure,' I answered excitedly. 'Hey, Granta, have you ever seen such nice tumshys?'
'Are you thinking what I think you're thinking?'
'Well, Mum could use a turnip and the farmer wouldn't miss one, would he?'
'That's true. Let's take that path down tae the left. Ralph, how is your geography?'
'Not bad. The teacher said I had a good grasp of the subject to a passable...ah...degree.'
'Let me ask ye, what's the population of Scotland?'
'Oh, that's easy. Close to five million. England is over thirty-five and a half, Wales is nearly two and a quarter million, and Ireland...'
'Let's no' cross the ocean just yet. In Britain, that totals what?'

I counted roughly on my fingers. Granta was going to be proud of me.

'Altogether,' I said proudly, 'altogether, that comes to - roughly - not accurately - roughly - fifty million.'

'Fifty million, eh? Now, suppose all of these people strolled up tae this field o' neeps and took one each, how many do you think the farmer'd have left tae sell?'

'Well, putting it that way...'

'Is there another way o' putting it? Look up there, two yellow yites. We haven't seen any Scotch canaries for a couple o' weeks.'

I wanted to tell him more about the populations of different countries; I was well up on that subject, but Granta was off on another topic. The implication in his theory didn't seem right but he had changed the subject so fast, I didn't have time to think about it. 'I'll get around to it later,' I decided.

'We've never been down here before, have we Granta?'

'No. Would ye like tae sit down for a wee while?'

'I don't mind. We can watch the birds.' A brilliant thought flashed through my mind. This will get us right back on to geography. 'Maybe we can count the different birds and then we would know how many there are.'

'A good idea, Ralph. Then you would be able tae tell what the population o' the different birds is in this neck o' the woods.'

He fell for my trap. Well, I thought he did. Then he said, 'None o' the birds eat turnips. You'll know that, of course.'

'Yes, I know. Talking about turnips...'

'You took the words right out o' my mouth,' said Granta. 'Taking turnips without the owner's permission is stealing...theft if ye like. Now, if five million people wandered into this field with the idea of stealing one turnip each, do you know what would happen?'

'Sure,' I said. 'A lot of them would be out of luck.'

'And that's no' all,' Granta exclaimed. 'The ones who were in luck would be out o' luck. They would be thrown in the nick for stealing, and they'd be up before Judge Thamson the next day.'

'Do you see these ants carrying dead insects back tae their nest?'
'Aye.'
'Where do you think they got them?'
'They found them, I suppose.'
'They killed them. These ants live by the law o' the jungle. They kill and steal and...if they were people, they'd all be up for murder. And they would hang by the neck until they were all dead.'
'But they are ants, and we are people,' I exclaimed.
'Exactly,' Granta announced, 'and we don't live by the law o' the jungle.'
It was time to change the subject; to get back to geography.
'Do you know, Granta, that the population of the United States of America is over a hundred and twenty million?'
'Aye, I know that.'
'How did you know?'
'You just told me. Let's walk on down this path for a bit.'
We wandered down a path not much used, Granta in the lead, I trailing five or six paces behind. I wouldn't miss these walks with Granta for anything, but sometimes I could kill him. Well, not actually kill him – that would be the law of the jungle, I suppose, but you know what I mean. We were about three hundred feet down the path when Granta turned about and clamped his hand over my mouth. It was so sudden it scared me. Then I saw it – a man and a woman fighting on the grass. The man had her pinned down and I could see her bare legs above her stockings. With his free hand, Granta motioned me not to make a sound, and he thumbed me to go back the way I came. When we were about three hundred feet away, Granta let me go and held a finger to his lips, signalling me to talk softly.

'Shouldn't we...g-g-get help?' I gasped. 'These men playing cards would come! I know they would!'

Granta was not the least upset. 'Just forget what you saw. There's nothing at all to worry about.'

'But he'll kill her, like the ants. Like the law of the jungle,' I shouted. Granta clamped his hand over my mouth again. 'Ssssh, not so loud,' he cautioned me. 'That's another kind of a jungle. They're nesting.' Then he changed the subject again. I couldn't help worrying about what I saw however.

'Look, there's a blackie's nest. If ye stand on that log, you'll be able tae reach in. See how many eggs she has.'

I was reaching for the nest when she passed us. She turned for a fleeting glance in my direction. 'Holy mackerel!' I shouted. Then I croaked, 'There are five eggs in this one.' My Hallelujah angel! The man with her followed a few paces behind. 'Nice day, Harry,' he said. 'Aye, it is that, Larry,' he said. The man looked up at me and smiled. Granta talked quite a bit on the way home, but I couldn't get my mind off my Hallelujah angel...nesting.

The next Sunday, I was ready for church before anyone else. I wanted to see if she was all right. She smiled a lot when she wasn't singing, and I noticed her glancing often at a man in the choir. He was the same man who was with her in the woods and he was smiling back. Suddenly I realized I didn't love her any more. It didn't matter much anyway. At school, we had a new art teacher. She was really nice. She resembled an actress in the movies whose name I don't remember. I didn't have to worship her at a distance. Miss Livingstone touched me a lot when she passed my desk. She also put her hand on the back of my neck when she stopped to talk. Her hand was always nice and warm. It was some time before I realized that she did the same with all the students, boys and girls alike.

I hated maths; I didn't understand algebra, but I was fond of art and English. Miss Livingstone used words I had never heard before, words like perspective, proportion, construction and balance. Of course I had heard of balance. I could balance a broom on my chin and walk right across the living room without touching it with my hands. This was a different kind of balance though. She was pretty old, about twenty-five or six, so I could never become serious about her. She gave me a halfcrown for drawing the best picture of a vase in the whole class. I was in love with her, but it wasn't the same as it was with my Hallelujah angel. Anyway, everybody in school was in love with her.

BAKER'S DOZEN

One Sunday afternoon, when I was out in the woods with Granta, he asked, 'How old are you, Ralph?'

'Seven and - April, May, June, July, August, Sep - seven and a half,' I said. 'Why?'

'Did you ever think of getting a job?'

'Uncle Henry said I could go into the coal mines when I'm fourteen.'

'I mean now.'

'What kind of a job?' I enquired.

'With Ovenstone the Baker.' My heart leapt.

'I can learn to be a baker like you, Granta?'

'Not right away. The message boy at Ovenstone is leaving this coming Saturday. They'll need a new boy.'

'Yes, I would like that but am I not too young?'

'If you want it, I'll put in a word for you, but you'll have to ask your Mum and Dad if it's all right.' They both agreed.

Granta swung it and I got the job. I was hired to start on Monday after the other boy left. Getting up at 6.15 am was a bit of a shock. I didn't realize that anybody in the world got up at that time. It was an even greater shock when I learned that Granta and some other bakers were up at 5 am so that people could have morning rolls for breakfast. My first job of the day was to deliver the rolls to a number of families, mostly professional people like doctors, bankers, store keepers and street cleaners. The shock of getting up so early was exceeded only by the discovery that, with the exception of the bakers and myself, everybody was still driving them home. Sometimes I would see a coal miner going to work on his bicycle but not often. It came also as a surprise that the people who ate morning rolls were astonished when I said 'Good morning'. I had begun to brush my hair back out of my eyes, so it wasn't that. I didn't have two heads so it wasn't that either. One Sunday afternoon I mentioned it to Granta. 'What's wrong with me?' I asked him.

'There's nothing wrong with you,' he answered. 'Are they all like that?'

'No. Just some of them.'

'They're snobs,' Granta announced. 'Pay no attention.'

'What's a snob?'

'A snob is a person who is afraid to talk to you in case other snobs get tae know about it.'

'They could whisper, couldn't they?'

'That would be cheating. That would be breaking the rules of snobbery. They would be ostracised.'

'What's that?'

'They would be outcasts. They would never be invited to play bridge with other snobs.'

'They could play at dominoes. And they could play pontoon on the Bing on Sundays.'

'They prefer things the way they are. And they prefer bridge,' Granta said, and I knew the matter was closed. Granta knew everything. Now I knew that a snob is somebody who likes to play bridge with other snobs. I said, 'Wouldn't it be better if they just nodded?'

'Your business is to deliver rolls and not to bother about the manners of the customers. And now the matter is closed.'

He wasn't always so definite but I could take a hint, so I said no more. As I said, they weren't all like that. Doctor MacLean and Mrs. Gault were especially nice. Actually, most of them were pleasant. I never tired of watching the bakers working. Granta was an expert at making shortbread. Marking it was a work of art. He placed his left palm on the centre of a disc of shortbread, and whirling it around slowly, he made the fluted edge with his right thumb, neater than any machine could do it. Nobody could do it as fast as Granta and he never made a mistake.

Jimmy Shand made the cream cookies. After baking them, he sliced them, spreading them on a wooden tray open. The he tossed a gob of cream on the bottom half, flicked them shut with his other hand, finishing the operation by powdering them with sifted sugar. The speed with which he sliced the cookies demanded the utmost concentration and the admiration of anyone who appreciated feats of skill. I walked up close to him one day to see if he had any fingers remaining on his left hand. They were all there. It was a miracle. Another operation which fascinated me was brushing the egg on cookies and certain loaves of bread. Bob Chalmers always did that. Bob poured some of the contents of a gallon can of egg into a tray, then, with a whitewash brush, he sloshed the egg across the tops of the loaves with one deft stroke. It was poetry in motion.

When they were empty, the egg cans were thrown into a large wooden bin inside the back entrance to the bakery. Sometimes, when a can was nearly empty, Bob would tip it up and an extra coat of egg would be brushed on a few loaves. When a customer saw it, she would want that one and no other. When two women saw a loaf with two coats, it was frightening. The tension could start a second world war, and the first one was only a few years over. Nessie, one of the girls at the counter, didn't help matters. She could never locate the loaf which the customers were pointing at. At first I thought she was stupid until I realized she was having fun, probably to relieve the boredom. I liked Nessie better than I liked Margaret because, when I bought a pennyworth of sweeties from her, I nearly always got more than I got from Margaret. I preferred cinnamon balls and raspberry toffees, but it was always best to choose sweeties from a jar which was nearly full because when it got low you didn't get as many.

Getting back to the egg cans. It is surprising that nobody thought of draining them into a bowl or something, because there was always about a cupful of egg in the bottom of the can. I was watching Granta marking the shortbread one day when Nessie came into the bakehouse. She yelled, 'Telephone.' Jimmy Shand started for the door. 'It's not for you, Jimmy. It's for Bob,' Nessie cried.

Ralph

Bob followed Nessie to the phone, and the other men started to tease Jimmy. 'Maybe your girl wants a change,' said Tommy Cairns. 'When are ye gonna bring her in and introduce us?' chortled Jock Black. Harold Duncan, who was as skinny as a knitting pin, said, 'Maybe Big Effie canna get through the door, that's why.'

'Oooo, I didn't know he was steady wi' big Effie,' said Tommy Cairns. 'Why don't ye share,' said Harold, rolling his eyes around like peeries. Jimmy was fit to burst. 'Oh, shut up,' he yelled. 'I wouldn't introduce her to you slobs. Besides, it's no' big Effie.'

They were still bugging Jimmy when Bob came back in. He looked annoyed and started to untie his apron. 'This is a helluva time tae go when I'm right in the middle of a job,' he grumbled.

'What's up?' Granta asked.

'Robertson's wants some egg cans.'

'Egg cans?'

'That's right. Empties.'

'Oh, that again?' said Granta.

'Seems we owe them a dozen empties,' Bob grumbled. 'I don't suppose there's a chance o' you taking them, Jimmy?'

'No chance at all,' said Jimmy sulkily. 'I'm tied up here wi' the cream cookies.'

Bob looked around at the others. They all looked busy. Some of them were busier than I had ever seen them. I didn't recognise this at the time as an elaborate piece of choreography. Glancing about me, I noticed that several pairs of eyes were looking straight at me.

'I'll take them for you, Bob,' I blurted out. 'I have about fifteen minutes before the pies are ready.'

'Let 'em wait,' Bob muttered.

'No, no,' I answered. 'Maybe they need them right away.'

'Let them send one o' their own fellas,' said Smitty, grinning like a halloween pumpkin. Smitty always looked like a pumpkin anyway. Bob gave Smitty a funny look. That should have tipped me off but it didn't.

'Maybe you could manage half a dozen, Ralph,' Bob said. 'They're not that heavy.'

'Oh, I can manage a dozen,' I announced. 'No problem.'
'Why not take a couple o' dozen,' Jimmy Shand called out, slicing the cream cookies.
'A dozen is all they asked for, and a dozen is all they get,' Bob yelled back.
When Jimmy was about to argue with him, Bob snarled, 'That's enough so shut up, you goddam sadist.'
Being a Baptist, I didn't know what a sadist was. I could imagine him sacrificing cats and sheep in the middle of the night and eating live frogs. He looked like that kind of a man. Bob was some years older than Jimmy and he had been with Ovenstone much longer, so he was able to put Jimmy in his place.
I found a piece of twine and tied up twelve empty egg cans by threading the twine through the handles and set out for the other baker on the High Street. As soon as I left, I forgot all about Jimmy anyhow. People in the street looked so friendly. Many of them smiled as I passed. One or two of them even stopped and watched as I staggered up the hill to Robertson's. Maybe they were thinking of helping me. I would have declined because I was determined to carry out any job I was called on to do. The load wasn't really a heavy one, but they shoogled all over the place, nearly falling off my back several times. At Robertson's they were surprised at first to see me with the cans they had asked for. 'Must be a mistake, sonny,' one of the bakers said.
'That's right,' said another, 'I told them that if they wanted any empties, I could let them have - how many have you got there?'
'A dozen,' I told him.
'Right. A dozen is what I said we could let them have.'
The man who said it must be mistaken. 'Some silly bugger musta got it all wrong.'
I screwed up my face and rubbed my fingers across my forehead. This was a trick Miss MacTavish told me about when I didn't understand something or other. She said it was method acting. 'Don't do it too often, though,' she said. 'Once or twice at each performance is enough to give it authenticity.' I must have given it authenticity, for nobody

mentioned it. To be honest, I hadn't given Miss MacTavish a thought at the time. It was a purely unconscious act. In another play I was instructed to scratch under my armpit. 'To move the lice around,' said the Lady Gwen, when I asked why.

'I haven't got lice,' I exclaimed.

'But if you had lice,' she inquired, 'wouldn't you scratch....Stanislavsky?'

'Who's Stanislavsky?' I asked Miss MacTavish.

'Just do it,' she growled angrily. I didn't like it but I did it. Some of the actors moved away and the audience laughed. Worse was to come. I was directed to scratch my backside. I balked at this, but I did it anyway. The audience howled with laughter. Even worse than that was to come. In another play we had a live dog on stage. 'The pants smell funny,' I said. 'They smell like a dog had peed on them.'

'They certainly do,' Miss MacTavish answered. 'Just put them on.' The dog, at the appointed time, followed me on stage, sniffing at the pants. Then he looked up at me and grinned. The audience reaction to this was so unexpected that I was taken off guard and he squirted all over the pants. I was told later that several women in the audience wet their knickers over this, they laughed so hard, but I didn't know if it was true or not. I asked Miss MacTavish for clean pants for the next performance.

'You ask too many questions, Ralph.'

'My grandfather said it's healthy to ask questions,' I replied.

'Your grandfather is not directing this play,' she replied sharply. I thought, 'Maybe he should be,' but I didn't say anything. Granta also told me I must learn when to keep my mouth shut.

Getting back to the egg cans – 'Well,' the baker said, 'better take them back, and take the other dozen they asked for.'

'I'll have to make two journeys.'

He ignored my remark. 'Follow me, and I'll show you where they are.'

He helped me string them together and hoisted them onto my back. Empty cans are certainly not heavy, but they are bulky and difficult to carry. They fell off three times going back down the hill, but everybody was kind, Mr. Black especially. He said that they should be balanced on both sides of my body, then they wouldn't slip off. 'Just keep your head and shoulders down,' he told me.

It was certainly easier, but some people began to pass drivelling remarks like, 'It's a growth of some kind.' 'Maybe it's an invasion from Mars.' 'Somebody should shoot it.' 'It's only a bread poultice.' 'Very funny!' I shouted, but they only laughed harder. All right for them: they weren't carrying the cans. When I arrived back at Ovenstone's, the first man I met was Bob Chalmers. He was carrying a tray of pies on his head. He was setting them out to cool. Bob was terrific with trays. No kidding! He could balance a full tray on his nut and walk anywhere without touching it with his hands. He could also make an about turn suddenly. Once I saw him make a full turn like a ball arena. 'Bob should be on the stage doing a variety turn at the Gaiety,' I thought. Boy, if I could do that! For weeks I practised, with empty trays of course, mostly on Saturdays after I had delivered the rolls. When I took a tray of pies to the baker's High Street store, I had to take the handcart. For three weeks I had been needling Bob to let me carry one on my head and I sensed he was weakening. The previous Wednesday he had said, 'O.K. Ralph, next Saturday' - that was today - 'but be very careful, especially on Saturday when there are more people rushing about and not looking where they are going.'

The egg cans? Right. Bob caught sight of me as I staggered in with my load.

'What the hell?' he cried.

'There's been some mistake,' I grumbled. 'They thought....'

'About as much as pigs can fly,' said Bob, cutting me off. 'Just throw them here. Here, let me help you.'

Placing his tray of pies on the rack, he took one of the bundles from me and tossed it into the box. 'Throw the other one in there,' he said. As I wended my way to the front shop, everyone in the bakehouse was very pleasant, giving me smiles and nods as I passed. Nessie was in the front as usual and she had the pies all ready in the proper tray. Nessie didn't look up. She was making out a receipt for a customer.

'What date is it, Ralph?'

I glanced at the calendar. 'April first,' I answered. Then my face started to burn when I realized what day it was and what I had been through. Everybody knew. I knew everybody knew. I glanced at the customer as she left. At least *she* didn't know. She could easily be the only person in the whole of Scotland who didn't know. I wanted to drop through the floor or simply drop dead or something. Even Vanessa was in on the joke. I was beginning to hate her when she said, 'Ralph, could you use some cinnamon balls?'

'I don't have any money with me,' I croaked. It wasn't my voice.

'Don't worry about that.' She filled a paper bag right to the top. 'There...never mind the penny, but don't tell anybody I gave you them for nothing.'

'No, I won't,' I promised, putting them in my pocket. How could anybody hate someone like that?

'The pies are ready. Maybe you should take them up right away.'

'Right. Bob said I could try them on my head this weekend.'

'Shouldn't you take the handcart?'

'Nope,' I whispered confidently. 'And thanks for the –' I tapped my pocket and whispered – 'cinnamon balls.'

My self-confidence was coming back fast. 'I'll show them I can take anything in my stride!'

'Take it easy, Ralph.'

'I will.' With the tray of pies on my head and what was akin to nonchalance, I was on my way.

ROBINSON CRUSOE

With the tray of hot meat pies on my head, I was sailing along High Street, Leven, on my way to the other shop, feeling very smug after the disastrous morning I had been through. I had a good, tight grip on the tray with both hands. What could go wrong? That was when Murphy's Law took a hand. Mrs. Murphy, a tall lady of more than ample weight - she was one of the Leven Sweet Adelines - came cruising towards me on the same sidewalk. Her son, Kevin, who was always eating, smoking, or mouthing off, was walking by her side. I knew he wouldn't step aside when we passed, so I decided to step off the sidewalk until they had passed. When he was almost abreast of me, he said, 'Hey, Ralph, got a match?' 'Smarty,' I sneered, giving him a two finger salute, and it wasn't the boy scout one either. I should have ignored him, for my attention was divided and both Mrs. Murphy and I stepped off the kerb at the same time. CRASH! Her hands were raised when she and the tray made contact. She did it only to defend herself. With only one of my hands holding the tray, it shot back and down. Somebody behind me caught it. Who else? Alex Noel. He happened to be walking right behind me, and only five pies bit the dust. This was the first time I was happy to see Alex. There he was, as usual, his hands stuck in his trouser pockets. I stared at him in disbelief and wonderment. Now, you tell me, how could he get his hands out of his pockets, catch the tray, then stuff his hands back in his pockets before I could turn around? I suppose that was, is, and always will be one of life's great mysteries.

'It wasn't your fault, Ralph,' Alex said, blowing the pies clean and replacing them on the tray. Kevin Murphy was grinning like he had done me a favour and he didn't raise a finger to help. I wasn't going to

Ralph

mention it, but after that I will. He had been downgraded twice. At nearly nine years of age, he didn't know the population of Scotland. Personally, I doubt if he knew the population of his own family. Mrs. Murphy was nice though and she apologised for Kevin. 'You lousy... twit,' I shouted at him. 'I have a good mind to.....' His face straightened and he beetled off in a hurry.

'Will you be all right now?' Alex asked.

'Yes, and thanks. It's a good thing you were there.'

Mrs. Murphy and I apologised to each other. Alex was on his way.

'Oh, Alex?' He turned back. 'Would you like some cinnamon balls?'

'Thank you, Ralph, but no. I never eat sugar except what is already in prepared food. Thank you all the same.'

I told you he was weird, remember? But I didn't hate him any more. I delivered the pies as if nothing had happened. When I returned to the bakery, there was another tray of pies ready for the High Street shop. Nobody mentioned my mishap but Bill was in the front shop.

'I think you should take the handcart this time,' he said.

News travels fast in a small town. Immediately after lunch, I had another pie delivery. This one was a weekly job which I enjoyed immensely for several reasons. One: I went by train, which was very enjoyable. Two: the railway cut right through the golf links, so I could see all my special places, the Salmon Bothy, the Bing and the sea, in comfort. Three: I was able to see Robinson Crusoe's house and statue at Largo, where I delivered the pies, and four: Mr. Greer always gave me sixpence.

Six dozen pies in a basket is quite a load, and from the railway station at Largo to Mr. Greer's shop was about a quarter of a mile. Robinson Crusoe's house was about halfway, so I stopped there for a rest. I never tired of looking at the statue, and I would gaze in wonderment at the stone carving with its fur clothing and rifle which he always carried with him on the island. Sometimes I would put down my heavy basket and contemplate the fur-clad figure standing guard in a niche above the door. This habit ceased when, just in the nick of time, I turned to see a dog sniffing at the pies. He was about to lift his leg when I yelled at him and he took off like a rocket. Thereafter, I delivered the pies first, then stopped at the statue on my way back. One day, to my astonishment, a man opened the door and stepped outside. Startled by the sudden appearance of a man with a heavy black beard, wearing dark blue clothing and a sailor's cap with a shiny peak, I jumped up and grabbed my basket. He was smiling, so I saw no reason to run. Besides, Robinson Crusoe wasn't a violent man. Besides which, he didn't have a musket, and besides, he wiggled a finger for me to come over to him, which I did.

'I have seen you several times,' he said, 'looking very intently at my window. Is there something you would like to ask me?'

'Are you.....?'

'Please go on,' he urged.

'Are you... Robinson Crusoe?'

'Do I resemble Robinson Crusoe?'

I compared him with the stone carving above the door. 'No.'

'Ah, the clothes,' he said, reading my thoughts. 'I'm sorry if I disappoint you, young bibliophile, but I am not Robinson Crusoe.'

'Oh.' Disappointment must have shown on my face for he looked sorry.

'What is a ....'

'A bibliophile?' he grinned. 'It can mean anything from a bookworm to a philosopher. It can also mean an inquiring schoolboy.'

'I'm a schoolboy and I deliver pies to Mr. Greer every Saturday.'

'I know. I watch for you, and I buy some of those delicious pies from Mr. Greer. A lot of people watch for you and they are very happy that you deliver the pies before you stop here. By the way, the dog is tied up now until after you leave.'

We both surveyed each other in silence. He was trying to read my thoughts. His grey eyes reminded me of Granta's, crinkly and sort of amused. I wondered if Mr. Greer knew about the narrow squeak I had had with the dog. 'Is Mr. Crusoe in?,' I asked apprehensively.

He looked troubled for a moment and I was beginning to feel uneasy. Then he smiled and answered, 'No, Mr. Crusoe is not in.'

'What about his man Friday? Is he in?'

He looked very grave. 'Man Friday has gone to his reward.'

I knew what he meant. The Reverend Alistair MacAndrew always told us when anyone went to his or her reward. I was wearing my cap that day, so I removed it and held it in front of me in respect for the departed. I thought I detected a faint grin on his face as his lips began to twitch. A horrible thought flashed through my mind. Maybe this man murdered Man Friday. *And Robinson Crusoe.* I felt my flesh crawl and I was on the point of running when he asked, 'Have you read Daniel Defoe's novel?'

'Who's he?' I was aware that my voice was thin and almost inaudible.

'He is the author of Robinson Crusoe' said the bearded man. He was smiling broadly. When he smiled he didn't look at all evil, so I stood my ground. 'I thought all authors were dead,' I ventured.

'Many of them are, including some who are still living,' he answered.

I didn't understand this, but I had heard Dad say much the same thing once and anyway, I was more interested in Robinson Crusoe and his whereabouts.

'You haven't answered my question, young man.'

'What question was that?'

'Have you read the novel, *Robinson Crusoe?*'

'Sometimes a man on the radio reads bits from *The Three Musketeers*, and *The Scarlet Pimpernel*, but I like *Robinson Crusoe* best.'

'Did anyone ever mention when he was born?'

'No.'

'He was born in the year 1676, and he died in 1721. His real name was Alexander Selkirk, and he was born in this house. If he were still living, he would be over two hundred and forty years old.'

I was crushed. 'But that was... before The Scarlet Pimpernel!' I gasped. This was, perhaps, the greatest blow in my whole life. I was hoping I could tell Alex A. Noel that I had met Robinson Crusoe. This would have beaten any of his rotten stories. April Fools Day?

'Mister, you wouldn't be giving me the flim-flam would you? I was caught this morning.'

'I assure you that what I have just told you is absolutely true.'

'Cross your heart?'

'And hope to die,' he said crossing his heart.

Well... I could always tell Smart Alex that his real name was Alexander Selkirk. Too bad about his first name, though.

But who was this man staying in Alexander Crusoe's house now?

'Excuse me, Sir, but are you related to... him?' I asked, pointing to the stone figure.

'No. My name is Rogers. There is a connection but no relationship.'

'Are you renting, sir?'

'No. I would like to show you inside but I have some important calls to make. If you are interested, maybe next week, I shall show you inside the house and tell you more about him.'

'That'll be great. What time is it, Sir?'

'Three forty-five,' he answered, looking at his watch.

'I have to catch a train,' I murmured. As I turned to leave, he was smiling. He had a nice face. 'Thank you, Sir.'

'Until next week then,' he said, and walked briskly away.

I could hardly wait for my next visit to Largo, but I caught the 'flu and Bob took the pies to Mr. Greer.

On my next three visits to Largo I knocked on the door of Rob - Alexander's birthplace, but there was no answer.

STUNG

Jock Munro was some three years older than I. I never got to know Jock very well. He was a surly individual and something of a loner. He was also very large and had a red face. The few times I greeted him, he looked at me as if I had just crawled out from under a rock, so with all of these features, it isn't difficult to see why I never got to know him very well. One day Jock stopped me in a passage at school. His method of engaging younger or smaller boys was to block their passage and stare at them for several seconds.

He said, 'You still with the baker?'

'Yes. Why?'

'You like it there?'

'Yes. Why?'

Jock had an uncle at the baker where I worked. Maybe he was after my job. 'I'm leaving the butcher,' he announced.

'Yes? Why?'

'You ask a lotta questions,' he growled.

'You started it,' I answered.

'I'm goin' to learn how to be a plumber,' Jock said. 'My old man says there is a great future in plumbing. You're never out of work and the money's good.'

'Is that so?'

Jock spat on the floor. That's another thing I forgot to mention.

'I just said so, didn't I?' he growled.

'So... what do you want?'

'I want to do you a favour,' he said.

'I'm not interested. What kind of a favour?'

Ralph

When Jock Munro did anybody a favour he always seemed to get the best of it. 'Of course, if you don't want me to help you, just say so.'

'I don't want you to help me. Now, let me pass.'

His attitude changed. 'Now, wait a minute, Ralph. My uncle says you are pretty good on the job.'

'So?'

'So I could put in a good word for you with the butcher before I leave.'

'What's it pay?'

'Five shillings a week.'

'That's what I get with the baker. Besides that, every Saturday I get a huge bag of buns and stuff to take home.'

'Pigeon feed,' cried Jock. 'I get a parcel nearly every day, and on Saturdays I take home a great big bag o' meat and sausages and stuff. Sometimes I get the end o' a roast.'

I didn't have a hanky with me, so I had to wipe the saliva with my sleeve.

'I thought you'd like it,' said Jock. 'The boss asked me if I knew of a good message boy to take my place, and I said I would find one.'

I had been with the baker for three years and I liked it well enough to want to stay, though not with any passion. I didn't fancy sausages as much as cream cookies, fly cemeteries and meat pies, especially when they were hot out of the oven.

'What's the catch?,' I asked Jock.

'No catch. If you get the job, you give me a set of Lucky Charms.'

I had been collecting a set of cigarette cards called Lucky Charms, but I was still three short of a complete set. I asked Jock if he would accept a set with three missing.

'No. I want a full set,' he replied. 'And a good tennis ball.'

'I don't play tennis.'

'Swap something with somebody who does.'

'*You* don't play tennis.'

'And six glassies.'

'You don't want much, do you?'

'And a *full* set of Lucky Charms.'
'Maybe I don't want the job,' I said.
'Better know for sure by tomorrow, because I have somebody else in mind.'
'Who?'
'Never mind who. You have a full set, haven't you?'
'Maybe I have, maybe I haven't.'
'Please yourself. I'll wait until tomorrow.'

I didn't like his attitude; his smug self assurance that he had a deal, so I contemplated saying nothing to Mum and Dad about the sausages and ends of roast. Mum would say, 'Grab it.' Dad would say, 'Now, wait a minute, Mum. Find out if Ralph wants to go there.'

When I got home, I felt it would be wrong of me not to mention this opportunity. Mum and Dad listened in silence until I came to the bit about the ends of roast beef. Mum said, 'Grab it.' Dad said, 'Now wait a minute, Mum. Find out if Ralph wants to go there.'

That would have been all right if Dad hadn't followed up with 'I expect Ralph will jump at the chance.' 'Sausages and roast ends,' Mum cried. I came in fast with 'cream cookies and pies and stuff.' Then I played my trump card. 'Jock wants a full set of Lucky Charms, and I only have a set with three missing.'

Dad was sympathetic. 'Ah yes,' he said, 'that is a problem.'
'It sure is,' I agreed. 'Well, he'll just have to look for somebody else.'
'Unless,' said Dad. 'Unless I managed to get the missing cards to complete your set.'
'I don't know where you would get them, and Jock has to know by tomorrow.'
'If I did manage to get the missing cards, would you be willing to go with the butcher?'

I glanced at Mum. She looked miserable. I felt rotten. What bothered me most was having to submit to Jock Munro's extravagant demands.

'I suppose so,' I whispered. Mum brightened up immediately.
'Where are you going to get the cards?' I asked Dad.
'Let's see. You lost a set at gambling I believe.'

'I wasn't gambling,' I protested. 'We drop the cards from a mark on the wall. If it lands on another card, you win all the cards on the ground.'

'I know the game well. Tell me, Ralph, do you know exactly where the card is going to land?'

'Oh, no. It flutters down before it lands.'

'Then it is a game of chance, not skill. That is gambling.'

Dad didn't approve of gambling and I must have looked very dejected.

'Don't look so melancholy,' he said. 'I am not forbidding you to play. It is a harmless game. I merely wish you to know the difference between a game of chance and one of dexterity.'

Dexterity. I liked the word. Dad used words that nobody else used in our neighborhood. Sometimes I didn't know the meaning of the word in itself, but the meaning of what he was getting at was always clear. Although Dad was disinclined to talk of his youth, I knew that he had spent the early part of his life in Switzerland and France. He spoke French fluently and had never entirely lost his European accent. It was fascinating to hear him talk, especially with Doctor Simpson who visited, usually with a friend. They would bring some gramophone records which they would swap for some of Dad's. Dad would produce a bottle of port wine and they would sit talking for hours, occasionally in French. When they saw me listening, they would talk in English and Dad would give me a small glass of port. I never entered into the conversation though. Most of the time, I didn't know what they were talking about. They mentioned names like Verdi, Wagner, Puccini and Bizet. Doctor Simpson, I noticed, fell asleep now and again, but when names like Jung, Freud, Adler, and Pinel cropped up, Doctor Simpson was the most lively in the group. Dad was sometimes able to guide the conversation back to music with names like Paderewski and Caruso. The only name I recognised at that time was Wagner, whose music I had to suffer for many years. I didn't understand why they didn't play good music like 'Margie' and 'Four Leaf Clover' until I was some years older and living on my own.

I did only once, when there was a lull in the conversation, try to become involved. I asked if anybody knew the population of Italy. They all said, 'No.' 'Germany?' 'No.' Then they started talking again. Well, if they didn't want to know, that was their loss.

'To whom did you lose your set of Lucky Charms?'

'Donny Kirk.'

'Will you go to Donny Kirk and tell him that I would like to talk with him?'

'Now?'

'Please. And ask him to bring with him his set of Lucky Charms.'

'Are you going to take them from him?' I asked.

'Certainly not. That would amount to anarchy. No doubt he has his price.'

I was leaving when Dad called me back. 'Ralph, did you notice that this is a request, not an order?'

'I think so.'

'You don't *have* to go with the butcher if you don't want to.'

'I don't? Maybe Donny isn't home, anyway.'

'There is one way to find out.'

Donny was in his Dad's workshop. 'You come for your revenge?' he asked, grinning in the most aggravating manner.

'No. My Dad wants to see you right away, and you have to bring my set of Lucky Charms.'

'*Your* set? You mean my set,' he almost screamed. 'I have two full sets now. Look,' he added with glee.

'Let's go, and bring one with you,' I said, looking as nasty as I could.

He left one set spread out on the workbench, padlocked the door of the shed and we went back to my house.

'What's the deal?' he asked on the way over.

'What deal?'

'How much is he going to pay for them?'

'Wait and see,' I snapped. We didn't speak for the rest of the journey.

'Hello, Donny,' Dad greeted him pleasantly. 'I believe you have a set of Lucky Charms for sale.'

'Maybe,' answered Donny.

'How much do you want for them?'

'How much do you wanna give me?'
'Well now, Donny, when one has something for sale, one puts a price on it.'
Donny tried to weigh up how much he might get out of Dad.
'... A shilling.'
Dad: 'Sixpence.'
Donny: 'It's my only set.... But seeing it's you... ninepence.'
Dad: 'Sixpence.'
Donny: 'You might say ninepence is wholesale. Ninepence.'
Dad: 'Sixpence.'
Donny: 'Ninepence.'
Dad: 'Sixpence. Take it or leave it.'
Dad lifted his newspaper and pretended to read it. Donny was unsure of his position. He decided to take a chance. 'No way,' he said. 'Bloody impudence,' I thought. Donny had turned towards the door, but seemed to be in no hurry to leave. I looked at Mum who was on the verge of tears. I felt awful. Then I blurted out, 'You lied! You have two sets.' Dad sat tight, reading, or pretending to read.
'O.K., sixpence,' said Donny.
'Fourpence,' Dad said, without looking up.
'Fivepence,' Donny yelled.
'Thruppence,' said Dad.
'Fourpence,' Donny screamed.
Dad got up slowly and folded his paper. 'Donny,' he said, 'you are a hard man to bargain with, but I admire your skill at it. Fourpence it is.' Dad shook hands with him and motioned me to take the cards.
'Do you want to check them, Ralph?'
I counted the cards while Dad and Donny, both looking very sad, stood by.
'They're all here,' I announced.
'You wouldn't like to change your mind, would you, Donny?' said Dad, looking depressed.
Donny brightened up and actually smiled. 'A bargain's a bargain,' he said. Dad heaved a great sigh and sat down with his newspaper.

Donny smirked at me and left without another word.

After he had gone, I said to Dad, 'I thought you did all right, Dad.'

'So did I,' he replied.

'Then... why did you offer to sell them back to him?'

'I didn't. I simply asked him if he would like to change his mind.'

'Oh. Then, why were you looking so unhappy?'

'There was no point in sending *him* home unhappy. Was there?'

And that is how I left the baker and became a butcher boy.

Being a message boy with a butcher thrust me into a world I never thought existed. A sirloin or a T-bone steak were epicurean delights, and they were not common at our table. A side of beef was a side of beef, not associated with a gentle cow, slaughtered, skinned, and cut up into roasts, steaks, soup bones and suet. I was aware, of course whence the various species of meat came, but I had never really given it any depth of thought. A chicken or a rabbit hanging from a hook in the butcher shop didn't look like a bunny or a cock-a-doodle-doo. It came, then, as something of a shock when I first visited the slaughter house and witnessed the process of creating the bulk of a culinary feast from beginning to chef. With a deft twist and a pull, a bird became somebody's dinner. A whack behind the ears, followed by a skilful slash with a knife and removal of its entrails, changed a bunny into a rabbit or a hare into a stew.

A burly man at the slaughter house looked at me and grinned. 'You'll get used to it,' he said. He threw me a piece of rope and said, 'Here, tie its forelegs together.' He then tied another rope around the hind legs of a cow and pulled the rope which ran over a pulley in the roof, thereby lifting the cow entirely off the ground. I stood transfixed. I couldn't believe any one man could do it. Taking the rope back, he said, 'Here, I'll show you how it's done.' After tying the fore-hooves together, he tightened up the rope even further and the animal was left dangling. But not for long. Burly then picked up a sledgehammer with a spike the size of a bullet on one side. He brought this down, with unerring aim right in the centre of the animal's skull. A large bucket was placed beneath its head, and its throat was cut. Blood gushed into the bucket, almost filling it. My stomach rebelled audibly. I thought I was going to be sick. In less than an hour she was killed, bled, skinned, gutted, hacked and cleaned into table delicacies. The mess had no resemblance to the cow that had mooed for mercy only an hour ago. Tongue, heart, liver, sweetbread, thrapple and lights were dumped into a container for me to transfer to the shop. This was my final duty for the day, and the proprietor, Mr. Douglas, a pleasant roly-poly man, said, 'Good lad. Now, I always give a new boy a parcel to take home on his first day.' He had a huge parcel of meat ready for me. I thanked him and left. On my way home, I was tempted to dump the parcel in somebody's garbage can but managed to control the urge.

When I arrived home with the goods, Mum was ecstatic.

'How did you enjoy your first day?' she inquired.

'It was all right,' I answered without enthusiasm.

'I knew you'd like it,' she cooed, fondling a large roast.

'I haven't started anything for supper yet, so I think we will have roast beef this evening. You would like that, wouldn't you?'

'I'm not hungry.'

Mum was immediately concerned. 'Are you feeling all right, Son? Do you feel you have a temperature?'

'No no. I'm fine.'

I swore to myself that I would never eat meat again, and I didn't – until the luscious aroma of roast beef weakened my resolve and I forced myself to eat with relish. I believe Burly knew of my distaste for slaughterhouse involvement, because he never tried to give me a job to do there again. One of my jobs was to crank the sausage machine. The girl upstairs made the sausages. She pulled a long length of animal gut on to a spout protruding from the machine. This was released as necessary when the machine spewed out the filling by cranking. Many people swore they were the best sausages in the world. I was able to boast that I helped make them. It didn't seem to dampen their hunger for our sausages. Another job of mine was to deliver to certain customers black and mealy puddings.

Toni's Fish and Chip Gardens was one of our treasured customers. Then there was Phemie.

STICKY LARGESS

Phemie was, without question, the most gruesome creature I had ever seen. She was about seventy years of age, just skin and bone. Her hair was screwed up into a knot on top of her head. She had a moustache like a doormat without the welcome sign, as well as the incursion of a beard, grizzled and grimy, blending in cunning camouflage with the green-black frock which was the only dress I ever saw her in. She smelled like rotten cabbage. The store was dark and narrow and had acquired the same aroma as its owner.

When I became a butcher boy, it was part of my job to deliver orders to regular customers. Toni's F. & C. Gardens was one of my favourites. Phemie's wasn't. I made a weekly delivery of tripe to Phemie. Not a pound, not two or three pounds, but a whole tripe, occasionally two. Do you think her ingestion of unvarying animal victuals was the cause of the resident aroma? She never bought anything else from the butcher, just tripe, which she kept in a cold cellar. The cold cellar was a small cave under the store, and I had to carry it down and place it on the shelf.

'Keeps for weeks,' she said. 'Nothing ever goes wrong down here.'

I believed her. A dead cat wouldn't have gone bad down there.

Her voice, high pitched and - well, to save me the trouble of describing it - harmonizing comfortably with her appearance.

The shop had one medium-sized window where she displayed trays of candies or sweeties and chocolate bars of half a dozen varieties. Phemie owned a dog and a cat. The dog was covered (or is it uncovered?) with a number of bald patches and it liked to rub itself against customers, who never came back again. The cat slept most of the day in the window amongst the sweeties. Both the cat and the sweeties were hairy for three reasons. Firstly, there was no window shade and the sun, which has no discriminations, beat down mercilessly upon the contents of the window. Secondly, the cat was in a constant state of moulting, and thirdly, the cat and the sweeties were in contact for a good part of the day. I don't recall anyone ever buying sweeties at Phemie's.

'Don't ever take Nell in there,' Granta cautioned me. I mentioned the moustache and beard to Granta and he said, 'She's certainly no oil painting.' Miss Livingstone had advised me to study paintings in art galleries, but I hadn't managed to get to any yet, so I couldn't compare. 'What is wrong with the dog?' I asked Granta.

'It probably has the mange', he replied. I didn't know what the mange was but it sounded dirty the way Granta said it. After that, I never took Nell there.

Phemie seemed to like me, for she always gave me a bag of sweeties from the window. I always thanked her, then took them home and washed them under the tap until all the hairs were gone. Nell loved them. She was a clever rascal but I knew she would never try to figure out why I didn't eat some myself. One day, when Phemie whacked the cat with a newspaper in order to get a handful of sweeties, a whole chunk of fur came away when the cat jumped. Some of the candies stuck to its fur. Phemie removed them and threw them back in the window. After that I told her I had stopped eating sweeties.

'Would you rather have a chocolate bar?' she asked me.

'Yes, if it's all the same to you,' I replied.

The chocolate was white and soft when the sun got at it. Soft or hard, it shaped like some part of the cat. Unlike the sweeties, the chocolate was imprisoned in silver paper and trapped in a sturdy paper sleeve with gold printing on the outside, sometimes a picture, describing how good the contents were. After careful inspection, I shared it with Nell. Phemie's main business was not sweeties, however, nor tobacco and cigarettes, which she always had in stock, but newspapers, especially Sunday newspapers. Early on Sunday mornings, great stacks of Sunday papers, as well as some comics and boys' weeklies, were dumped on her front door. The *News of the World* and the *Sunday Post*, as well as the *Vanguard*, my favourite, were among them. Other shops picked up some of them, paying for them in cash. She told me she didn't like cheques. 'Some of them bounce higher than a sorbo bouncer,' she claimed. I wouldn't know about that, because we didn't use cheques. How she paid for her newspapers was a mystery. I imagined somebody creeping into her place in the middle of the night and leaving quietly with a suitcaseful of money. Once in a while, a banker would visit her to have a 'private talk', but he never stayed long. Maybe it was the odour. Maybe it was the three old codgers who occupied the long, narrow bench along one wall of the shop. They all smoked pipes of different varieties. One of them - let's see if I can remember their names - yes, it was Rab. He smoked a clay pipe. Another one, Pete, smoked a corncob. The other, Jock, smoked various wooden pipes. They were always smoking and talking, and they would blow a waft of acrid smoke at the dog when it came too near. Granta claimed that the stink would blind a skunk, which was never, to my knowledge, actually tested, and that he never went in there without a gas mask, which I agree was necessary but unbelievable.

One day I asked Granta if what I heard was true. 'What did you hear?'

'That Phemie has hair on her chest.'

'How in God's name would I know?,' he spluttered. Granta could be very direct when he wanted and he wasn't above using the Lord's name in vain. If the Reverend Alistair MacAndrew could hear him sometimes, he would have given him 'what for'. Granta never used filthy language though, just ordinary swear words, and it was only when he got angry about important things like something the Prime Minister should have done about it, or something one of the bakers should not have done. He was smoking his meerschaum when I sprang the question on him. That is what made him splutter. I suppose I should have known better. Dad said that if Phemie wasn't making so much money handling newspapers, she could make a reasonably good living in a carnival side show. Anyway - the three old codgers stuck it out. They were always there. I heard - this is only hearsay, you understand - that the owner of the property behind her wanted to buy part of her land behind the shop. The lot was narrow at the back door, fanning out for three hundred feet to a line two hundred feet wide. She didn't grow anything except weeds, mostly dandelions, real whoppers. The man who owned the property behind her was a brother of the Magistrate, and he wanted to build a couple of houses which he would sell to his friends for more than they were worth. Well, here's what happened (hearsay remember), The LAW was very strict about closing time and if you were caught a minute or two late closing shop, you were certain to land up in court. Storekeepers, unless they were related to the Chief of Police or to the Magistrate, were very careful, for they were frequently caught. This meant a fine of up to twenty-five shillings or seven days in the slammer. What storekeeper would spend some time in the slammer in preference to paying the fine? Phemie was five minutes late closing one day and a policeman nabbed her. The Magistrate fined her ten shillings, which wasn't very smart considering his brother wanted to buy some of her land. I was delivering her tripe one day, and Jock – or was it Rab? No it was Jock – was urging her to sell.

'You getting a rake-off or something?'

'Guid heavens no, Phemie. Whatever made ye think o' that?'

'I'll never sell tae that greedy sonofabitch, and don't you ever mention it again, dae ye hear?' The balding dog rubbed itself on Jock, but this was a moment for discretion, and he had to wait until Phemie's back was turned before he engulfed it in a cloud of nicotine. I would not have been surprised to learn that the dog had become addicted to tobacco. The three old codgers generally agreed with her. Pete said she would be wise to hang on to the property. A penetrating look from Phemie pricked Rab to agree. Then Jock made a monumental blunder.

'I can see it now, Phemie, and I was wrong,' said Jock. 'It would be wise tae hang on to it, for in a few years time it'll be worth a guid lot mair. Aye, on second thoughts, it'll be wise tae keep it, at least until ye get rid o' that dog.'

I thought Phemie was going to blow a gasket.

'What dae ye mean 'until after I get rid o' that dog?'

'Maybe I didnae put it right. I only meant, until you might decide tae... get the vet tae... put him tae sleep.'

'Are ye finished?'

'Well, he is gettin' auld. And.....'
'And..... what?'
'He could have just a wee... touch o' the mange.'
'If he has the mange, he probably got it fae you and yer stinkin' pipe,' Phemie yelled. 'And you get oot o' this shop and don't ever show yer face in here again.' As Jock departed, followed by Phemie's malignant stare, Rab and Pete transferred their pipes to their pockets. Before Jock's banishment, the three codgers were always talking and smoking, sometimes bantering with Phemie. They always stopped abruptly when I entered with the tripe, and this is why. When I started with the butcher, Granta told me to get his tobacco, giving me the money to pay for it. 'There's no use two o' us getting infected,' he said. When I asked for the tobacco, the gum beating stopped. When Phemie asked how Nell was, or how I liked being with the butcher, the symphony of tongues started up again. One day Phemie asked, 'How's your Grandpa?' There was immediate silence. All eyes turned on me. Granta was a popular man and it was gratifying to see how interested these men were in him.

'Couldn't be better,' I said.

The old men didn't look as happy as they should.

'He hasnae been in for some weeks.'

'No, he's busy with the dogs,' I lied.

'And yer Grandma?'

'She's fine.'

'I heard she's been poorly.'

'She's much better now, thanks. She's bearing up pretty well.'

The old men looked happy to hear this, and the orchestra started up again.

'I'll gie ye a bag o' sweeties for yer Grandpa,' she said, reaching into the window. The gums fell silent again.

'Ah - ah, I don't think he likes those,' I said quickly.

'Oh. What kind *does* he like?'

'A few of those, and a few of those,' I said, pointing to the bottles with the glass lids. I got a nice bag of cinnamon balls and some black balls, so both Nell and I had sweeties for the next two days.

Ralph

Tragedy was not far into the future. Granny became very ill and was admitted to hospital, where she died within a week. Mum was more upset than anyone but Granta, on our walks, would hardly say anything. I didn't ask what was wrong with Granny, because she had always cautioned me that 'little boys should be seen and not heard'. Death was something that happened to other families and when it happened to ours, it came as a great surprise to everybody.

The Rev. MacAndrew looked happy when he mentioned what a fine person Granny was, and promised that she was happier than she had ever been. I wondered if there was a place where she could make mince. The Rev. didn't say a word about the pan drops and I was glad he didn't. Granta was miserable enough as it was. It must have been on his mind though.

One Saturday, about two weeks after the funeral, Granta decided to accompany me on my round of delivery. 'I need the exercise and some fresh air,' he announced. Boy, this was like Christmas, having Granta go with me on my rounds.

'I'll get some tobacco at Phemie's,' he said. I was stricken with guilt. I had said nothing about the sweeties Phemie had been giving me for Granta for several weeks, so I decided to make a clean breast of it.

Granta said that it was dishonest and in an earlier age people had been strung up by the thumbs for less. Pretty severe punishment for such a small oversight, I thought. Anyway, I'm glad I didn't live in an earlier age. I must have looked worried though, for Granta said, 'Don't worry about it. I'll tell Phemie they were very enjoyable, but I'll no' say who enjoyed them.' That was the first time I saw Granta smile since Granny died. I - we - delivered the tripe. The old codgers fell silent when we entered the shop.

Phemie fixed them with a drill sergeant's eye and said, 'Buzz off'. The old codgers, working their eyebrows at each other, struggled to their feet and staggered out.

'How are ye bearing up, Harry?' Phemie inquired, searching for clues in his face.

'Well enough, Phemie. Well enough.'

'Ralph,' she cooed, 'would you be a good boy and take the tripe to the cold room?'

I beat it out the back door. When I got back, Granta was sitting on the bench. He looked shaken.

Phemie smiled at me. It was a horrible sight to behold.

'Thank you, Ralph,' she crooned. 'Here is your chocolate.'

I thanked her and Granta rose. As we were leaving, she said, 'Think about it, Harry. That's a' I ask. Think about it.'

'I have thought about it, Phemie,' Granta said, and we left.

We walked in silence for a while, then Granta said, 'I think I'll get ma tobacco at Anderson's from noo on. He never visited Phemie again. I continued to deliver her tripe but she never asked after Granta and she never gave me sweeties for him or chocolate for myself again. I wasn't grief-stricken about it.

Phemie lived for many years after that. I was in the Army when I heard that she had been found dead in her bed. She was hugging a pillow case full of paper money. Her mattress too was partly stuffed with honest lucre. Only one person attended the funeral, her only living relative.

When I heard the story, I felt sorry for the old crone. My grief, however, was slight, momentary and unreflective.

I don't recall ever having heard her name being mentioned again.

OEDIPUS REX

I was close on thirteen, still at school, when I was summoned to appear in Juvenile Court. The charge? Accosting a woman in the street. If you expect something very naughty here, you are in for a disappointment, so just skip this chapter.

Seven years earlier, I had been given a no-nonsense warning by Constable Taylor for urinating in public. For one thing, I didn't know he was watching; for another, as I explained to him truthfully, I couldn't make it to the lavatory inside the picture house. It was jammed with boys of eight, nine, and even ten, who simply pushed the younger or smaller boys aside. Trying to get out was about as difficult as trying to get in. It was at the Saturday afternoon matinee. *Elmo, the Mighty* was the main attraction. It was a serial, and I could hardly wait to see how he would escape certain death. My pocket money was threeha'pence. A penny went towards the cinema and the other ha'penny was squandered on sweeties.

A few of us bought black balls. When we sucked away the outside, which was striped black and white, we got to the inside which was all black. After we had sucked two or three of them, we stuck our tongues out at each other. This brought exclamations of admiration for the blackest tongue. Getting back to the lavatory: that week's instalment of *Elmo*, always last on the programme, ended where Elmo, pursued by a gang of rotten outlaws, was thrown by his horse when it came to a great gorge in whose bowels rushed a mighty torrent of water, boiling and frothing in an incontinent rage. Elmo looked around him hopelessly. Then he noticed a huge tree trunk, about twenty feet long and three feet in diameter at the thin end, and we had to wait until next week to see if he could lift it. As if that wasn't enough, the instalment finished with a sweeping and lengthy panoramic view of the gurgitating cataclysm below. Most of the audience didn't wait for the National Anthem. Instead, there was a mass exodus of young humanity heading with savage determination for the lavatory.

Miraculously, no one was trampled to death and injuries were slight. I fought my way through the seething mass, only to find the last few feet impassable. I battled my way, against the flow, to get outside and into the corner opposite the blacksmith's shop. There, without hesitation, I went.

That was when I heard those damning words, 'Caught ya!' There were about a dozen of us there, and we turned off our taps as soon as we could and buttoned up. Looking up at Constable Taylor was like gazing up at a church spire. We were cornered. We all looked sheepish as Constable Taylor gave us a good dressing down. When he had finished, he stepped aside tight-lipped and frightening as we passed him in funereal procession. Then, when we were out of his line of vision, we ran like hell up Mitchell Street, where we parted without a word, still running.

This time it was different. 'Accosting a Woman in the Street'. Did you ever hear anything so stupid? At thirteen years of age? Perhaps. But not at my age, in our town, at that time, in history. Did I gripe? Surely I griped. Here's what happened: Tom Drysdale (whose father owned a small hardware shop near the bridge, which I knew, even at that early age, never to refer to as 'small') – Tom and I were standing at the corner of Mitchell and High Streets shooting the breeze, when I saw Mum walking towards us on Mitchell Street. She had been visiting Granta at Taydon Cottage and was hurrying home to prepare supper. I recognized Mum right away. Tom didn't. I said, 'Let's hide in this doorway and we'll grab an arm each when she passes.'

'Like hell we will,' answered Tom.

'But it's my Mum!' I chuckled. 'Don't you recognize her?'

'So it is,' answered Tom, peering into the semi-darkness. 'O.K., I'll go as far as the bridge then I'd better get home.'

We hid in a shop doorway. When Mum reached us we grasped an arm each.

'Oh You spalpeens!,' she cried. 'You gave me such a scare.'

Oedipus Rex

No one within a block would have had to strain their ears to hear her as we peppered her with terms of endearment such as: 'Can we see you home, sweetie?' 'What ya doin' tomorrow night, honey?' That sort of thing. That was before 'Come wiz me to ze Casbah'. I'm sure we would have used that too. Mum had a great voice. It wouldn't be described as stentorian exactly, but when she called my younger brother Henry, the two syllables captured both ends of an octave.

'Let go of my arms,' she cried, trying to shake us off. We hung on, ignoring all her protestations until we reached the railway bridge; then we let her go. 'You two had better be on your way before I call the police,' cried Mum in a lion-tamer's voice. Then she added in a more confidential voice, 'Stovies'. 'STOVIES!' I slurped, 'Lovely, lean, pork sausages, in saintly repose on a field of onion rings!'

I glanced at Tom who was drooling. 'And underneath, scads of potatoes, thinly sliced.' Tom wiped his mouth with his sleeve. 'Boy, am I hungry!' he groaned. 'Shut up!' (Mum had taken off around the corner and was now out of sight.) 'I haven't finished yet. Potatoes. Wallowing in a sea of savoury sausage succulence.' Tom raised his fist as if to belt me one in the mouth. He then fled. Took off like a snowball out of hell. I was drooling myself at the thought of stovies for supper when, Wham! I was in the iron grip of a bobby. One huge paw had me by the back of the neck. The other fist held a truncheon at the ready.

'What's up?,' I yelled.

'What's up?' he repeated, shoving me against the wall of a house.

'I asked first,' I answered, pretending not to be scared. That truncheon looked pretty wicked. He produced a notebook and a pencil.

'Don't get smart with me or I'll use this on you.' Wetting the point of his pencil between two pouty lips, then flexing his arm like some monarch about to sign a new Charter of Liberties, he grunted, 'Name?' I told him my name. He jotted it down in his notebook.

'Address?' He scratched that down also. As he scribbled, he mumbled, 'Accosting a lady in the street.'

I exploded. 'That was my mother,' I protested. 'Ask her.'

'I've heard that before. Now then, what's the name of the other man?'

'What man?' I screamed. 'He's a schoolboy, the same as me! Thirteen. What are you gonna do?'

'Tsk tsk tsk tsk tsk. Ever heard of the Borstal Institutions?'

I thought he was just trying to scare me. Nevertheless, I felt my legs turning to jelly. 'You're sixteen if you're a day, and that's where young buggers like you should be. Now, what's the other fellow's name?' I could hardly believe what was happening, but I was beginning to regain control of myself.

'Well!... what's his name?'

'Find out for yourself,' I replied.

'We will,' he said gruffly. 'You will be notified when to appear in Court.' He walked away. I was so bewildered by what had happened in about two minutes or less that I stood for a moment benumbed. I was aware that I looked older than thirteen. Indeed, less than two years after that, a well intentioned lady asked me how my wife was keeping. She was referring to my mother. Right now, I felt about forty. When the policeman was at a safe distance, I yelled, 'I think you escaped from *The Pirates of Penzance*,' then I ran, hell for leather for home.

I told Mum and Dad what had happened. Dad said, 'Don't worry. He was probably only trying to frighten you. However,' he said, 'if you do go to a training school for a couple of years, remember... there will always be a home for you when you get out.'

Mum was more sympathetic. 'A first offence is never more than one year.'

'Very funny,' I said.

Dad added, 'Do you think Granta would bake a cake that will hold a file?'

'Of course he will,' said Mum. 'One big enough to hide a hacksaw in.'

'Right. And on visiting days, we'll smuggle them in.'

'That's very funny, but that policeman wasn't joking,' I grumbled.

The following day, a bobby arrived with a summons for me to appear in Juvenile Court. Dad was not at home. Mum was indignant. The policeman was amused and said it should turn out all right.

When Dad arrived home, he examined the summons. 'This ought to be fun,' he announced. I didn't see it as fun. I was about to be harnessed for the rest of my life with a criminal record.

I have forgotten the magistrate's name. He was a gray-haired man of about sixty, with unblinking blue eyes and long slender fingers. The atmosphere in the court was so quiet and sombre that it was scary. I felt weak. I imagined I heard the strains of *Lohengrin*. The opening bars of *Finlandia* would have been just right to fit in with the magistrate's movements as he mounted the few steps to the bench and plunked himself down on the chair. I suppose that was the beginning of Dad's gramophone records taking possession of me. The magistrate made himself comfortable on the chair, banged his gavel three times on the bench, then rested his elbows in front of him. Pressing the finger tips of each hand on those of the other hand, he viewed us through the spaces. I wondered if he was trying to see how we would look behind bars. Two other boys were tried before me. They had deliberately thrown stones at somebody's window, breaking it, and they were fined enough to replace the glass.

When my turn came, the policeman told his story. I was then asked if I was guilty or not guilty.

I said, 'I'm guilty all right, Sir, but it was my mother.'

Dad interrupted. 'Not guilty, Your Honour.' The magistrate lowered his hands and I felt better.

'Is the lady involved in the court?' he asked. Mum stood up.

'Please remain seated. Are you the boy's mother?'

'Yes, I am.'

'Are you the lady this youth is accused of accosting?'

Mum glared malevolently at the constable.

'I most certainly am,' she announced with a degree of conviction which any judge in his right mind would have accepted as gospel.

'M-hm,' was his only comment. Then he turned to the constable, his caged hands in front of his face again. 'Now, Officer, look searchingly at this – at the accused.'

The Constable gave me a quick glance, then faced the magistrate.

'What did you see?'

'The accused, Your Honour.'

The cage tightened, and for some seconds I couldn't see the magistrate's face. The cage, again. 'Would you say, Officer, that this youth lives a prisoner of an Oedipus Complex?'

The Officer considered this carefully. The magistrate was seeking his opinion. 'That is something on which I would not care to give an opinion, your Honour. However, I have seen the outside of their domicile which is a rental in an eight-family stucco block, situated....'

'Thank you, Officer....'

'south of Union Street....'

'Thank you, thank you,' said the magistrate. Then he covered his face with his hands, lapsing, I suppose, into deep thought.

After a reasonable period of consideration, I surmised he had reached a verdict. Peering at me through the bars again, he asked, 'Young man, what do *you* feel about the Oedipus Complex?'

'Well.... ah....'

'And don't claw your backside.'

'Sorry. Miss MacTavish said....'

'In a court of justice?'

'Amm, what was the question, sir?'

'Do you have an Oedipus Complex?'

I looked at Dad who wagged his head slightly.

'No, Your Honour. I have a bicycle, and pigeons and a dog.'

'What is his name?'

'She's a girl. Nell.'

The magistrate turned his cage on the constable. 'I think, Officer, it behoves you to be more careful with your charges. I think we could have nabbed him on..... well, never mind.'

Turning to Dad, he said, 'Mr McCaa, tell me what *you* think about the Oedipus Complex.'

'In relation to the boy?'

'In relation to anything.'

'Well, I suppose in their early years, many boys have an unconscious response to paternal discipline, but....'

'But?'

'But.... in my son's case, he has so many birds and animals demanding his affection that....'

'Enough,' the magistrate cried. 'Case dismissed. Mr. McCaa, would you be so good as to see me in my chambers - alone? Court is dismissed.'

Dad asked Mum and me to go on home without him. 'I shan't be long,' he said. Mum and I were worried.

'What did he want you for?' I asked when he arrived home.

'He wanted my opinion of a very excellent sherry he had just acquired.'

I didn't know whether to believe Dad or not, but I was glad it was over.

The strangest things happen. On his next visit to Dad, who do you think Doctor Simpson brought with him?

SECONDARY EDUCATION

I didn't like school much. I never could understand algebra. I was also incapable of understanding why anyone else liked algebra. Don't sneer. I know what an isosceles triangle is. Although I had to look up the spelling of isosceles in my dictionary, I can spell desiccator and consanguineous off the cuff. I liked English but Shakespeare was something weird. Shakespeare used words nobody has ever heard of, and at thirteen years of age, I didn't see many of the implications in his allusions. We studied *Julius Caesar*. When I say studied, I really mean memorized. Miss Greigson was very strict. She was also very thorough – about memorizing. It didn't seem to matter very much whether we understood it as long as we memorized it.

When Miss Greigson gave one of us a dressing-down, she showed great consideration for our feelings. Instead of embarrassing us before the whole class, she took us outside where nobody could hear and, for about five minutes, we were told how lazy, shiftless, stupid, delinquent and inconsiderate we were. One exception was Amy Lister. Her verbal assessment lasted little more than a minute. Amy was able to produce tears whenever she wanted to and she would return with a smirk on her face, followed by a slightly concerned Miss Greigson. So Miss Greigson wasn't as hard-boiled as one might think. Her curt commands, however, gave that impression. She never said 'Sit down', or 'stand up'. She said simply 'Stand', 'sit', or 'come'. Whether it had to do with her preoccupation with Shakespeare or her two Dalmations, I don't know. However, she never said 'heel'. She liked me to recite, I think, because I was asked to perform more than anyone else.

'Ralph?' she would say.

Ralph

'Yes, Miss Greigson?'

'Stand.... Take it from 'Friends, Romans, etcetera.'

Then I would recite, 'Friends Romans Countrymen lend me your ears I come to bury Caesar not to praise him the evil that men do lives after them the good is oft interred with their bones so let it be with Caesar.'

'Thank you, Ralph. Sit.' I didn't have to memorize beyond this point because she always stopped me. Once in a while, another teacher would enter to tell her that the Headmaster would like to see her. That was good for six and a half minutes or more. When we were sure that she was well on her way, all hell broke loose. I or Pete Forsythe, who was also good at memorizing, would stand on our desks and declaim, 'Friends Romans Countrymen lend me your ears,' whereupon six or eight boys would try to unscrew their ears, urging us to accept them. We would pocket some of them, rejecting those with a nasty smell or those that were too limp. The girls liked our performances; some would applaud and we would take a bow. The girls never participated as actors, which puzzles me now, seeing that nine out of ten members of amateur drama groups are female. They were a good bunch though. None of them snitched. I think, in retrospect, Julius Caesar would have appreciated us - as lion fodder.

Despite this buffoonery, I was somewhat introversive. I didn't care for team games, which seemed unproductive, uncreative and, in many cases, too violent. While I didn't think of participation in sports in these terms, I simply had other interests. My disinclination to enter into the field of sports landed me then, and later, in lots of trouble. Arguments over my refusal to participate ended occasionally in fist fights. Apart from the time I burst George Lane's gumboil.

I never hit anyone first. It was a mystery to me why anyone believed that pushing or hitting me would induce me to do something in which I had no interest. When attacked, it usually ended in retaliation. Then my aim was to draw blood. Nothing ended a fight like the sight of blood. Unfortunately, instead of reducing the number of challengers, others were stimulated to become the ones to clobber me. Generally, these gladiators were older or bigger boys than me. One warrior, well known as a bully, shoved me hard, which made me stagger back and fall over my own feet. He was a good head taller than I and maybe thirty pounds heavier. He came at me again, his arms outstretched. He had a longer reach than I, so I kicked him in the groin. He fell in a heap, screaming and holding his groin. George Lane, who was in the audience, said, 'That was a goal, Ralph. I'd like you on our team.' Most of the audience were grinning. No one tried to help the bully. Then they wandered off. I felt like helping him to his feet but his eyes were not in the least friendly, so I left him where he was. I mentioned this to George who said, 'If someone kicked you in the goolies, how would *you* feel?' I understood. During my short time at school after that, I was never challenged again by any boys.

I was, however, a favourite target of our history teacher. He was a couple of inches shorter than me and not, in my opinion, a good teacher. I was involved in *his* history to some extent. He was the most prolific exponent of flatulence I have ever known, and a master at covering it up. Out of class, some of the boys referred to him as 'Old Thunderbum'. The crude word for flatulence was never mentioned in our house and, while my parents were not guilty of prudery or over-fastidiousness, 'that' was referred to with the enigmatic and inoffensive name of 'pumping'.

We were educated not to 'pump' in company. We were not forbidden to 'pump' at all, so the instruction was not unreasonable. Having clarified the parity between flatulence and pumping, I shall now refer to our history teacher's dexterity in the act of 'pumping'.

We always knew when it was about to happen. He raised his taws or, if you prefer it, leather strap, high above his head and as he pumped, he brought it down on his desk with a loud bang. He tried, sometimes unsuccessfully, to synchronize the two with vocal emphasis on a word or phrase. Success resulted in only a few smiles. Miscalculation brought a few barely concealed giggles. On one occasion he erred in his timing so painfully, it kindled a ripple of giggles impossible to conceal. I was not one of the gigglers. Maybe I grinned, for he rushed straight for me in the second back row of desks. Raising his strap above his head, he brought it down with force. I bent my body to the left in order to avoid the impact, and it caught me across the right ear. My head was ringing. Tears welled in my eyes; not tears of self pity but tears of anger. I rose and glared at him. He looked appalled at what had happened. I am willing to believe that it was meant for my back. I ran from the classroom.

'Come back here,' I heard him shout as I ran. It was nearly lunch time so I went home. Mum said, 'You're early?'

I told her what had happened. She was angry but she asked me what I had done.

'Nothing,' I told her. 'He just picked on me.'

'Wait until your father gets home, then maybe you'll tell him what you were up to,' Mum said.

'That'll be too late. I'm going to the police,' I said, and ran out of the house.

Guess who was minding the store? Oedipus – alone.

'Run along, sonny,' he said, without letting me finish my account of the incident. 'You must have deserved it.'

Lunch time was nearly over. There was no use going to the Headmaster. He was always in agreement with the teachers. I trudged back to school to find the classes lining up outside, ready to march inside in columns of twos. Three or four teachers were stationed outside to direct the classes when to move. It wasn't difficult to slip past the teachers outside. Our history teacher was not outside so he must be in the classroom to make sure we didn't get up to any high jinks. The classroom was empty. A few moments later he arrived. I have now and again wondered what would have happened if he had said something like, 'Ralph, I'm sorry I caught you across the ear with my strap. It was meant for your back, which would not have hurt you. It won't happen again.' We shall never know. What he said was, 'What are you doing here, boy? Get outside with the rest of the class.'

Before he spoke, I was more than a little afraid and felt like running. Instead, his attitude triggered new resentment which turned to anger. It could happen again, by God! I grabbed him by the throat and backed him up against the blackboard. Clenching the fist of my other hand, I said quietly, 'If ever you hit me again, you maggot, I'll bash your nose.'

His face turned grey and he slid to the floor in a sitting position, his back against the wall. I ran outside and joined the class which was on its way in. We filed in and took our seats. The teacher was sitting where I had left him. Two of the girls rushed to him.

'Are you all right, Sir?' one of the girls asked. He didn't answer.

They helped him over to his desk where he sat for a moment in silence. He didn't become his usual loud-mouthed self for several days, and he never looked me in the eye again. Funny thing, too. He never 'pumped' again.

WORK - INITIATION

I had been with the butcher for three years. Besides putting on some weight, owing to the generous nature of my employer, I had stretched considerably. Mr Douglas was very generous and when sales were low on certain items, he would wrap a few of them in a wax paper for me to take home. This bounty was, in fact, enough to enable my mother to dispense with the necessity of buying any extra meat for our small family.

My Uncles Bob and Henry were both miners, and they assured me that if I got into the coal mines I would never be out of work. I didn't like school anyway, so I worked on my parents to let me leave and go into the coal pits. They were not at all keen. Dad was out of work temporarily, and if I got special exemption to quit school - for I was only thirteen and a half years of age - there would be no more free packages of meat. It wasn't easy, but I persuaded my parents to apply for my termination of schooling because of hardship. It wasn't long before I realized this was one of the greatest mistakes in my life. It was not pleasant work; not nearly as pleasant as working for the butcher, and there were no more free lunches, so to speak, although I always got a bargain when I shopped for meat. I was now getting ten shillings a week in place of the butcher's five shillings. This made the change a rotten move, because I had been taking home free, more than five shillings' worth of meats. It was against the law for anyone under the age of fourteen to go down the pits, so for six months I worked on the pit head, where I handled tubs, or small waggons in which the miners dumped their coal. The coal was then thrown on to a conveyer belt which disappeared into a wired-in cage. Here several girls 'sorted', that is, they picked out any 'red' or rocks from the coal, which was tipped mechanically into a railway truck. Where I worked, there were six girls – well they were shaped like girls, but they were monsters in disguise. I am not going to pretend the cage in which they were imprisoned for several hours had anything to do with their species; the cage was rather to keep out any horny stallions who could not resist the liberal invitations with which they were, from time to time, bombarded. At a dance, or indeed, almost at any time outside the cage, they were like girls; inside the cage, monsters.

I had been there two days when one of them cried, 'Hey, kid. C'mere.'

I went over to the gate.

'Push the gate. It's open.'

I wondered.... no. No. I sensed danger, but I had no idea what sort of danger, so I pushed open the gate which swung shut on a spring. 'Yes, what is it?' I asked.

'How old are you, sonny?'

'Why?'

They exchanged grins and they had closed me off from the gate.

Four of the girls backed me into a corner and, without warning, yanked open my fly. I was close to panic. Two monsters grabbed an arm each and kicked the feet from under me. In a flash I was on my back. The other two rushed in and pinned a leg each to the ground. They were strong. I struggled helplessly. 'What are they going to do?' I wondered. 'Are they going to rape me?' At thirteen and a half, I was still uninitiated. Number five started groping and in half a trice she had me out, naked for all the world to see.

'Not bad,' sniggered Monster Six. 'I'm gonna keep an eye on this one. How old do you say you are?'

'I didn't say,' I yelled. 'You let me go or I'll... I'll...'

'You'll what?,' asked Monster five, grinning. Then I saw Monster six coming towards me. Now, it was all clear. She had a short stick in one hand. One end of the stick was covered with about two pounds of axle grease. I was about to become the victim of a ritual which all, or nearly all, of the young fellows were subjected to, sometimes on their first day on the pit head. I was desperate and, frankly, terrified. Monster Number

Work - Initiation

Six, the one with the grease, shouted 'Bull's eye,' and took aim. A split second before she connected, I jerked my right leg free and kicked. It caught her in the stomach and she lay there, moaning and holding her belly. When she didn't get up, the loud guffaws from the others changed to oaths. Two of them rushed to the assistance of the stricken monster whilst one still held on grimly to the pinioned leg.

'Let go!' I yelled, pointing a menacing finger at her.

She started to unscrew the foot from my leg. This was my only chance of escape and the pain was excruciating. Pulling both legs in to me, I drove my free foot square into her mouth. I realize this was a terrible thing to do and I am not proud of it. It was a purely reflex action. If I had it to do again, I would certainly not have kicked her in the face. I would have mashed her abdomen. Anyway, it dislodged her grip and I fled with my loose bits showing. Only when I was outside the cage doing up my fly, did I realize that I had an audience. One man shouted, 'You're lucky, kid. You're the first one I seen got away.' I glanced back at the monsters. The one I had wounded in the mouth was sitting looking at the blood on her hand. They all seemed to be yelling at the same time. I had heard their language before, but never as loud. One of the older spectators said, 'You're not out of the woods yet, kid. Better make a run for it.' I followed his gaze towards the cage, where the monsters were making for the gate, then I followed his advice and fled.

I had no more trouble with the bare sex, and while it was a miserable drag on the pit head, it seemed to have passed quickly enough and it was time to go below. I became articled, though perhaps that is not the correct term – apprenticed to a contractor who had a gang of men working the coal face. My job was to keep them supplied with empty 'tubs' and to keep the full ones on the move to the pit bottom.

A pit, in case you don't know, goes straight down; a mine travels into the earth's bowels at an angle. The earth's bowels, though not structured in any way similar to the human counterpart, is, nevertheless, just as hot and wet, and I see no reason why it should not be referred to as bowels. The difference to be emphasised is that where our bowels absorb nourishment, the earth's bowels discharge nutrients in the form of cool, clear, delectable and irresistibly seductive water, seeping, sometimes gushing, from its ruptured canals. After a shift of eight hours, especially then, these fountains, sweeter than a mother's milk to any infant whether it be endowed with two or four legs, gratified a thirst eager to be quenched, in spite of the certainty that a crop of boils would follow. We got boils on our arms and boils on our tum, boils on the neck, sometimes boils up the lum. And that was when it really hurt. Many a miner has eaten his dinner standing up.

Ours was a pit. Where I worked, we were not allowed carbide lamps, which shot a jet of naked gas from the centre of your forehead. Instead, we were supplied with electric lamps, the heads of which were attached to our caps, and from the light a cable three or four feet in length connected with batteries which we attached to our waist belts. One day – it may have been a prank of my younger brother, or maybe it was a leftover from Halloween – when I opened my piece-box for the usual inspection, there lay a packet of sweetie cigarettes. These cigs were half as thick as a real fag, and were in a wrapper which resembled a packet of Woodbines. It was routine, where there was gas present, or the possibility of the presence of gas, to make a search of our piece boxes for matches or cigarettes. On the day shift we were searched by Callipers. I cannot remember his family name, and I doubt if Callipers, the moniker by which he was referred to but never addressed, was his baptismal name. Rather, he acquired the appellation because his legs were curved like two bananas. It wouldn't have surprised me if they had looked like two bananas, because his head resembled, as near as it is possible for a human head to resemble, a watermelon. It was large, bald and shiny, but of a different colour. His watermelon was red, but not as red as mine that day. Upon the unmasking of the villainy, Callipers pounced.

'Ahhh-ha,' he cried, reeling away from the murderous box in terror, but not before he managed to nip the packet of sweetie cigarettes from the box and dangle it at armslength for everyone's inspection.

'What have we here? What, pray, do I behold?' He was dramatic if nothing else. 'What pray, upon my soul? Indeed, indeed!' – stuff like that. As for myself, I was mortified; speechless. Callipers wasn't speechless.

Work - Initiation

I truly disliked violence, but at that moment I would have liked to knock him speechless. Then came his pièce de résistance:

'I... am... non... plussed.'

In fact his favourite condition was being nonplussed. On this occasion, he managed to hold on to his sanity until he was nonplussed, after which he returned the wretched felon to its lair. With trembling fingers, Callipers dropped it, withdrawing his arm with lightning speed and staggering back against the wall. In the gale of laughter which followed his act I said, 'Get stuffed.' His burlesque terminated with unexpected suddenness.

'What? What? What's that?' he cried. The mood changed.

'What did you say to me?' I had no desire to make an enemy of him.

'I said, "that's tough".' His face was saved, but he wasn't finished with me yet.

'Tell you what,' he cooed. ' I have a four year-old grandson, a real loveable little bugger. You give me a half of them for the kid and I won't report you to the management this time.'

I wondered if his grandson had callipers like Callipers' callipers. He ran his hands over my pockets.

'You can take them with you,' he said. 'I'll trust you not to smoke them.' Actually, there were a couple of men who did smoke in the forbidden area. They didn't carry matches, but managed to secrete cigarettes, which wasn't really difficult. They got a light by placing a thin wire across the battery of their safety lamps, creating a short circuit which turned the wire red hot. It gave me the willies when I thought of what might have happened had there been a sudden upsurge in the gas content of the atmosphere. No, I didn't snitch, nor did any of the others as far as I know. What should I have done? It could have been a matter of life and death. I could have given them one warning: 'Stop, or I report it.' Forgive me or condemn me. I was a few weeks over fourteen years of age.

THE COALHEAVERS

The two smokers were brothers. They were not very much alike except in nature: they liked to torture someone they thought couldn't or wouldn't retaliate. They were, I would guess, eighteen and twenty and they chose me as a target for their amusement. At noon we all stopped for lunch. The brothers would disappear to some spot out of sight for their smoke, not too distant from me but well away from the coal face. For some reason, they didn't make much effort to hide their illegal and dangerous antics from me entirely. After they had satisfied their appetite for nicotine, they sat beside me. One day they chose to sit either side of me, at a distance of some twenty feet. One spoke so as to draw my attention away from the other, who then threw a small lump of coal at me. Then, when I turned to face the pitcher, the other threw a chunk of coal. I couldn't catch either of them at it, but it could be no one else. After five or six lumps had been fired, I had had enough.

'You're asking for trouble, both of you,' I said.

'What did we do?' said one.

'Are you threatening us?' growled the other.

'That's right,' I replied. 'I'm threatening you.'

A couple more pieces were thrown. One landed near me, the other hit me. I said nothing but moved off. That evening, I had to know if I was as accurate as I was when I was nine and ten years old. Taking an empty can down to the beach, I found that I could hit it almost as well as I had ever done. I put in a half hour's practice.

I saw a bottle bobbing about in the water but, tempted as I was, I refrained from smashing it. Someone might walk on it at low tide.

The next day I collected several chunks of coal and at lunch time I sat beside them. Sure enough, they took up positions. The battle was about to begin. If I were an army commander, I would never be caught with both flanks exposed. The enemy's arsenal was not lethal, nor was it meant to be. Mine could be, but it was not intended to be. Klunk! A chunk landed on my left and I obligingly looked at it.

'Boy, I hope there isn't going to be a cave in,' said the right flank.

'I hope not,' I answered, looking at the roof 'Do you remember, yesterday I gave you a warning?'

My remark was met with loud laughter. Another chunk of coal landed at my feet. Then another from the opposite side. One of them must have adjusted his sights, for the next one caught me on the shoulder. I rose quietly, picked up two anthracite cannon balls, and took aim. It hit one of them on the side of the head as he turned away.

Screaming revenge, he jumped up and was about to rush me but my raised arm stopped him. Turning abruptly, I was facing his brother rushing at me. My second shot parted his moustache and he dropped. I grabbed two more hunks of coal and faced the other one who was on his way towards me.

'I never miss,' I cried.

If he had been on a tether four feet from me, he couldn't have stopped more extempore. The upper half, that is. The lower half, conforming to the laws of compulsive energy, continued on its course, dragging the lower portion of the upper half, namely his butt, along the ground. It was pretty rough, and despite the weight and stability of the moleskins he was wearing, it hurt. With no intention of prolonging the battle, I lifted my arm above my head as if to bash his head in with my remaining ammunition.

'No! No, don't!' he yelled, scrambling to his feet.

Both of them left the field of battle cursing and vowing that this was not the last of it. That evening, I went round to Henry's house and told him what had happened.

'That's serious,' he said.

'They threw rocks. I threw rocks.'

'If they report you, you're finished in the coal mines.'

'In that coal mine?'
'In every coal mine. You'll be blacklisted.'
'They threw first.'
'It's two against one. Besides, even if you are believed, they would say it was a game. A bit of fun, chipping little bits of coal at each other. You lost your temper.'
'Hell, whose side are you on?'
'Cool it, kid. And watch out for the hot lamp.'
'What's that?'
'Two fellows sit together, then one of them moves off, he may even sit beside you. He leaves his lamp beside the other man's...'
'So?'
'The other twerp still sitting, directs the flame of his lamp on the handle of the other.'
'And?'
'And you are asked to bring it over. Naturally, you grab it by the handle.'
'Well, thanks, Henry, but it can't happen where I am.'
'Why not?'
'Because we don't use naked flames in the Circle Dook.'
'The Circle Dook is gas free. Has been for 6 months. Next month you...'
'Are you shooting me a line?'
'It'll happen. Don't forget I warned you. Be... careful.'
'Thanks. I'd better be going.'
'Just a minute, Ralph. When are you going to join the Club?'
Henry was an athlete, mainly a weight lifter. He was also a fairly good boxer. He managed the Club and he had been at me before to join.
'I don't want to box,' I said.
'It would be a good thing if you learned how to defend yourself.'
'Well, thanks, but no thanks. I don't want to fight. Goodnight.'
As I left, Henry cried after me, 'Have a word with George.'
No more trouble with those two, I thought. How wrong I was.
About a month passed without incident, then one day at lunch, when

we were using carbide or tallow lamps, they sat opposite me. After they had eaten, one of them rose and came over to me. 'Hey, man,' he said, grinning and offering his hand, 'No hard feelings, eh?' He sat beside me, talking about soccer, that sort of thing. I lost my appetite. Something was wrong. It was a gut feeling. When I finished eating, I closed my lunch box and rose.

'Hey, Ralph, now you're on your feet, do you mind handing me my lamp - right over there.' So, this was it. I went across to the other one. The lamps were close together. Too close. Before I got too near, the other goon lifted the lamp and held it out to me, handle facing me. Grasping the lamp by the top half, I felt the heat from the handle. Taking it across to the owner, 'Here's your lamp,' I said cheerfully, shoving it close to his face. He bent over, covering his face with one hand, palm outward. I jabbed the handle into the palm of his hand and held it there. He screamed and leapt to his feet. The lamp seemed to stick to his hand for a moment.

His accomplice rushed to his aid. I skedaddled. This was no time for a showdown at the old Circle Dook. As I disappeared into the twilight to the accompaniment of oaths, outrage and threats of retribution, I was not happy with the outcome, but I did to them only what they had intended to do to me.

Henry was at the gymnasium that evening. It seemed appropriate that I tell him what had happened, so I went there. He listened in silence, then he said, 'They haven't finished with you yet.'

I felt my insides turning over. 'What'll they do?'

'I don't know. But you should come here and learn how to defend yourself. Have a talk with George. There he is now. C'mere George.'

Only two days before, George and I had gone fishing for mackerel from the jetty and he had urged me to join the Club.

'What kept you?' said George, grinning. 'Hey, fellas, this is Ralph McCaa. He's my chum, so make him welcome.'

'Now, hold on, George. I just came here to talk to Henry.'

'Oh.' George was obviously disappointed. Turning to some of the younger members who had come over to make me welcome, George said,

The Coalheavers

'Sic 'im.' A couple of them growled like angry dogs and pulled snarling faces. 'Okay, down boys, down,' cried George, shielding me with his body against menacing natives.

I said, 'Look, George, all this clowning isn't....'

Henry stepped in with his dry patter. He said to George, 'I've just been telling Ralph he should learn to defend himself.'

'He's right,' said George, 'and if anyone bothers you, you can knock his block off.'

'But George, I don't want to knock anybody's block off. And I can defend myself just fine, thank you.'

'Okay, Ralph... hit me.'

'I don't want to hit anybody, except you, maybe,' I said, grinning at Henry.

'Why me?'

'Because you keep nagging me about joining the Club.'

Henry was only five feet nine, but he was built like a bull. He was wearing oversize boxing gloves. Henry rarely smiled, but now his face crumpled into a diabolic yet comical smile. So, that is what he looks like when he smiles, I mused. A few titters told me that mine was not an isolated surprise.

'Put the gloves on him, George,' Henry ordered.

'They look like pillows,' I objected.

'That is what they are called,' George said, fitting me with the gloves. Henry was ready. 'O.K., Ralph. Hit me.'

'How can I miss?'

'Try not to miss.'

'You asked for it,' I answered. 'Well, put 'em up.'

'I don't have to,' Henry answered. 'Hit me.'

I swiped and missed. I swiped again and missed again. Henry looked bored. 'How can I hit you when you don't stand still?' I griped.

'All right,' he said, crouching. 'I'll hit you. Defend yourself.'

He connected with a right hook to my jaw. I swiped again. Missed again. Henry let me have one to the right jaw. It wasn't really hard, just humiliating. It made me nervous and, I confess, a trifle irked when he was able to do this and I wasn't able to make contact even once. I swiped three times and missed three times.

I felt like a dinosaur trying to connect with a weasel.

Henry wagged his head in sympathy.

'I'll help you,' he said. 'here's my jaw.' He thrust out his jaw, letting his hands hang loosely by his sides. 'Now, hit me.'

This is it, I thought. Without warning, I brought up a torpedo. He pulled in his head several inches. My torpedo whirled me around in a full circle and I landed on the floor.

Everybody, led by George and Henry, laughed like a pack of hyenas.

'Take off these pillows and I'll show you,' I growled.

'No can do. I might hurt you,' Henry replied. 'You know, Ralph, those blockbusters you bring up from behind your backside aren't any good except in Western movies.'

'O.K. You win. Teach me.'

George said, 'You've just had your first lesson.'

Then Henry rubbed my face in it. He said, 'You may not believe it, kid, but I could hit you three or four times before you got that club within a foot of me.'

'The hell you can. Give me lighter gloves.'

'George, fit him with lighter gloves.'

Sheer bravado, impudence made me say that, but it was too late to withdraw. The laughing hyenas were gathering round as George fitted me with match gloves. Henry kept his pillows. He wasn't smiling now.

'Ready, Dummy?' he grunted. He crouched behind his gloves and looked more menacing than before. He seemed to have disappeared behind the leather. I tried to copy his stance, but it wasn't comfortable.

'Stop shuffling about and try to hit me,' he said, jabbing me on the shoulder.

'This time I won't miss,' I thought. Bringing up my torpedo for a knockout delivery, I ran into a storm, staggered by a rat-tat-tat between the eyes. I had just inherited the promised settlement. I staggered back, blinking and slightly stupefied. Then I got Henry's face in focus, only a few inches from mine. He blew on me, like blowing out a match, and at

The Coalheavers

the same time he gave me a slight push on the chest. I staggered back, losing my balance, then landed on my backside on the floor. As the fuzziness in my head was clearing, I heard laughter. What could I do? I waved my arms across each other, indicating I had had enough, and joined in the merriment.

On my way home with George, I told him about the coal throwing and the lamps. 'You'll meet them everywhere,' said George.

'What happened, George? When I was a kid I hated lots of people, other kids, but that was child's hate; not real hate. Now, I don't hate anybody. There are some people I don't like. And if someone picks on me, I retaliate.'

'They're bullies, Ralph. Generally, when they are alone, you'll have no more trouble. However, when they pair up, two against one...'

'Are you working on me again?'

'Stay with the other men. Go in with them, leave with them. Stay with the group until you get on the tram. That way, you'll be safe. Safer.'

'Oh, for heaven's sake, George, I've told you a hundred times, I'm not interested in joining your lousy Club. When do you go there?'

'I'll pick you up on Thursday. Goodnight, Ralph.'

'Hmm.'

BETTY BLUE-DRESS AND SARAH

At fifteen, time stands still. I still had Nell. I still went for walks with Granta but he seemed to be failing. In the past five or six years he had become more frail and he staggered a little. He was an auction addict and occasionally I accompanied him to the auctions, which were held each week. My thoughts were racing over events far removed from dancing. Far removed from boxing and the coal pit. Most thoughts were happy, some of them were sad. A whole long life, in a period where measurement of time stood still.

I laughed aloud when I thought of the last time I had accompanied Granta to the auction room. He had bought a carpet which I helped him carry home. He had retired and lived alone in a small, two-bedroom cottage.

'Where do you want it, Grant?' I asked when we got home.

'In that bedroom,' he said, pointing.

It was like walking on an upholstered floor. There were already five carpets on the floor, the edges of which were about eighteen inches from the door. We had to squeeze through.

'What do you want with *another* carpet?'

'It was a bargain. Help me move the bed.'

It took a bit of doing, but eventually we got the sixth carpet colonized. At that sale, the youngster who held up various items for inspection had waved a white chamber pot in the air.

'This,' cried the auctioneer, 'is a genuwine antique poe, used exclusively by Queen Anne Boleyn, who carried it with her everywhere she went. What am I bid?... Let's start at a shilling. ...Sixpence...?'

'Tuppence!' one woman cried.

The auctioneer gave her a withering look. 'Missus,' he said, 'you'll never clap your backside in this for tuppence.' He got threepence.

A little later. 'Now we have a sexual table.'

'Where's the mattress?' cried one man.

'There's an end table coming up later,' shouted the auctioneer.

I never knew whether this was rehearsed or not, but it was hilarious.

Granta had stopped breeding dogs but he kept one for himself, a Scottie called Tam. Tam had provided several bitches with handsome pups and Granta was very fond of him. I still had Nell, and the two dogs got along very well together. They fell in love now and then, but Granta's antipathy towards an imperfect harvest thwarted their designs.

Accompanied by George, I went to the Club on Tuesdays and Thursdays but I saw little of him otherwise. George played soccer and liked to be with crowds. I didn't care for team sports, nor did I crave the company of lots of people. It came to me in a flash, I think, that I was a loner. I was never lonely. I just liked to be alone much of the time. The men at the Club were a friendly bunch but they were all older than George and me and they were very attentive when Henry instructed them. Friendly, noisy and jocular outside the ring, inside the ropes they were assassins, machines.

Henry started my training with stance, how to move about without losing my balance. Skipping and shadow boxing were part of the exercises. He taught me how to bob and weave, how to spring out of a crouch, and how to jab at a defenceless bag with my left. I was getting bored with all this workout and I said so. I would like a sparring partner.

'Ask all the questions you like,' said Henry, 'but don't presume to give me advice and don't challenge my answers. It won't be long before you are going to be sorry.'

Was this a threat? I wondered. One evening, without warning, Henry said, 'George, bandage Ralph's hands and your own and wrap him up.' I was wrapped up all right. Headguard, mouthpiece, six-ounce gloves. I donned the works. It wasn't long before I *got* the works.

George was rigged out in the same way and he was weaving about like a ping-pong ball with the hiccough.

'O.K., George, you know what to do. I'll referee.' We climbed over the ropes. No more torpedoes. That was a thing of the past. I wouldn't hurt George, though. He was my friend. 'Shake hands! Into your corners! Box!' were Henry's crisp commands. I went after George, but he was slippery as a fish. If I could just make contact, but he kept backing away. His gloves were everywhere I aimed.

'Break!' cried Henry. 'How do you feel, Ralph?'

'I would have got him if you hadn't stopped us,' I said.

'You think so?'

'Yes, I think so.'

'Your confidence exceeds your ability. George, you had better floor him. Try not to hurt him. Corners! Box!'

George came at me like a bullet. Jab, jab. Right cross, left hook to my ribs. Crouching, I managed to block a few, but I was being pasted. My head, my ribs, everywhere. George had ten arms. The blows stopped. Now I counter-attacked. I straightened out of my protective crouch and got a solid one on the side of my head. I hit the deck with a thud, dazed. Looking up through my woosiness, I was aware that George and Henry were helping me up to my feet.

'That's it. Next time you'll do better,' Henry said, and he walked away. On our way home I said to George, 'That was a helluva pasting you gave me.'

'Just think, Ralph, the mess you would have been in without protection.'

'Without the headgear, yes.'

'That, and if we weren't friends and if Henry hadn't been referee.'

'There are an awful lot of 'ifs'.'

'Another year and you'll be able to take care of yourself,' George said.

'Are they all as good as you, George?'

'Henry would say not. He says I have the killer instinct.'

'Have I got it?' George didn't answer. 'Well, have I?'

'No. ...But you will be able to take care of any two louts who want to take you on – outside the ring.'

'Without a frying pan?'

'Without a frying pan. Say, what are you doing on Saturday?'

Ralph

'Nothing in particular.'
'Like to come dancing?'
'Where?'
'The Palais de Dance.'
'With girls?'
'What do you think? Shorthorn stots?'
'I've never tried dancing.'
'With shorthorn stots?'
'Those, too. And girls. ...I'll think about it.'
'Ralph, how old are you?'
'Fifteen and a half.'
'Hey, psst.' He motioned me to hear something in confidence. I bent my ear to him. 'You don't have to sleep with them. Just dance.' I raised my fist in mock answer. 'I don't know. I... '
'Fine. We'll pick you up at seven. A bunch of us all go together.'

On Saturday I went to the Palais de Dance with George and four others, two of whom I knew at school. It was one of the most miserable evenings I ever spent. The entrance to the dance hall was festooned with signs. 'Ties Must Be Worn.' 'Dancing in Shirtsleeves is not Permitted.' 'Objectionable Language will Not be Tolerated.' 'Anyone Breaking these Rules will be Ejected.' I supposed that meant he or she would be kicked out. Whether one had to break all the rules or just one of them, I never found out. Another sign, more prominently displayed, read: 'Anyone Fighting Will be Ejected and Will not be Allowed Back in Future.' Again, I supposed they meant 'any two or more persons fighting.' I was being picky – perhaps it was my mood. This being my first visit to a ballroom, I said I would like to sit and watch. The male of the species wandered over to the females and nodded towards the floor. The lady would then rise, indicating acceptance, or she would decline the invitation by a negative shake of the head, whereupon the man would give someone else the nod.

George was a real killer on the floor. He had style. He could glide like Caesar Romero and dip like Rudolph Valentino. The dip came at the end of the dance. Their eyes met as the lady was bent over backwards and the man hovered above her. I bet if the management could have read what George was thinking, he would have been 'ejected' and not allowed back in future. George urged me to get up and dance. I wasn't keen but he insisted.

'That one over there is a terrific dancer,' he said pointing.

'Where? ... Oh, yes. Suppose she doesn't want to dance?'

'Then try somebody else.'

He pulled me up by an arm and I stood there like a wet leek. It was a nerve-wracking moment. The orchestra started up – weeeeeh.

'The one in the blue dress. Go on,' said George, giving me a shove.

I sauntered over to the blue dress as nonchalantly as I could and nodded. Stony-faced, she rose and we stepped on to the dancing area. I didn't think it was my fault that two road hogs peppered into me and landed on the floor. I helped the lady up and the man, who had scrambled to his feet, raised a fist and was about to drive it in my direction. I pointed to the 'no fighting' sign and he changed his mind. Blue-Dress didn't bat an eye. I slipped my left arm around her waist and was reaching for her left hand with my right. She removed my left arm and pulled my right one around her waist.

'I'm sorry, I'm not very good at this,' I murmured. 'Do we shove off now?' She looked slightly stricken. We took a few steps and I trod on her toes. 'OW!,' she cried and left me standing alone.

I was in a state of near shock. A couple of dancers bumped into me. The lady glared as though I had assaulted her. The man said, 'What's the matter, buddy – you lost?' I apologized and threaded my way back to where I had been sitting. Nothing would induce me to try it again. I looked over at Blue-Dress. She was smiling at a young man standing beside her. She rose and they danced away together, to get lost on the crowded floor.

When the dance was over, George joined me. 'I saw what happened,' he grinned. 'You found it funny?' I snapped back.

'Listen, Ralph, next dance I'll be the girl; you are the man. You'll soon get the hang of it.'

'Are you out of your mind?'

Ralph

'I didn't know you were a quitter, Ralph.' That remark bothered me.

'I'm not a quitter, but two fellas dancing together! You're crazy.'

'We all start that way. It's just until you get the hang of it. By the way, I'm glad you didn't tangle with that chap.'

'Lucky for him that sign was there.'

'Lucky for both of you,' said George with a smug grin. 'That was Lenny Cassiday.'

'Len... you mean... '

'Yeah. I mean the Welter Weight contender.' The orchestra had started up. I was so flustered I didn't realize that I was on the floor with George as a partner.

'For God's sake, George!'

'Just until you get the hang of it.'

'They'll throw us out.'

'No, they won't.'

I kept looking about me to see if everybody was laughing at us. Nobody seemed to be aware of our existence. Then one bruiser came over and put a great hand on George's shoulder.

'Ya gotta dance with the women,' he growled.

George explained that this was my first time and he was teaching me.

'Well, make it fast. I'll be keeping an eye on yous pair,' he said.

On the journey home, George said he would teach me some of the steps and rhythms before next Saturday. Then I could dance with girls.

'There won't be any "next Saturday",' I told him.

We came to Toni's Fish and Chip Gardens. It was years since I had been there. 'We always stop here for something to eat,' said George. I had just enough to buy some chips. My pay from the pit always went to the house, except for half a crown which I kept for pocket money. After buying feed for the pigeons, there wasn't a lot left.

'We eat it on the way home,' George informed me. 'It costs more if you sit down and it's a crummy place anyway.'

The Gardens had changed. It didn't look as inviting as it had last time I was there. The odour of fish and chips, though not unpleasant, was overpowering. I wondered if the flypapers were the same ones that were there nine years ago, they were so thick with flies. The music was deafening, competing unsuccessfully with the babble of voices of customers gulping down mounds of food. People bumped into me without apology. Prices had risen. I bought a few chips. On the journey home we were a noisy bunch.

'Do you fellows ever take girls home?' I asked.

'No,' said Jacko Jackson. 'You take 'em home and they think they're engaged.'

'Or they want to go steady,' added Curly Carlson.

'And if you don't, you're likely to get a black eye,' said Andy Laing.

'Like the one Jacko got,' George chuckled.

'I did not,' Jacko shouted.

'That's right, Jacko. She bit your lip, didn't she?' said George.

'Why didn't you bite her back?' I suggested.

'How would you like to have your mug rearranged?' Jacko answered.

'Easy Jacko,' George warned him. 'This lad's a tiger at the gym.'

We bantered a lot like this on the way home. As we neared our respective destinations, we peeled off in ones and twos. When we were alone, George said, 'Sorry you're going to quit, Ralph.'

'I didn't say I was going to quit,' I retorted.

'Maybe not in so many words... but it's obvious.'

'I don't see anything obvious about it.'

'You're a natural for ballroom dancing, but forget it.'

'The one in the blue dress. What's her name anyway?'

'Betty.' 'Betty what?' 'I don't know. Just Betty is all I know.'

'Betty Blue-Dress, eh? Well, Betty Blue-Dress is gonna ask me to dance sometime in the future, then I'm going to turn her down.'

'That's the spirit, Ralphee. But I don't think you have the guts.'

'Don't you?'

'No, I don't believe *you* have the guts.'

That devil was baiting me and I couldn't back out.

'You teach me the steps,' I said gruffly.

'Goodnight, Ralph.'

'Goodnight, George.'

Ralph

Gotcha, I said to myself after he had gone. I had managed to bait him to bait me. ... I think.

On Tuesday at the gym, George was slow to shower and change after practice. 'Are you going to stay all night George?' Henry asked.

'You go on home and I'll lock up, Henry. Ralph'll wait for me. O.K.?'

'O.K., but make sure the door is properly locked. Ralph, you check, just to make sure.'

'Sure,' I answered.

'See you both on Thursday. Goodnight.'

We wished Henry goodnight and he was gone.

'Now,' announced George, as if he was about to unfold a plan for the invasion of a foreign country, 'we start with the foxtrot. Then the waltz. Pull the drapes.'

I hoped to heaven no one knew what we were up to. Two guys dancing alone. 'Geeze!' I pulled the drapes. 'What about the door?'

'It locks itself. Now, watch. Take great big strides. Betty has nice long legs.'

'I won't be dancing with Betty whatever the hell her name is – Blue-Dress.'

'Of course. Now watch.' He danced alone for a couple of minutes..

'Now, we'll do it together. I'll be the girl.'

We danced. Two sissy boxers dancing with each other.

'Now, the waltz. It goes 1 2 3, 1 2 3.'

We tried it, and I got that quite easily.

'What about dipping and stuff like that?'

'Ah, that is tabled for Thursday,' answered George.

'Tabled? I didn't say I would do this on Thursday.'

'You'll like it, Ralphee. Wait and see.'

'And quit the Ralphee, unless you want another fat jaw.'

'That's it for now. Pull back the drapes. And be prepared to stay late on Thursday.'

'Maybe I'll skip it.'

'You won't. And stop griping.'

On Thursday, after the workout, George said, 'I'll lock up again

Henry. I want to work on the heavy bag. You wait for me, Ralph.'

'Don't overdo it,' cautioned Henry. 'Better a little at a time. Goodnight boys. Take it easy.' Henry left.

George closed the drapes, then sat on a bench hugging his knees.

'What's up?' I asked.

'Nothing. Just wait.'

There was a gentle knock on the door. George was up like a jack-in-the-box. Doffing an imaginary cap, he bowed low as he ushered in the visitor. Like a gallant cavalier, he kissed her hand, then presented her, 'Lady Sarah Kirk.' She lifted the scarf which hid her face.

'Well, stone the crows,' I cried. 'Sarah!'

'In person,' she gurgled. 'You are the victim?'

I nodded, grinning. This was more like it. Sarah was George's older sister. She was nineteen. Sarah was slim, brunette, with nice long legs - like Betty Blue-Dress. If a smile wasn't there, one was about to emerge. At fifteen, I didn't feel she was so old.

'All right, all right, let's go,' cried George. 'I'll be the orchestra.' Then, like a bona fide master of ceremonies,' Take partners for a waltz.' It was such a pleasant and unexpected surprise that I didn't move.

'All right, then. Ladies and Gentlemen, the next dance will be a waltz. LADIES' choice.' Sarah slunk over to me, waving her fanny like Nell when she saw a bone coming her way. She breathed perfumed lozenge into my face and whispered, 'May I have the pleasure of this waltz?'

'Is that what I say?' I gulped.

'No,' she purred. 'You can either say, 'Delighted,' or you can say, 'Shove off, dogface.'

'Delighted. Delighted,' I cried, before any calamity had a chance to strike. George started up the orchestra. 'Dum da ra rum, dum dum - Da ra ra rum, dum dum, dum dum....' After the third time around the floor, George tapped me on the shoulder, 'May I cut in?'

Sarah and I looked at George, then at each other. Together, we gave him the 'thumbs down' sign, discouraging any further intervention. These thoughts all passed in a flash, and I realized I was home. And that is how I got hooked on ballroom dancing.

Ralph

I soon got lots of partners but Betty Blue-Dress wasn't one of them. I'll teach her to walk away and leave me like a fool, standing on the dance floor. Then - one Saturday - a waltz, ladies choice. Betty Blue-Dress walked over to me. She was smiling. There was no question. She was looking right at me. This was my moment of revenge. The moment I had been waiting for. Still smiling, she said, 'May I have the pleasure of this waltz?' I leapt to my feet, slipped my right arm around her waist and whirled her off into the crowd.

Served her right! Right? We danced a lot that night, and other nights. Sarah became one of our group. No, she wasn't a Groupie. The term 'Groupie' had not yet been coined and if it had, Sarah would not have been considered a Groupie. She had to mix, as one of us, but we never forgot she was a lady. It was great fun to have our own girl to tease but when we got inside a dance hall she was on her own, except that we kept an eye on her. Sarah was not engaged and she had no special boy friend, so she enjoyed being with us, the only girl in a noisy, but in no way unruly, group of youths.

One week we decided to try another dance hall. It was smaller than the Palais and not as well disciplined. Three loutish men, the worse for drink, took a notion to become possessive of Sarah. After two or three dances, she decided to stay with us. The three louts became objectionable and it was necessary to tell them to buzz off and not bother Sarah. There were four of us and, though much younger, we were sober - none of us drank alcohol - and we were fitter.

On weighing us up, they decided to take our advice and they didn't bother Sarah any more. Minutes later, a huge pot-bellied man sidled up to me and suggested that we slip away early. 'I run the dance,' he said. 'I'm not telling you to leave. It is just a suggestion. Those three are rough bastards. You should ....'

'So are we, if we want to be,' I told him. 'I appreciate your warning, but we'll leave when we're ready.'

'Suit yourself,' he responded and disappeared.

The three louts were watching us a lot and whispering.

George said, 'I think they're cooking up some trouble.'

'We can handle them easily if we stay together,' I answered.

After a couple more dances we had had enough and we left. It was really Sarah who was the most anxious to leave.

'I don't blame you, Sis,' George said, 'They reek of beer.'

'That is only part of it,' answered Sarah. 'They have too many hands.'

'That was a lousy place,' said Jimmy Westlake, who had joined the Club recently and showed promise as a fighter. 'I'm glad it's over.'

'It isn't over yet. We're being followed,' whispered George.

I glanced behind but no one was in sight.

'Imagination, George,' said Mel Brooks. 'There's no one there.'

We stayed together until George and Sarah reached home, then Jimmy and Mel left. They lived only a block or so away.

'Ralph, you can stay with us for tonight if you like. We have a spare bedroom,' George suggested. 'You have quite a bit to go yet.'

'Thanks, George, but I'd better get home.' We bid each other goodnight.

We were all aware that it had been a bad choice of dance hall. It was the last time we would ever go there. As I walked the High Street, I was aware of footsteps not very far behind me. I quickened my pace. So did they. I could have handled one, maybe even two, but three? No thanks. I broke into a run. They did the same. Outrunning them easily, I resumed walking. They must have taken a short cut for they bounded out in front of me near home. I turned about and bolted. There was a lane quite near, so I turned in there hoping to lose them. From the lane I got back on to a main street. I had gained a considerable distance but they were still chasing me. I dodged into another side street and landed in the arms of a policeman. He gripped one of my arms with one hand with his other above his head holding his truncheon ready to crack my skull.

'Three drunks are after me,' I croaked, 'Listen.' He listened.

Fortunately the clatter of feet convinced him. Then they stopped. The policeman said, 'Step outside the lane and when you are sure they have seen you, dodge back in behind me. O.K.?'

'Sure.' I felt my heart pounding. I did as he asked. One of them yelled 'There he is. Let's get 'im.' They were running and shouting at the same time. I darted in behind the policeman. Seconds later the leading lout turned into the lane. The bobby brought down his truncheon hard on his skull. He dropped in a heap. The second lout was close behind. The truncheon cracked him on the shoulder which made him scream. He fell beside his companion, scrambled up and ran, followed by the third lout. 'What's your name?' my saviour asked. I told him. 'You live around here?' I gave him my address.

'Glad I was here. Do you want to lay a charge?' 'No, but thanks for your help.' 'You're welcome. Do I know you?' 'I don't think so,' I said. I started for home. Looking back, I saw he was walking slowly in my direction – alone.

I suppose the lout he had clobbered with his truncheon over the skull survived. Frankly, I didn't care.

BIG MIKE

Remember the Charleston? Remember the patent leather shoes with toes that snaked out about four inches beyond the big toes, their shark-nosed nebs pointing accusingly at anyone on a dance floor imprudent enough to be without them? The length didn't matter so long as you could squeeze into them. Getting into them was a labour; getting out of them was a masochistic nightmare which we bore bravely, if not painlessly, in order to be in the fashion. Those were the good old days. Henry didn't see it that way.

'If I ever got my hands on the bugger who thought that one up,' he said, 'I'd string him up on a flagpole and leave him there to dehydrate.' George wasn't too helpful. 'Isn't it the fellas who wear them you should condemn, not the one who thought of it?' he suggested.

'There aren't enough flagpoles,' Henry grumbled.

'Right. Right,' said George. 'Besides, they'd smell like hell after a while. Heh heh heh.' Do you remember I told you Henry smiled only once in a while? Well, this wasn't one of them. He said we were a couple of morons to wear such stupid things.

'An accusation without a solution is worthless,' I countered.

'The solution is obvious,' he said. 'Wear decent shoes.'

This was the one thing about Henry which I found hard to accept. He didn't seem to understand about the times and the fashions.

I said, 'I wouldn't be found dead at a dance without patent leather shoes.'

'There are two other solutions.'

'Go on.'

'Give up dancing,' he said, as calmly as if he were saying 'Give up heroin. Kick the habit.' That would have been easy. But to give up dancing! He must have gone stark, raving mad.

'You've scrambled your marbles,' I said. 'What's the second one?'

'Give up boxing.'

'Now you are making sense. That... I will consider.'

He didn't reply.

'Besides, I'm getting fed up with all this skipping, shadow boxing and bag punching.'

Henry became really nasty. 'Go on, ruin your feet. What you do in or out of the ring wouldn't hurt a fly anyhow,' he jeered.

'Let's get into the ring and I'll show you,' I said, hoping he would refuse.

'No thanks, Ralph. I don't want to clobber you when you aren't able to defend yourself.' His calm was infuriating. Then he surprised me. In a loud voice he called out, 'Anybody want to get in the ring with Ralph?' One man raised his hand. 'Anyone else?' Henry called. George raised his arm. 'I'll have a go.'

'I offered first,' said Big Mike. Big Mike was a beefy individual. His face looked like it had been in a collision with a double decker. His nose resembled a turnip - mashed. Big Mike had joined the Club only a few weeks ago, and he was rough, especially with other people's faces. Maybe he wanted to restructure others in his own image.

'You've got a big mouth,' George said under his breath.

'All right Mike, you and Ralph. George'll referee,'

'Look, I was just kidding.' I said.

'I know,' answered Henry, 'but as George says, you've got a big mouth.'

We got dressed for the bout. Mike objected to the pillows. Henry shut him up. 'You wear what I say. Take it or leave it.'

Neither George nor I had spoken to Big Mike; not for any particular reason, we just hadn't got around to it. I noticed, though, Mike had been looking at us a lot. Several times, when I turned unexpectedly, he would be staring at George, sometimes at me. He looked formidable and mean. We climbed into the ring. George was there before us. I said, 'We haven't really had a chat, have we?' offering him my gloved hand. He ignored my salutation and turned his back on me.

George said, 'Shake hands and go to your corners.'

Mike turned, slapped my gloved hand and ambled to his corner.

George looked at us, then called out, 'Box!'.

He came at me like a charging bull. I didn't expect it and reeled as he hit me square on the mouth, cutting my lower lip. George got between us. Henry cried, 'Hold it. You don't have to be so rough, Mike. He's not ready for that yet.'

I dodged and Mike backed me into a corner. Mike stood in front of me grinning, his guard hanging loose by his sides. I hit him where he had hit me, square in the mouth. The blow jerked his head back but he didn't even blink. He kept on grinning. Maybe Henry was right when he said I couldn't hurt a fly. Of course, Mike wasn't a fly. Suddenly the grin vanished and he looked savage as he delivered a blow to my mouth again, followed by a smashing hook to my jaw.

George was between us in a flash, and Henry leapt into the ring.

'All right. That's enough. Out of the ring, both of you,' he yelled.

Had I not been wearing a headguard, I'm sure my jaw would have been broken. As I climbed down I saw George, his bare fists clenched, facing Big Mike. Mike was grinning.

'Put on the gloves and I'll take you, too,' I heard him say.

George said nothing and walked away. I could see that it irked him, for he was in a rotten mood on the way home. I asked George if he had ever seen Big Mike before.

'I can't say I have. Have you?'

'There's something about him,' I replied.

The following week, George took him on and didn't fare too well. Henry stopped the bout. 'What is this - A grudge fight?' he growled. George wanted to take on Mike again but Henry wouldn't hear of it. Mike sidled up to me and whispered, 'Wanna get your revenge?'

'No thanks,' I whispered back.

'Scared?'

'No, I'm not scared.'

'I'll tell you what you are. Chicken, gutless.' This in a voice so low, nobody but me could hear him.

I was boiling with anger but it didn't work. I knew I was being baited. That weekend George and I were running. I stopped suddenly.

'What's up?' George cried, pulling up a few steps ahead of me.

'Cripes!, do you know who this Big Mike is?'

'Nope. You already asked me that.'

'He's the jerk you hit with the frying pan, ten – eleven years ago.'

'Are you sure?' he asked in astonishment.

'Well, aren't you?'

'I didn't really look for anything.'

'That's him all right,' I insisted.

We started to run again. When we stopped, George said. 'It figures.'

'What figures?'

'He was about sixteen then. We were under eight. Right? He is about twenty-seven. Don't you see, Ralph, it's me he's after. He wants to massacre you, then he knows I'll want to take him with or without Henry's permission.'

'Hell, I don't want to tangle with that clot.'

'Scared?'

'Maybe. Sparring is one thing. Grudge fighting, street fighting is something different. I don't want any part of that.'

'Maybe you should leave the Club.'

'I've told you before, I don't back up.'

George said, 'I'll talk to Henry. Maybe he'll get rid of him.'

'No, George. *I'll* talk to Henry. O.K.?'

George was silent. 'O.K., George?'

'O.K. Ralph. But don't get any glaikit ideas.'

We finished our roadwork and nothing more was said about it. I saw Henry that evening. 'Does everybody go to the Gym every time it is open?' I asked him.

'No. Most come only once a week. Some twice.'

'Is it possible to go when the Club is closed?'

'It could be,' he replied cagily.

'Could I have a key?'

'You didn't come here to discuss the price o' bloody oranges, Ralph, what's brewing?'

Trapped, I told Henry about the hold-up eleven years ago.

'Are you sure? Absolutely sure?'

'That's him all right. No question.'

'Lying son of a bilge.'

'Who – me?'

'No no. Mike. He told me he was attacked by four construction workers with shovels.'

'Bull. Anyone can see his mug is shaped more like a frying pan than a shovel. Heh heh, Wait'll I tell George.'

'You seem to think this is funny. I advise you to take it seriously.'

'Sure, I'm taking it seriously, but....'

'But what?'

'Well, there's no point in being serious about it, is there? Do I get a key?'

'No. He's mean and he's tough – and I know what you have in mind.'

'I know that,' I answered.

'You're no match for him.'

'I could be.'

'I'll think it over.'

'What you are saying is....'

'What I am saying is, I'll think it over. Take it or leave it.'

Henry meant it and left me standing alone. My big mouth. I didn't want to mix with Big Mike anyway. Henry would turn down the idea. On Sunday morning I was feeding the pigeons and cleaning out their house when George appeared. He came straight to the point.

'Hi, Ralph. Nice morning.'

'I noticed it myself.'

'Got any new birds since I last saw you?'

'Since yesterday? So, Henry wants to see me.'

'That's right, Ralph. At the Club.'

'On Sunday morning?'

'Right now.'

Locking up the pigeon coop took longer than usual. I don't mind admitting it, I was scared. When we arrived at the Gym, Henry was pounding the heavy bag.

'So you decided I take on Big Mike?' I twittered, hoping Henry wouldn't notice how bleached my voice was.

'That depends.'

'Depends on what?'

'On your answers to a few questions.' Henry removed his gloves.

It shouldn't be too difficult to fail his interrogation, and I would be off the hook. 'Shoot,' I said.

'You'll have to work hard.'

'I know that.'

'And you will do exactly as I say. Understood?'

I didn't reply. Henry looked almost as mean as Big Mike.

'I said 'Is that understood.' Answer me!'

'Yes, Sergeant. Understood.'

'You will train by yourself, under the supervision of George. He knows what you have to do. And... AND, you will discontinue wearing those pointed shoes altogether.'

I exploded. 'Now, wait a minute. That's hitting below the belt. I think... I think...' Like Callipers, I was nonplussed.

'I don't give a damn what you think. Already you are going back on your word.' Henry was angry. I had been tricked again. He had given me a way out. Or had he? He continued. 'I want an answer.'

'Yes, Sir, Captain.'

'Make it clear to me,' he said. 'Yes, you will, or no you won't wear those stupid shoes.'

I looked at George, whose eyebrows had disappeared into his scalp.

'No, Herr General, I will not wear those stupid shoes.'

I treated Henry to the smartest salute I knew how.

'Thank you for the speedy promotion,' Henry said, perfectly dead pan.

'George will have a key. He will tell me if you break any promises.'

Big Mike

George, grinning like a cream-fed cat, crossed his heart.

When Henry was out of hearing range, George said, 'Ralph, did anyone ever tell you you had a big mouth?'

'Yeah... You and my grandfather.'

To think I could have wriggled out of it, and I bungled it!

Henry had returned from somewhere in the store room.

'All right, you win. When do I start?'

'Right now... if you want to,' answered Henry.

If I want to. Here was another opportunity. Why didn't I grab at it? Maybe I needed to see a shrink.

'All right. After today you take your orders regarding training from George. He will report to me and I will observe your progress, if any, from time to time.'

George let me away with nothing. He insisted I pound the heavy bag hard and low, especially with my left hook. 'Why my left hook?' I inquired.

'Because I'm telling you to. Hard and low.'

George was nearly two years older than I, but he looked two years younger. I looked two years older than my age. I suppose he thought at seventeen and a half he was grown up. He wouldn't spar with me, saying that I would pull my punches. I griped about the gruelling work he made me do, and promised that one day I would work on him hard and low. He was unmoved. And he was relentless in his training. He also threatened that if I didn't do as I was instructed, he would report to Henry and the match would be off. No one will ever know how much I wanted to wriggle out of this match, but I couldn't or wouldn't back off. One evening, after a gruelling workout, I said to George, 'I'm changing jobs.' He was surprised.

'Have you had any more trouble with the two louts who tried the lamp trick on you?'

'No. But I just thought I would like a change. I'm going to the Dubbie.'

'The Dubbie? There's no tram goes there.'

'I'm going to ride the pushbike. You know, George, I'm beginning to hate this bloody place. And I hate not being able to go to the Saturday night dancing.'

'No Ralph. What you hate is the thought of a match with Big Mike.'

'That, too.'

'That, period.'

We closed up the Club and George said, 'I'm not going your way tonight, Ralph. I promised I would look in on my brother on Carwell Ave. Here, read this. It's specially for you.' He produced a half sheet of paper which looked like it had been in his pocket for about a week.

'Oh, no. Not another one of your crummy poems?'

'Goodnight, Ralph.'

'Yeah... Night, George.' I opened the paper and read:

> O pride, you foolish vanity,
> Defying all the laws of sanity;
> Take on Big Mike and you'll get plastered,
> Worm out of it, you stupid bastard.

I'll kill him! No. Not Mike. George.

On the way home, alone, I started thinking about the dancing that I missed so much, and how it had started one night at the Club.

EENIE MEENIE YES OR NO

Before I arrived home, my thoughts were on other matters. I was sure I would not be followed, and if I was, I was equally sure I could take care of two louts who were half drunk, one possibly injured. My mind was filled with the possibilities of the forthcoming bout with Big Mike. By the time I had got home, I had it all figured out. Did it matter who won? Not to me. It was a grudge fight. But at the same time it was what is called a friendly fight. I would take a fall. George had assured me he was to be the referee. I would hit the canvas early in the first round. George would stop the fight, announce Mike the winner and the match would be over. No, I couldn't do that. Why not? Some people would know. Does it matter? Why should I care. I intended to give up boxing anyway. But I would be known as a quitter. So what? Some of the fellows at the coal pit were coming to see the fight. What if they were betting on me to win? That's their business. Maybe they would be betting on Mike to win. Great. I would be playing right into their hands. But – suppose they were betting on me to win? I would get my face rearranged so they could win a few shillings? No way! I would take a fall. Then I would be ostracised. Who cares? Mike was out to change my appearance. Maybe I was good enough to change his. Anything would be an improvement on what he had now. But he was tough. Where could I hurt him? He didn't have a weak spot that I knew about. The only answer was to take a fall in the first round. I'll go down in the first. Then I would have gone through all this gruelling workout for nothing. No, I'll face it. Perhaps he's not as tough as I think.

He really shook me though when... Yes, now I had it all worked out. I'll take a fall in the first round. I wish I could get the damn thing out of my mind.

When I arrived home, my parents were still up. Dad was listening to one of his records – Tannhauser. Mum was knitting – she was a splendid knitter – and pretending to enjoy the music.

I made some tea, and a three-inch sandwich at which the fourth Earl of Sandwich would have been green with envy. There was some cold mince in one of the kitchen cupboards. This brought the sandwich up to four inches in thickness. 'Anybody want tea?' I asked.

'No, thank you. We had some about an hour ago,' Mum responded.

'How did you like the new dance hall?' Dad asked, as I munched greedily.

'Oh,' I shrugged.

'Were there many people there?' Mum asked.

'Oh, yes.'

Dad: 'Don't you tire of dancing?'

I: 'No.'

Mum: 'Did you see a girl home?'

I: 'Sarah.'

Dad: 'Is it further away than the Palais de Dance?'

I: 'No.'

Dad: 'Do you like it better than the Palais?'

I: (munch munch) 'No.'

Dad: 'Why is that?'

I: 'I'm giving up dancing.' (munch munch)

Mum: 'Giving up dancing? ... I thought you liked it.'

I: 'I do.' (munch)

Mum: 'Then why are you giving it up?'

I: (munch munch, swallow) 'Henry.'

Mum: 'Henry? What does Henry have to do with it?'

I: 'Shoes.'

Dad was beginning to show some aggravation. 'Ralph,' he said, 'will you try to answer our quite pertinent questions with sentences of three or more words?'

'Of course – Dad.'

'Well done. Now, try four words.'
'I'm in training – boxing.'
'Do you intend to make a career of boxing?'
'No. I'm giving it up after the fight.'
'Good. Boxing is all right for numbskulls like....'
'Alex Noel?'
'Like Big Mike.'
How did Dad get to know about Big Mike, I wondered?
'I think I'll go to bed.'
'I put the hot water bottle in your bed,' said Mum. It should still be warm.'
'Thanks, Mum. Goodnight.' Mum held out her cheek and I kissed her goodnight. 'Goodnight, Dad.'
'Goodnight, Son.'

The hot water bottle was still warm. It was one of those cylindrical stone things that took up about the same bed space as a person. One was careful not to drop it on one's foot. Such carelessness could mean amputation. I eased it over to the side of the bed and stretched. I couldn't sleep right away. The fight was still on my mind. I would take a fall. Well, I would sleep on it.

Sunday was one of the most miserable days I have ever lived through. It was even worse that the previous Sunday. What has happened to Sunday lately? It used to be the best day in the week. I was now aware that my Hallelujah angel wasn't really fighting, but it wasn't that. Anyway, she was no longer my Hallelujah angel, and she was no longer an angel, anybody's angel. I cleaned out the doo-coop as usual, watched my favourite tumbler doing its acrobatics in the sky, and I wished I were in Timbuctu or New Guinea. Heaving a great sigh, I said to myself, 'Snap out of it, Ralph. This frame of mind is anything but healthy.' I was just beginning to adjust when – there he was again. Alex Knowall. It sent me right back into a tailspin.

Alex wasn't a bad sort, really. Objectionable, but not a bad sort. I suppose he was unaware of it. He had gone off to University a couple of years ago. I had thought he was in Edinburgh but no, here he was again, his hands dug into his trouser pockets as usual, his spectacles sliding slowly but silently down his nose. Maybe they were trying to escape. He was surveying me like a horse dealer trying to sell me a used car. It was his superior attitude that cheesed me off. You know that 'God help you, how did you ever get into such a mess' attitude?

'Hello, Ralph.'

'Hello.' No point in being unpleasant, I thought, but I needed Alex Knowall about as much as I needed a dose of castor oil. Questions, so many questions. And assertions. He asked questions, then, when he got an answer, he contradicted you with an assertion. When he got started, sometimes he wouldn't hear a bloody word you were saying. This time he was at his worst. No, I haven't forgotten he saved the tray of pies, for which I will always be grateful, but I considered that I had paid for that before the event. Someone had to break the silence so I asked, 'You're not in Edinburgh?'

'I'm here,' he answered, looking at me as though I had just said, 'You're not on Mars?' Then he said, 'How did you get into such a mess?'

'Mess?'

'Everybody knows about it.'

'About what?'

'I hear that you are going to have a grudge match shortly with a person by the name of Big Mike.'

'I can handle it,' I said expressing a show of serene confidence.

His specs had reached the point of no return, and slipped off his nose. They had always looked like part of his body, so my reaction in trying to save them was that fraction later than Alex's own reflex. He caught them in mid-air without even taking his eyes off me. How could .... Practice, I suppose. He started to clean them with a handkerchief.

'I thought you were in Edinburgh - studying law.' I said.

'I want to - whether you like it or not - I want to give you some good advice.'

'Did you drop out or something?'

'A grudge fight is not a good fight, especially when you are so young and your opponent is so mature.'

'Your folks'll be disappointed if you don't stick it out.'
'*Your* muscles are not fully developed. *His* are. Believe me, it is sheer lunacy to go through with it.'
'It's not everybody gets the chance to go to university. It's not everybody can afford it.'
'I know that your pride is in conflict with the courage to call it off.'
'If law is too tough for you, take something else, something easier.'
'Call it off, Ralph. Make some excuse, any excuse, but call it off.'
'Have you thought of a trade? There's good money in a trade. Jock Munro's father says there's a great future in plumbing.'
Alex wiped his glasses again and peered at me like an absent-minded professor. He hadn't heard a damn word I said.
'If your pride won't let you throw the fight, call it off.'
'Throw the fight?'
'In the first round. *Early* in the first round. And thanks for the advice, Ralph. I'll think about what you said if you promise to think seriously about what I have just said.' Alex stuck his hands in his pockets and shuffled off. George appeared.
'Hi, Ralph. Wasn't that Alex Knowall I saw leaving?'
'Yeah.'
'He's on summer recess, I suppose.'
'I suppose.'
'Has he qualified in law yet?'
'He quit law.'
'Quit? What's he going to do?'
'Medicine, or ....'
'Or what?'
'Plumbing.'
George gaped at me as if I were from outer space.
'What are you gaping at?' I asked.
'Ralph, whether you like it or not, I'm going to give you some good advice.' He sounded just like Alex Knowall.
'Get out of it... Forget this fight,' George barked.
I heard Granta's voice calling Nell. Nell pricked her ears and stared at

me, awaiting instructions.

'All right, Nell. Go on.'

Granta's slightly stooped figure appeared. Nell rushed past him to greet Tam, her pal, giving Granta a friendly prod with her nose as she rushed past him.

'I'm gonna take a walk up Spinkie Den through Cockmalane. Do ye feel up tae it, Ralph?'

'Of course I do. You go ahead, Grant. I have to lock up. I'll catch up with you.' Granta disappeared with both dogs.

'Want me to come, Ralph?'

'No, George. This is something special and ....' I hesitated.

'Say no more. I understand. He is getting frail, isn't he?'

'Don't ever tell him that. Will you lock up for me, George?'

'Sure. See you on Tuesday?'

'We'll see,' I replied, and walked off sharply to catch up with Granta. I glanced back to give George a wave. He was staring at me, looking extremely happy. I waved and shouted back at him. 'Don't count on anything. One way or the other.'

I was around the corner when I heard him shout, 'You stupid, dumb, ignorant .... Ahhhhh.'

I retraced some steps until we could see each other.

'Don't forget to see the birds are all in before you lock up. Cats!' I yelled.

Granta and I wandered up Cockmalane to the house with the monkey puzzle tree - the biggest I have ever seen - on the lawn. Then we turned right until we reached Spinkie Den. I believe it has now been improved upon and is called Letham Glen. I'm sure the change of name and the improvements pleased many but - Spinkie Den, what a delightful name! There is something magic in the name - Spinkie Den. I suppose it is pure nostalgia, and I mustn't gripe. I wonder, too, if the gigantic monkey puzzle tree is still living. There were exciting paths, winding erratically by the little stream which wandered aimlessly, it would appear, in the valley, emerging eventually into the sea where the Thistle golf links started. Ducks waddled about in the stream in front of the Club House and small fish took an exploratory trip up the mouth of the stream when the tide was in. In Spinkie Den a rustic bridge crossed the burn. When one stood quiet and still, it was possible to see trout waving their tails at one in the shadows. At a particular place, gone now I'm sure, Granta lifted me up by the armpits to see how many eggs were in a robin's nest, warning me to look but never to touch. Our walks through Spinkie Den were done mostly in silence now. Observing Granta's laboured breathing, I could see that he was having some difficulty, especially when the path was very uneven and large roots of aged coniferous trees, bare and shoe-worn, crossed the paths.

On this walk I said, 'Do you think we should turn back, Grant?'

'Too much for you, laddie?'

'Well ... yes, I've had enough. But if you want to go further, I'm game.'

I took his hand and we 'helped each other' where the going was rough. We must have been a comical sight. It was not important.

'How are you getting on in the pit, son?'

'I'm changing over to another one. I would like to leave but we need the money.'

'How much do you make?'

'Fourteen shillings a week. I keep half a crown.'

'Did you know that Andy is in the Isle o' Man?'

'Yes, I know.'

'He gets five pounds a month, plus board and lodgings.'

'That's not bad, Grant.'

He gripped my hand and squeezed it. 'It's no' as dangerous as the pits,' he said, looking hard at me.

'No, it couldn't be.'

'If ye wrote tae him, maybe he could get ye a job.'

'What about our walks on Sunday, Grant?'

He heaved a gargantuan sigh. Then he said, almost in a whisper, 'Nothing stands still.' We walked.

My uncle Andy was only three years older than I. We had spent some time together, holidaying in a pup tent around Fifeshire. We got on well together. Andy was employed as an attendant in the Mental Hospital in the Isle of Man. Andy had invited me to spend a holiday with him in the I.O.M. He said he knew of a place where I could stay free of charge. I told Granta about it on the walk home but he didn't seem to want to talk about it, so we finished our walk mostly in silence.

We reached his house where he had lived alone since Granny passed away.

'How about a cup o' tea,' he asked.

'I'd like that. I'll make it.'

Granta fell asleep in his easy chair. The house was clean but he never remembered to open windows on a good day and it smelled musty. Mum visited frequently to keep an eye on him and to tidy up. Then the house got a good airing.

I woke him gently and he took the cup of tea which I held out to him. I had made sure it was not hot enough to burn him.

He sipped noisily.

'Did ye sugar it?' he asked.

'Two teaspoonfuls. Is it all right?'

'Did ye heat the pot?'

'Yes, Grant. Is it not hot enough?'

'Pour out half and fill it up from the pot.'

I took the cup and saucer and did as he asked. When I brought it back he was fast asleep again.

This time I let him sleep.

THE GUTBUCKETFUL

On Monday morning I went to work with mixed feelings. This was my first day in a new coal pit. This one was a mine actually, not a pit. Many of us rode bicycles, some in groups, some alone. Those who lived near the mine walked to work. The most compelling reason for biking it was that there were no tram cars or buses on that route, and the nearest point of disembarkation from a public vehicle left a good mile to walk. There were other reasons for biking: 1. It allowed one to travel at one's own pace, fast or slow. 2. It saved the tram fare. And 3. A bonus which I was unaware of until I went there, free coal if you were willing to carry it. The coal company didn't seem to mind this mode of pilfering, for it was done openly with no pretence at hiding it. It was a relief not to have to rely on a tramcar any more. I lived half a mile from the tram terminal. While most of the drivers stopped or slowed down when they saw, in their rear-view mirrors, someone running to catch up, one driver, a wretch whose name I prefer not to mention, got his jollies by starting up when I had almost reached his vehicle. When I ran, he would speed up; when I stopped, out of breath, he would slow down. It was a game he enjoyed, speeding and slowing down, then accelerating when the brass rail was almost within my grasp. Many a time I was left, out of breath, cursing him and wishing upon him the most direful and barbarous torments. He was responsible for some of the most luminous language I have ever uttered.

Once I got used to the five-mile bike ride, I enjoyed it, short-lived as it was. The crisp clean unpolluted air of early morning was delicious and invigorating. This was, indeed, a beautiful morning, designed for sensitive and whole-hearted appreciation. My thoughts, however, were divided.

Ralph

My apprehension, when I considered the damned bout with rotten Mike, bordered on fear. I should be devouring the landscape, counting the trees and marvelling at the fields bursting to deliver their bounties to the many industrious farmers along the country road. My mind should be rejoicing, untrammelled by the anxiety I had for events to come, when I glimpsed the occasional shimmer of the Firth of Forth as the sun sneaked over the horizon and blushed over the grateful earth. This morning I didn't even remember passing the giant monkey puzzle tree at Cockmalane as I rode silently past it to my destination.

The pit bottom was dry and hot. As I crammed into the cage with nine or ten others, I felt the waft of hot, almost sticky air envelop me. The contrast to the sweet air above made a fitful companion to my frame of mind. Laughing and bantering was on the lips of only a few. These were the older men who had spent many years at the coal face. They had accepted, with resignation, this life of dreary toil, until old age, ill health, sometimes death, demanded their retirement.

Young Pete Rintoul was standing next to me as we descended into the depressing atmosphere. We nodded affably but solemnly to each other. Pete's job was to fill the cage with full tubs of coal and to unload the empties when they were returned. He was also obliged to help me with coupling and uncoupling the tubs which were sent down empty to the men at the coal face and returned full of coal. On leaving the cage, the miners left for their various locations. Pete and I sat down and waited for the whistle which commanded us to get off our butts.

'What kind of sandwiches have ye got' asked Pete, after the preliminaries of introducing ourselves to each other.

'Corned beef,' I answered.

'Mine are hard boiled eggs and onion. Wanna swap a couple – later?'

'I don't mind.'

We got along well together. It was about two weeks later that Pete asked 'How's it going, Ralph?'

'How's what going?'

'You know. Your training for the fight.'

'I didn't mention anything about a fight.'

'I know you didn't. But everybody knows about it. Any chance of seeing it?'

'No date has been mentioned.'

'You must have some idea. Are *you* ready for it?'

'That's up to Henry,' I said. It was time to change the subject. How the hell did they get to know about it here? Everybody seemed to be urging me to get out of it - except those who were betting on the fight. Adding even more to my misery, was the fact that everybody who was betting was putting his money on me to win. I changed the subject.

'I have never asked you, Pete, but why do you wear gloves?'

'To save my hands.'

'That's obvious, but why do you want to save your hands?'

'I thought you knew. I play the fiddle.'

'No kidding? So do I. I made it myself.'

'You made a fiddle?' he said, incredulously.

'Yes. A one string fiddle with half a coconut shell and a long piece of wood which I whittled. I play 'Home Sweet Home', 'Margie' and 'My old Kentucky Home' without making a mistake. I'm working on 'Jock o' Hazeldean' and 'Charlie is Ma Darlin'.'

Pete looked stupefied. I thought he was so impressed that he was speechless. 'What do you play?' I asked him.

'Scales - mostly. I take violin lessons.'

'Oh. Your's is a real fiddle then?'

'Yeah. But I made a gut bucket, and....'

'What's a gut bucket?' I asked.

'.... and my old man said, 'If I buy ye a fiddle, will ye stop that bloody .....'

'What the hell is a gut bucket?'

'Well.... it's hard to explain.'

'Try.'

'Well.... ye start with a zinc tub.'

'Go on,' I urged.

'Well.... ye bore a hole in the bottom - in the centre. That's where the gut is attached.'

'Then what?'
'Well.... ye get hold o' a broom handle....'
'And?'
'Well.... then ye attach the other end o' the gut tae the broom handle – then ye play it.'
I was fascinated. 'What do you play it with? A bow?'
'Well.... ye can....'
'Pete, do you have to start every sentence with "Well?".'
'Well.... no, it's a habit, I suppose.'
'I suppose. Go ahead, I'm interested in this gut bucket. Where were we?'
'Well.... Ye can play it with a bow or ye can pluck it wi' yer fingers.'
'How do you get the different notes?'
'Well.... ye pull the broom handle tae get the higher notes and....'
The whistle went. 'I'll talk to you later,' I said. We both got up and started to move the tubs around as necessary. Our two counterparts on the previous shift were not the most energetic types. They left a clutter of tubs, both full and empty, for us to take care of. I didn't mind. The time went faster this way. We didn't have a chance to talk until lunchtime. We exchanged two sandwiches.
'Looks like we both have sausage,' I said.
'Well.... maybe you're right,' Pete replied, staring my sausage sandwich in the face.
I was more thirsty than hungry and, with the exception of about half a cup, I drank nearly all of my cocoa. I was contemplating what I would ask Pete about the gut bucket when I heard tubs moving at the top of the incline.
'What's that?' I cried, jumping up in alarm.
We both rushed to the top of the brae in time to see four tubs hurtling down the slope. Pete had helped me with the couplings. Between us, one must have been missed. BUMP, BUMP, BUMP, CRASH! Then silence.
'My God, Pete, we missed a coupling!' I yelled.
The tubs had jumped the rails, so there was no danger to the men

below. We rushed down to the tubs, which lay in a cloud of coal dust. That was when we discovered there were four of them. Pete looked grey beneath his blackened face. 'I... I thought you had done that one, Ralph. Will I go for help?'

'We'll manage,' I shouted. 'Look, you go back and grab an armful of pins, and hurry up.'

Pete scrambled up the incline to get the pins while I surveyed the jumbled mess of empties. It wasn't long before we had them lying in a row, parallel with the rails. We stuck the two-by-two wooden pins into the spokes of the wheels as we got three back on the rails. Tubs are stout wooden boxes, small wagons really, about five feet long and four wide. They are mounted on two pairs of wheels, each pair being welded to the axle, leaving a side play of about three inches. This is why, at any great speed, they wobble and are likely to jump the rails. It also helps when tubs are off the rails but in contact with, or nearly touching, the rails. It is usual to lift one end of the tub while someone pulls the wheels and axle over, letting the whole thing down on the rails.

The last one was too far away to pull the wheels above the rails.

'All right, Pete. Heave this end over nearer the line.'

Pete heaved, then the tub slipped on his gloves, which were glossy with usage. The tub came down, missing the rails, and squashed my right forefinger which was in the spokes of the wheel.

'God Almighty!', I screamed. I gaped at the mutilated finger in disbelief. I felt no pain, but the end of my finger was like a blood-soaked fan. The nail, the flesh and part of the bone of the first digit were gone.

'You and your bloody fiddle and your bloody gloves!' I yelled, 'Well, don't just stand there! Get some water!'

'Where?' Pete croaked weakly.

'My flask! Fetch it!'

Pete scampered off to bring my flask with the dregs of cocoa. Why I stood there instead of running for it myself, I'll never know.

I poured the residue of my cocoa over the wound. It was even worse looking than before. Between coal dust, blood and cocoa dregs, it resembled a squashed acorn.

'How the hell did you let go of it?' I yelled accusingly.
'Well....'
'You and your goddam 'Wells'. Oh, never mind. Get.... get.... get.... clear the cage!'
'Well.... the cage is only supposed to be used for tubs,' whined Pete.
I was near to being apoplectic with rage.
'Piss on the tubs. And piss on your fiddle. And piss on you!' I yelled. 'Jump to it!'
Pete jumped to it and emptied the cage. I pressed the starting button and slammed the scissor gate. As the cage slowly disappeared up the shaft, I heard Pete's voice, plaintive and penitent: 'Ralph – if ye want it, ye can have ma gut bucket.'
I wondered if the first aid man would be at his post. A small card on the door read 'Knock and Wait'. Maybe they were operating on some poor slob. I knocked. There was no answer. Oh, what the hell! My case was urgent anyway. I knocked, opened the door and rushed in.
'Hey, hey,' said the elderly man who was propped up in a chair and reading a newspaper.
'It's my finger,' I croaked. Having had time to realize the real significance of the calamity, my voice seemed almost to have disappeared.
'Did ye no' see the sign?'
'I knocked.'
'But ye didnae wait.'
'There's no time to wait. I need a dressing on it now,' I said.
'Aye. Well, ye've come tae the right place, laddie.'
He sipped his tea, wiping his walrus moustache on his sleeve.
'Well, young man, what can I do fur ye?'
This man had me flummoxed. I gaped at him in disbelief. Shoving the wounded finger under his nose, I said, in the most controlled voice I could muster, 'I would like .... to have .... this wound .... cleaned and dressed.'
'Dear me,' he said, observing it over the top of grimy glasses. 'That.... is a nasty one. Lie doon on yon table while I get some hot water.'
I lay down on the long narrow table, which was covered by a near-

The Gutbucketful

white sheet.

'Try no' tae get blood on the cloth,' he said, filling the huge iron kettle from the cold tap.

'Why don't you just use cold water?' I asked.

'Cold water in hot water bottles? Laddie, were ye last in line when they handed oot the brains?'

My voice had come back. 'What do you want hot water bottles for, anyway?' I yelled.

'Tae keep ye warm, of course.' He raised a warning finger. 'And don't you get uppity wi' me. Now, dae ye feel you're going tae faint?'

'No. I just want a dressing on this wound so that I can see a doctor and get medical attention.'

'What dae ye think you're gettin' noo? And I'll thank ye no tae raise yer voice.'

'Don't you understand? I need proper medical attention.'

He looked at me coldly. 'Young man, I have had first aid training long before ye were born, and I ....'

'You forgot to light the gas under the kettle,' I interrupted.

He ambled over to the stove. 'Geeze,' he said, 'I lit the wrang one. Heh heh heh.'

I watched apprehensively, wondering when he would do something which would blow us both to hell before I could escape – without the dressing. He lit the other gas ring then moved the kettle on to it. He then lit the one from which he had removed the kettle and shunted the thing back to where it was, turning off the flame that wasn't being used.

I relaxed momentarily. 'Now, let me see,' he mumbled, opening a glass cabinet on the wall. After some consideration, he selected some cotton swabs, a roll of pink lint and a brown bandage. Placing them on the table beside me, he asked, 'Are ye all right?'

'No, I'm not all right.'

'Aye, well don't worry,' he said in a confidential tone. 'I have seen lots o' men, big, strong, husky lads pass right oot when I started tae dress their wounds.'

I was not surprised but I refrained from saying so. I had a feeling he was touchy. He waddled over to the kettle and patted its bulbous exterior to test its warmth. After warming his hands for a minute or so on its bulging abdomen, he selected from a cupboard below the glass cabinet, three stone hot water bottles. He carried these, one at a time, to the stove. His back was facing me. Scratching his backside with one hand while he alternately patted the kettle with the other, he started to sing 'Scots wha hae wi' Wallace bled, Scots wham Bruce hae often led....' As I mentioned, his back was to me and when he reached, 'Welcome tae yer gory bed,' I grabbed at the opportunity. Quietly, I snatched the lint and brown bandage and I slid silently off the table. I slipped away stealthily, closing the door gently behind me. Imagination? Maybe. But I wasn't up to taking a chance that I might bleed to death in the same way that so many gallant men led by King Robert The Bruce at Bannockburn had done - haemorrhaged.

Outside, I tore off a strip of lint, covered the wound and wrapped it with the bandage. With 'life or death' urgency, I mounted my bike and fled. I held onto the handlebars with one hand, holding the damaged finger above my right ear in case it should start to bleed. It was some five miles to the doctor's office. On the way there, I got several one finger salutes from complete strangers who thought I was giving them a sign of recognition. After the seventh one, I pulled my hand in close to my chin. Hell, it was beginning to ache.

When I reached the doctor's office, he was in but happily he had no patient in the surgery. He was very efficient. He soaked my finger in an antiseptic solution, removed the pink lint, then dried my finger, which had a layer of congealed blood on it.

'I'm afraid I will have to trim away the ragged edges,' he informed me. He squirted something on the wound, ether I think, then, with a pair of scissors, he cut off the fan.

'That can't be saved, and it will only retard the healing,' he said, seeing my concern. The doctor stitched the wound and applied a dressing. The pain was gone, but so was the point of my finger. I groaned.

'That's all we can do for now. The bone is exposed. Later it will have to be amputated at the first joint,' said the doctor. I was too stunned to

speak.
   'Go home and lie down. If it begins to pain, take two aspirins. That'll help. I want to see you tomorrow at two o'clock. Right?'
   'Thank you, Doctor.' I went home.

THE BIG FIGHT

The assassination of the Archduke Franz Ferdinand in 1914 could not have triggered more of a kerfuffle internationally than did the accident to my finger locally. Mum was in tears. Dad wanted to know who was responsible.

'It was my own fault,' I told him. Granta was sympathetic but he wondered if it would prevent me from helping to roll his dog pills. Some people, perfect strangers, stopped me in the streets to inquire about my hand. At first I enjoyed the notoriety, but it was soon apparent that the concern was whether or not I would be ready for the fight with Big Mike. Mike was advertising it all over the place, urging people to bet on him if they wanted to make an easy bob or two.

I didn't go near the Gym of course. The day after the accident, I saw the doctor again. He changed the dressing and seemed to be well pleased with what he had done. He told me that I should now have the dressings changed at the hospital.

After a week of dressings at the local hospital, the doctor there said that I would have to go to the Royal Infirmary in Edinburgh, where they would remove the bone fragment that protruded so stubbornly through the flesh. Fortunately, compensation paid for it. Shortly after my arrival at the Infirmary, I was wheeled into a surgery where two young men and a statuesque young woman were talking. She sat on a high, antiseptic looking stool and crossed her legs. All three wore surgical gowns and they had masks around their necks. I was lifted on to the operating table, as if I couldn't get there myself.

A tray with scalpels, scissors and other gadgetry used to cut people up was placed on a small side table. What if they opened me up and stole something for another patient?

'It's just my finger,' I said.

'Yes, we know,' answered the blond, giving me what could be considered, at my age now, a wanton smile. Lying on the operating table, my eyes were on a level with her knees.

'Who is going to do the operation?' I asked.

'I am,' she replied, dangling her legs. 'Relax, it won't take long.'

They slipped the masks over their mouths. One of the men disappeared behind me.

She's so young, I thought. I suppose she knows what she's doing.

She was at my side. A mask was suddenly clamped over my mouth. I heard her voice say, 'Just count to ten, slowly.' Boy, she could win a beauty contest anywhere.

'Count. Are you counting?'

'And those legs. One - two - three - .... I'd like to get her on the floor at the Palais de Dance in Edinburgh. I bet she does a mean tango. She'll know how to use her head too. A sudden twist facing her partner, then a jerk in the direction of the next step. Probably everybody would stop to watch us. With trams like hers, she ought to be a professional ballroom dancer, not a doctor.'

Someone was slapping me gently on the cheek. My eyes felt bleary but when I got them in focus, it was she - the legs. I looked around me. This was not the surgery. It was a room with other patients. 'The operation is over?'

'All done,' she said with an antiseptic smile.

'Then I can get the six o'clock train?'

'You have missed that one. You will be staying here tonight. You may leave in the morning.'

'I see. Thank you for everything, Doctor.'

'You're very welcome. And thank *you* for everything.'

'I beg your pardon?'

'Maybe we shall meet again some day.'

'Oh?'

'When you are a little older. I do a mean tango. And I have nice long

The Big Fight

legs.' She threw me a wink that pulled her cheek up, causing her nose to wrinkle. I felt the rush of blood to my face. Good Heavens! Did I say all that aloud? I buried my face in my hands. When I found the courage to look up, she was gone. I had no more trouble with the wound and the stitches were removed several days later at the local hospital.

There was a long battle over compensation, during which time I received benefits during sick leave. One day, the Union president called me in to his office to tell me with great pride that the Union had won their case with management. For the loss of one digit from the forefinger of my right hand, I received a settlement of eight pounds sterling.

In a few weeks, my finger had healed nicely to the point - if I may be excused the expression - where it was not even tender to the touch. I visited the Club, not to start training, but to say 'hello' to the boys. I had been to a couple of Saturday night hops at the Palais, which meant I had had to wear my pointed patent leather shoes. So, I would be crippled before I was twenty. It was worth it.

I didn't have the courage to face Henry wearing those shoes so I put on a pair of blunt-toed shoes which had gone out of style three years ago. I wasn't so stupid as not to notice that Henry's eyes darted directly to my feet. Henry greeted me coldly, I thought. A curt nod was all I got from him. George was skipping and he just grinned. He didn't miss a skip. From some of the others I was welcomed back with, 'Hi, Ralph.' 'How's it going?' 'How's the finger?' 'Nice to see you back.' That sort of thing.

'What brings you here?' Henry asked.

'My finger is O.K. now. I can start training.'

'Training?' As if he had never heard the word.

'For the fight, of course.'

'You're not going to fight.'

'But I have an obligation.'

Henry sniffed and wrinkled his nose. I knew this from experience to mean 'No argument.'

'You see....', I began.

'I said, 'No argument',' he rasped.

It would be difficult to describe the relief I felt at being denied the opportunity to cut Big Mike down to size, but I knew Henry meant business when he said 'No', so it seemed safe to insist.

'Are you denying me the opportunity to clobber Big Mike?' I demanded.

'You got the message.'

'But everybody's expecting it. I can't let down all the fellows who....'

The nose wrinkle again. 'I'm running this place and that's an end to it.'

He was so definite, I thought I'd chance one last blast of hot air.

'You could postpone it until I'm ready, couldn't you?' I did a little skipping without the rope. A funny smile spread over Henry's face.

'All right, kid,' he said. 'George can whip you into shape in about four weeks.'

I was stunned. 'On second thoughts,' I stammered, 'if you really think I'm not up to it, we could, you know.'

'No, I don't know. Your finger is all right, isn't it?'

'Well.... yes and no.'

Henry's face pretzelled into a corrugated ambush.

'Of course, if you want to crawl out of it, just say so.'

Skewered on my own big mouth!

'Get outa here,' Henry hissed.

I said nothing and took a hike over to George who had finished skipping. Glancing around at the others, I noticed Big Mike tenderly rubbing his right side over the floating ribs. Somebody must have belted him there, I thought. I left with George, who was unusually silent.

'You know the fight is off, don't you?'

'No,' George answered.

'Henry just let me off the hook.'

'Right. But he didn't let Mike off the hook.'

'What do you mean?' I asked George.

'I'm not supposed to tell you. Henry is going to take him instead. Mike wasn't too happy, but Henry called him yellow and a few other things, with everybody listening.'

'Like chicken?'

'How do you know that?'

'That's what he called me. You were standing near us and overheard

The Big Fight

him. And you told Henry - right?'

'I let it slip one day. Mike won't have me as a referee, so we're getting that chap from Dunfermline - whatsisname.'

'Fotheringill?'

'That's him. The fight is on Friday.'

'This Friday coming?'

'That's right,' murmured George. 'For heaven's sake, don't let on I told you.'

'Henry certainly fooled me. I suppose I can see the fight,' I said, gleefully.

'As long as you didn't hear about it from me.'

Henry was shorter in height than Mike, but he was built like a bull. They weighed in about the same. Everybody was there. The ref. did his speil and they were in their corners. The bell went and they sprang at each other like two wild animals. Mike was out to change Henry's identification. Henry was after Mike's ribs. Henry received a couple of nasty blows, then delivered a piledriver to Mike's right side. Mike winced and tried to keep out of reach. I never heard such silence except in the woods. Henry went in, ignoring his opponent's blows, and delivered two more torpedoes to his right side. Glancing at the tense faces that emitted a tortured 'Oooooo', I whispered to George, 'So he does have a weak spot.' Mike was obviously distressed. I was about to learn, with electrifying unexpectedness, the meaning of 'killer instinct'.

Within the next five or six seconds Henry drove three more into his victim's right side. The referee pointed Henry to his corner. Mike's legs crumpled weakly and he began to fold slowly to his knees. Then Mike fell on his face. It was incredible. He hadn't lasted even one full round.

'Call an ambulance,' Henry growled and leapt out of the ring.

When Henry, George and I were alone, Henry said, 'That's the last dirty fight I'll ever get into.'

'Henry,' I said, 'I don't like him any more than you do. In fact, I hate his guts, but be honest, he didn't fight dirty.'

'Not him, you moron,' Henry grunted, giving me a scornful look.

'I fought dirty. He has some liver ailment. He wanted to call it off.'

ALL THE COMFORTS OF HOME ETC.

If there was not actual rejoicing, there was no weeping, wailing or gnashing of teeth when I said I was finished with the coal pits. My finger was healed and trouble free but I would regret the loss for many years to come. I still do. Dad was in steady employment, but my contribution to the family budget was, if not actually a necessity, a subscription much appreciated and, I think, owing. I must find a job. But where? I couldn't hang around my parents' necks and not contribute something to the household. These were my thoughts, not my parents'. Granta had suggested that Andy might be able to get me in beside him, but he didn't realize I was not yet sixteen. I looked older and could have passed for eighteen where no birth certificate was required.

Andy wrote to his sister that he was coming home for a week or so. He had split his three weeks vacation and would take the other two weeks later. I decided to talk to him, although I wasn't sure that I wanted to be an attendant in a mental hospital.

'Why not come back with me?' said Andy. 'I'll show you around, then you can decide for yourself.'

'I don't think I can afford it. Food and accommodation as well as the fare would leave me practically broke.'

'If I got you free accommodation and helped you with the fare, would you come?'

'I can manage the fare and food myself. I'm free. Should I go back with you?'

'No. Let me arrange for a place to stay first. It'll be all right but I shouldn't take anything for granted. A week from now maybe?'

'That'll be fine,' I answered.

As promised, Andy sent me a letter to say it was all fixed up and that I had a place to stay free of charge. I had to sell my motor bike, but I had taken that into consideration when I decided to visit Andy. The motor bike was a Bradbury. It had oversize wheels and four gears. On the open road where it was flat, or where there was a slight incline going downward, I could run it in high gear. Then it was as silent as anyone could wish. I mentioned to Dad that I was going to advertise the bike for sale.

'You'll do nothing of the kind,' he said. 'How much do you need?'

'Maybe four pounds will do.'

'Do you want to make it more?'

'No. That is about what I would get for the bike. But I don't want to borrow.'

'All right, Son, I'll buy the bike and when you have the four pounds you can buy it back. How's that?'

'It's terrific. I don't know what else to say . . . except thanks, Dad.'

I got the railway train to Liverpool and got to the ferry just in time to see it leave the dock. Fairly tight on funds, I didn't want to spend money for an overnight stay in Liverpool, so I decided to walk around the city until morning when I would catch the first boat. About two hours later I began to tire and realized that I was lost. It didn't matter, except that the further away I got, the further I had to walk back. I heard footsteps around the corner. Then two policemen came walking leisurely towards me. 'Good,' I thought, 'I'll ask them for directions.' I waited for them to catch up with me.

'Excuse me,' I said, 'but I think I'm lost. Can you tell me if I'm on the right street and in the right direction for the ferry?'

'You're a long way from the ferry. What are you doing in this neighbourhood?' asked one of the bobbies.

'Just walking until it is time for the first ferry in the morning.'

'Where are you from?' inquired the other.

'Leven.'

'Leven? Where's that?'

'That's in South America, isn't it?' said the other.

'It sounds more like a Japanese name,' said the first to speak.

'Do you speak English?' he inquired, looking at me suspiciously.

'I thought I did,' I answered. 'Do you?'

They both burst into boisterous laughter. What could I do but join them?

'Why didn't you go to a hotel for the night?' one of the bobbies asked me.

'Or the Y.M.C.A.?' said the other.

'I wanted to save what money I have for the Isle of Man.'

'If you want it, you could sleep in a cell at the station. It's a few hours before the ferry leaves.'

'Well, thank you, but I don't fancy being locked up. No offence meant.'

'Well, come along with us and we'll point you in the right direction. By the way, you shouldn't be walking here alone. This isn't Leven in the Kingdom o' Fife.'

'So you knew all the time where it was.'

'Aye. I started school there but left when I was about seven years of age. Maybe I know your parents, What's your name?'

'Ralph McCaa.'

'Hmm. The name doesn't ring a bell. Well, Ralph McCaa, do you see that bright light yonder?' he said, pointing. 'When you get to that light, turn left and stay on the main street and you'll come to the ferry.'

I thanked them and went on my way. It seemed forever before I was able to board the ferry, and it was a welcome relief to know that I was on the last leg of my journey. Andy wasn't there to meet me as he was working, but I had no trouble finding him.

'While you are here, you may as well meet the Old Man,' said Andy.

'The Old Man?'

'That's what we call him when he doesn't hear us. He's a Scot from Aberdeen. He likes, for reasons known only to himself, to hire men from Scotland and nurses from Ireland. Be on your Ps. and Qs. He can spot anyone trying to fool him right away.'

'Then I can't fool him about my age.'

'What age are you?'

'I'm nearly sixteen.'

'If he asks you, say you're not eighteen yet but you hope he'll remember you and . . . well, something like that.'

Eventually, I was confronted by 'The Old Man'. He was an imposing figure, quite elderly, and with a grim expression similar to the old-time preachers who promised only agony in this life and damnation in the next. He was a religious man with a stentorian voice which thundered out the hymns on Sunday during the service which the mental patients attended, dressed in their dark clothing. He was interested to know if I went to church service on Sundays, and to which church. There was probably no bigotry involved, because his attendants, I learned later, were mostly, but not all, Presbyterial, and the nurses mostly of the Roman Church. Of course, I didn't know any of this at that time and I answered his questions as vaguely as I knew how without lying. 'Age? Come back in a couple of years, Mister.'

'Sounds promising,' Andy said when we were alone.

'It sounds promising two years from now,' I griped. 'What do I do meantime?'

'Look around. You never know your luck. Meantime, let's see your landlady. She said she would be happy to put you up free of charge. I told her you were going to work with me.'

'But nothing has been actually promised!' I proclaimed.

It was a private, two-storey house where lived a childless couple, both about forty-five years of age, I guessed. I didn't know where the husband worked but he was always on the night shift. He came home for meals, then disappeared. He seemed to wear a smirk when we were introduced. He had no comment of any kind to make during the meal. When he had finished eating he said, 'I have to run, dear.'

'What about supper, dear?' she asked him.

'I'll grab a bite out,' he answered, and left.

When he had gone, she engaged me in small talk but seemed to be measuring me with an eye for a suit of clothing. She showed me a bedroom and asked if I would like it.

'It is perfect,' I assured her.

'You'll have supper with me,' she said.

'I'll be eating out. It wouldn't be . . .'

'Of course, but this evening you will dine with me.'

'It's very kind of you. I want a word with Andy. When should I return?'

'Any time between seven-thirty and eight-thirty,' answered my charming hostess. I sought out Andy and we talked about the prospects of getting some kind of employment.

'Have you got settled in all right?' Andy inquired when we had exhausted talk about a job.

'Oh yes. Everything's fine.'

'She is very nice, isn't she?'

'She certainly is. She asked me to have supper with her, just for tonight, that is.'

'Sounds promising.'

'What do you mean?'

Andy ignored my question. 'Now, listen Ralph. If anyone should ask you, you're eighteen.'

'Why? Who's going to ask?'

'Nobody. It . . . well, it sounds more . . . more grown up. Know what I mean?'

I didn't know what he meant, but why argue over it?

She was a marvellous cook and I enjoyed the meal. I offered to pay for it but she wouldn't hear of it. The journey had tired me, having gone without sleep the previous night, and after a chat about nothing in particular I said I would like to turn in.

'Of course,' she said, 'then you can have a good breakfast in the morning.'

I thanked her for her kindness and retired. I fell asleep almost immediately but was awakened by a gentle knock on the bedroom door.

'Come in.'

My hostess entered. She had a blanket in her arms. 'Are you warm enough?'

'Just fine, thank you,' I assured her.

'I brought you an extra blanket. It can be chilly in the night.'
'You shouldn't have troubled. I'm perfectly . . .'
That was all I managed to say. She had thrown the blanket over me and, leaning over me, she placed her hands on my cheeks and kissed me on the lips.

I froze. It was so unexpected.

'I would be terribly unhappy if you caught a chill,' she said, and slipped in beside me.

I was petrified. Heading the multifarious thoughts that rushed to my mind was the urgent, though hardly noble thought: what if her husband should walk in? Not in the boxing ring, not on my motor bike, not in the pits, not anywhere at all have I as much as winced. But now – I began to tremble.

'What's wrong?' she whispered.
'I don't know.'
She looked at me. Her face was serious. 'Ralph . . . how old are you?'
'Eighteen.'
'That is what Andy told me. What is your true age, Ralph?'
'Eighteen,' I said hesitantly.
'You can confide in me. I promise I won't tell anyone.'
'I'll be sixteen next birthday.'
'Fifteen,' she said with a sigh. She slipped out of bed as easily as she had joined me. 'I have many faults, Ralph, but child molesting is not one of them. Goodnight. Sleep well.' She left as silently as she came. Next morning she had set a place at the table for me. I couldn't look her in the eye but I mumbled, 'I'll find some other place to stay.'

'Good gracious, why?' she exclaimed. 'You're a nice boy, Ralph. Stay here. I would like you to.' She was aware of my embarrassment and left the table. Cheerfully she said, 'See you later,' and disappeared. I met Andy in Douglas as prearranged.

'Did you sleep well?' he asked.
'Yes, I did.'
'She's a good looker, eh?'
'I would say so . . . yes.'

'And generous.' Andy's eyes looked searchingly at me.

'Most generous,' I assured him. 'She insisted I have breakfast with her then fend for myself.'

'Breakfast, eh? That's all?'

'I think that was very generous of her. I tried to pay for it but she wouldn't hear of it.'

Disappointment was written clearly on Andy's face.

I continued to stay there but there was never any mention of the burlesque incident of that first night. Indeed, another blanket, one of taciturnity, enveloped the whole thing. It wasn't until two years later that I learned that her husband and she had been estranged for three years and, much to her joy, he had vanished with another woman, which provided her with grounds for divorce.

Andy and I went to Douglas often, dancing occasionally to Jack Kerr's orchestra, swimming, movies, just enjoying ourselves. Too soon the holiday was over and I returned to Leven feeling rather deflated.

'Come back in a couple of years,' the Old Man had said. That's promising, but what about the two years between now and then?

AN INTERVIEW

Back in Bonnie Scotland, the outlook for employment wasn't too bonnie. I did a few odd jobs which I found very unrewarding in every way. There was nothing for it. There was no difficulty getting work in the pits. I had many walks with Granta but they became shorter with each passing month. These rambles were, however, more enjoyable than ever, perhaps because I felt I had a responsibility for his return home, as he had for mine when I was a tadpole. One Sunday, when we had gone further than usual, we sat on a fallen tree to rest.

'I hope I haven't tired you out, boy,' he said.

'Not really,' I answered, 'but have you ever seen such a beautiful tree trunk to sit on?'

Granta turned his blue eyes on me and they crinkled even more than usual. Then he turned away and chortled somewhere in the roof of his mouth. 'Aye, it might no' be here tomorrow,' he murmured.

'It'll be here for a long time and we'll sit on it often, Grant.'

He looked at me seriously. 'Did ye ever hear about the boy who sat on a tree trunk so long he took root and started tae grow branches?'

'No, Grant, I don't believe I have.' I grinned.

'Neither have I. Nor has anybody else. Are ye ready?'

'Whenever you are.'

George and I went to the Palais pretty regularly, as well as going to the Gym. I was not serious about the Gym though, and missed many of the nights I should have gone there. Dad had become very interested in birds and we built an outside aviary, where we collected many foreign birds. Some of them were quite exotic, but my favourite was the budgerigar.

I took it upon myself to do the gardening. Between that and my growing interest in the aviary, time passed quickly. Andy had come home for a holiday and reminded me that the two years were almost up.

'Why don't you come out again and talk to The Old Man?'

'He has probably forgotten all about me.'

'On the contrary. He has asked about you several times.'

'He did?'

'Come out after I get back,' said Andy. 'Maybe I can soften him up a bit.'

The motor bike had been a source of trouble lately. Not the bike itself, but the law relating to it. Constable Oedipus had not forgotten the embarrassment he had suffered some years ago. First, he nabbed me for speeding. I was fined five shillings. That hurt. Some months later he collared me again. Dad was riding pillion and his coat-tails were obscuring the licence plate. Ten bob or three days in jail. Damn nearly a week's work in the pit. That hurt even more, but I paid it. The old girl, the Bradbury, was almost part of myself. I had paid four pounds ten shillings for her and I sold her for six pounds. That was after Andy had written to say: 'Come right away.'

Right Away meant in the near future where I was concerned.

I didn't smoke or drink, but it seemed that a pipe would make me look older, more mature, and give me a kind of dignity. After a couple of weeks, it was not too abominable. I even began to like it. I wondered what I looked like with a pipe. It was electrifying. Looking myself straight in the eyes, puffing gently on the pipe lodged firmly in the left side of my mouth, the effect of the slightest smirk, accompanied by the elevation of the right eyebrow, gave me maybe not a suave, but a dignified, an illustrious stamp. A mirror does not lie, I told myself. Here was my passport to a new career. I followed Andy about three weeks after his instruction to 'Come right away'. He was unable to get me accommodation free of charge, so I stayed at a Youth Hostel. Arrangements were made for me to meet 'The Old Man'.

'You may have to wait for some weeks before you get in,' Andy said.

An Interview

'You should have come right away when there was an opening.'

Andy was tied up at work with something when I was called to meet The Old Man, so I saw him on my own. Removing the pipe from my mouth, which denoted good manners, I said brightly, 'Good afternoon, Sir.' He looked at his pocket watch. I stuck the pipe back in my jaws and treated him to my most irresistible smile.

He stared back at me. 'It is exactly fifteen and a half minutes before noon. Afternoon begins at twelve o'clock. You smoke the pipe?' he said.

'Yes, sir. Do *you* enjoy the pipe yourself?'

'Mister,' he answered gravely, 'I do not smoke or drink or swear or fornicate, and I'll thank you not to smoke in my presence.'

'I'm not crazy about it myself,' I croaked, trying to stuff the smouldering instrument of mortification in the breast pocket of my jacket, which contained a handkerchief. Somehow I missed it. Just inches before it would have hit the carpet, I snatched it out of the air. If you think that is impossible, it is. Try it. I tried, when I was alone. Four times. It is impossible. If I had missed, and it had bounced off the carpet, it would undoubtedly have left a burn.

'You can go now,' he commanded, 'before some monstrous accident occurs.'

'Thank you, Sir,' I said and bowed. Not a deep bow, just a little one in respect for his position. I was so astonished at what I had done, however, that I just stood there and stared, not knowing what to say. He stared back at me. After about three hours, actually three fast seconds, he said, 'I didn't do it. You did.'

In utter confusion, I turned and fled. It put me off smoking for a week. When I saw Andy later he asked, 'How did it go?'

'I think I buggered up the whole shebang,' and I told him what had happened.

'It sounds promising.'

'It always sounds promising. How do you figure that?'

'The Old Man likes to think of himself as a kind of Buddha, scaring the hell out of everybody.'

'He struck me as being more like Genghis Khan.'

'He's not that bad,' said Andy. 'Pretend you're a Baptist next time you meet him.'
'I am a Baptist.'
'I know, but pretend you are anyway. He is very religious.'
'Yes, I know. He doesn't do anything.'
'Don't you believe it. He has six children. Do you like it here?'
'I'm sure I would get to like it.'
'Well, hang around,' said Andy, 'you never know your luck.'
One thing I did know was that I would never go back to the coal mines. As I had nearly two weeks to go before I would run out of cash, I might as well enjoy it here.
It was obvious to me I had blown any chance I might have had of getting a job at the Hospital, so I relaxed and roamed, walking, swimming, stopping to listen to the entertainers who sang the latest pop songs to the accompaniment of a piano; everything that didn't cost money. I wondered how the lady-of-the-blanket was getting on. Fully a week had passed before I had the courage to visit her.
'Ralph!' she exclaimed when she opened the door, 'I heard you were here. It must be, oh . . . two years?'
'Almost to the day,' I answered, 'I should have come to see you earlier.'
'I'm just about to make a pot of tea. Come in and have some,' she said giving me a pat on the cheek like a mother with her small boy.
'How is your husband?' seemed like a nice way to open the conversation.
'I have no idea, Ralph. He skedaddled with his girlfriend some time ago. I thought he would never go. I'm getting a divorce.' She was smiling happily about the whole situation. And she was reading my thoughts. 'Ralph, Honey, two years ago was too soon. Now it's too late. I met a charming man of my own age. We love each other. We are going to be married as soon as my divorce comes through.'
'I'm delighted to hear this. What I mean is, I'm glad it has a happy ending for you. I know it will for him.'
'Thank you, Ralph.' She kissed me on the cheek. 'Sugar? Cream?'

An Interview

'Both, please.'

Next day, after work, Andy sought me out in great excitement.

'What's up?' I asked.

'You start here day after tomorrow. You impressed him, Ralph.'

'Impressed? I did just the opposite.'

'He scared the daylights out of you, didn't he?'

'Do I have to face the old curmudgeon once again so soon?'

'Not at the moment. I'll show you the ropes. In about a week or so he'll ask you how you like it here.'

'What do I say? I like the grub.'

Andy spread his hands in a gesture of perplexed incomprehension.

'Tell him the truth. Say what's in here,' said Andy, tapping his breast. 'Tell him you feel you are doing fulfilling and compassionate work. Tell him exactly how you feel about working here.'

'But suppose I don't feel fulfilled and ahm . . .'

'A little embroidery wouldn't hurt you. Don't overdo it, though.'

'I suppose not. All the same, it seemed to me that *you* were overdoing it.'

'I was just giving you the idea,' Andy said, grinning. 'By the way, you'll like the grub.'

I wrote home to say that I had landed a job beside Andy and that I would not be home for about a year. It was all so different from anything I had ever done, opening and locking doors everywhere we went throughout the building. For a few days I was caught in the disquiet of a depression of sympathy for these derelicts of society, living behind locked doors, prisoners of circumstance not of their own making but of fate, both designed and uncontemplated by forces beyond our control. Fortunately it was some weeks before the Old Man got around to asking me how I liked it here. By then my depression had lifted and I saw that I could indeed actually enjoy working with the patients of a mental hospital. At the same time, I felt sure I would not spend my life in this environment as the Old Man had done. It wasn't until much later that I realized he very carefully chose the time to ask new attendants 'how they liked it here'.

Ralph

The job presented many lighter moments as well as darker ones. For example, once a week Archie, a deaf mute inmate, took a horse and buggy on his own to a mill some miles away to collect a week's supply of meal and flour. Although he couldn't hear, he was expert at reading lips. One day I asked him if I could ride with him. I wanted to see the mill. Archie nodded in the affirmative and I sat beside him on the buggy. About halfway to our destination I nudged him and asked if I could take the reins. He smiled and handed them to me. I think the nice old mare could have been told to go on by herself and she would have collected the meal and delivered it all by herself. For no reason, I flicked the reins on her back. It wasn't a heavy whack but it was unexpected. She bolted, wondering, no doubt, what she had done to deserve such treatment. A motor car coming towards us came close to being sideswiped. Archie grabbed the reins and brought us to a halt, shaking his head at me in just reproach. He leapt to the ground and Daisy and he nuzzled each other in silence. As he returned to his seat on the buggy, Daisy turned her head, following him with her eyes. I wouldn't bet my life on it, but I imagined I heard her mouth: 'Don't let that damned fool have the reins again.' I travelled with them, Archie and Daisy, several times after that but I never asked to drive again. When we came to the place where Daisy had bolted, Archie used to look at me as if to say, 'You poor slob, this is the place - remember?' Sometimes I would cover my face in my hands with shame. Sometimes I would shake my fist at him. It was all in fun, however, and we would both laugh, Archie in a high-pitched squeak which was all the voice he had, I with a hearty, unrestrained guffaw.

Jackie, born an idiot, cried out in silence for affection. He had no visitors and he would stand and smile, nodding, sometimes waving at some of the other inmates' relatives. As gently as we could, we guided him away from these family groups, who were sometimes upset by, if not resentful of this uninvited attention. One day, while walking through the wards, Jackie decided to claim me as *his* relative. Throwing an arm around my neck, he fell into step with me - pals, while he smiled at the other inmates, who paid no attention to him. Out of earshot, I stopped, disengaged his arm, and told him never to do that again. Jackie's face was full, his body overweight and his head above his eyes resembled a coconut. His eyes were small, but they expressed deep and distressing hurt. He rushed into a corner and faced the wall. I felt I should restore his confidence. Going over to him, I put my hand on his shoulder. He pulled away, angry and disappointed. I assured him he was a good boy and that everyone liked him, including myself. 'Let's walk to the door together, Jackie. Good friends. Everyone is watching.' Placing an arm around his shoulder, I practically pulled him from the corner. He looked around him at the other patients and their visitors, all unaware of the drama that had taken place right beside them. Satisfied that his dignity had been re-established, we walked joyfully to the door, where I patted him and left him smiling. Poor, lonely, bewildered creature that he was, wandering endlessly about the wards looking for - somebody!

Every two weeks we had a dance for the patients. The male attendants danced with the female patients; the nurses danced with the male patients. Some of the inmates didn't dance, or didn't want to dance, but there were those who found their favourite partners on both sides. Patients didn't wait to be asked to dance. They made a run for their favourite partners. One young woman occupied herself during the dance by inspecting my clothing, removing any specks of lint or other superfluous substance from my jacket. She never spoke, but she kept me spotless.

An old woman, a chatterbox with whom I always had a dance, told me regularly how well her children had done in life. She was so proud of them. I wondered why they didn't ever visit her. She said that some day she would take a holiday and visit them, laden with presents for *their* children, darlings, all of them.

I cannot swear to it, but I think my decision to leave came after I attended my first post mortem. It was two days after a patients' dance. On the mortuary slab lay the body of the old woman. The top of her skull had been sawn off, exposing the brain. She was cut open from her neck to her groin. I am not squeamish and, had she been a complete stranger, I might have been untouched. Poor woman, she had no children; in fact she had no living relative.

The patients were well taken care of. Epileptic fits, bowel movements, and any aberrations, mental or physical were faithfully recorded, and drugs or medicines prescribed and administered as necessary. They had walks in the countryside, they were given various jobs to do, and they were more than adequately fed and clothed. Yet, in this wilderness of timeless separation from what is normal in the world outside, there were no pets. The monotony for some must have been painful. Some readers will criticize me as being unqualified to make judgements. And they would be perfectly right. However, this is meant not as a judgement, but as a layman's opinion.

For us, the staff, it was a different life. Andy, Billy Q. and I were pretty close pals, especially after the first two years. Andy was always ready for any kind of hellery, provided it did not include death or dismemberment. Billy Q. was almost as eager to participate.

It goes without saying that some of the attendants and some of the nurses dated each other. Complaints began to surface that couples were being followed by some locals, who hid where they could watch and listen to lovebirds when they found a snuggery or somewhere nice to lie. Headed by Andy and Billy Q., a kind of vigilante group was organized. I was chosen, with one of the nurses, to act as decoys. We talked and laughed enough to be heard, then we found a roost. The plan was that I should whistle at the right moment, then eight or nine fellows would pounce on the enemy and deliver a few black eyes. Our attention had strayed from business to pleasure, and they jumped the gun. I had some explaining to do. Anyway, we were never bothered again. Besides, I was not anxious to get mixed up in a free-for-all.

Another time it seemed unavoidable. The three of us had a favourite pub where we stopped for a pint when the weather was hot. One day, three young men who were sitting at a table sidled up to us at the bar. One of them said, 'Hey, how are you?' Andy said we were just fine and turned back to the bar. Another one grabbed me by the shoulder and pulled me around. 'How's about buying us a drink?' he said. I removed

An Interview

his hand and told him to 'Buzz off'. He grabbed me by the shoulder again and tightened his grip. Andy, Billy Q. and I finished our drinks, then I nodded to them. If it had been choreographed and rehearsed for a Western movie, it could not have been neater. As one man, we turned and drove our fists into the three grinning faces. Then we walked out.

ANOTHER INTERVIEW

After the P.M., I think I knew that I would never spend the rest of my life in this environment. Still, there was nothing to prod me into making a move. I had no trade and the thought of going back to the coal mines was out of the question. Another year had passed almost unnoticed and I had not prepared for the examination to come after three years service. 'There is no point in taking this examination,' I told the examiner. 'Then, I shall have to fail you,' he said. This was the prop I needed to resign. I gave a month's notice and arrived back in Fifeshire, out of work. I had been away only three years, yet everything looked different. The streets looked narrower, the people older. It didn't occur to me immediately that I looked different to those I hadn't seen for three years. The awful truth sank home. I was twenty-one. What would another three years do to me? I would be twenty-four and that was close to a quarter of a century. Also, the food at the hospital had been so rich and so plentiful that I had put on weight. In four more years I would be an old man – no, I would be a fat old man of twenty-five. After greetings with everybody, Mum and Dad, Granta and others, I walked the High Street of Leven – alone. I stopped to gaze into shop windows but I saw nothing. My mood was gloomy and introspective. A group of kilted soldiers were coming towards me. They were a noisy bunch, laughing and jostling each other and whistling to passing girls. They came abreast of me and I had a sudden thought.

'Hello,' I said. 'Black Watch, aren't you?'

One bandy-legged young lad looked me down and up.

'That's right,' he said, 'what's it to ye?' He was not impressed with what he saw any more than I was with what I was looking at. He was skinny, some inches shorter than I, and slightly tipsy.

'How does one go about joining the Army?' I asked.

The skinny one walked right around me, then stopped in front of me.

'Ye've got tae hae a bonnie arse tae wear a kilt,' he advised me.

He was smiling and meant no harm. I should have said, 'I can see how you qualified.' Instead, I thought it would be more fun to give him some of his own medicine. I said, 'Tell me, how the hell did *you* get in?'

The smile vanished. 'Pit up yer dukes,' he cried, raising his fists for a fight. His feet were in a poor position. He had no control over his balance. A sawed-off copy of myself when I joined the Club some years ago.

'I asked a civil question,' I grumbled, 'but if that's the way you want it, O.K.' Taking a fighting position, covering my face with my clenched fists, I scowled as fiercely as I could behind an exaggerated crouch. Then I did a little dancing, weaving and feinting.

One of the others yelled at my challenger, 'Hey, big mouth, pack it in before ye get kill't.' Wee Bandy backed off. He said, 'I was only kiddin'. What dae ye want tae know?' I laughed aloud at the collapse of the encounter.

I said, 'I just wanted to know how you go about joining up.'

'Why did ye no say so in the first place?' he said. 'Ye can jine up at the Black Watch Depot in Perth.'

'Thanks. Look,' I said, kicking his feet apart into position, 'when you put up your . . . dukes, anchor your feet like that. Then you can spring forward or back without losing your balance. Got that?'

'Aye. Ah'll remember that. If I had known that five minutes ago, Ah wid have slaughtered ye.'

'Undoubtedly,' I answered, holding up my open hands in a posture of self protection.

'Hey, Mister, when ye jine up, maybe ye'll gie me some mair tips?'

'Maybe. If I am in a better mood than I am today.'

The incident had cleared away my gloomy thoughts. I walked away briskly. Some fifty feet apart, I turned to wave. They returned my salute,

Another Interview

shouting wishes of good luck. It was then I had the jocund urge to deliver what might be the ultimate insult.

'Take care,' I cried, 'and when ye see the enemy, dinnie pee yer skirts.'

When all five of them sprinted towards me, shouting revenge, I ran like hell, outdistancing these likeable young men easily, despite my accumulated suet, the result of three years of drinking hundreds of gallons of fresh creamy milk.

The following day I took a bus to Perth and, asking directions, headed straight for the barracks, cradle of that famous regiment that, in World War I, had earned the name, 'Ladies from Hell'. As I walked from the bus, I was aware of the precious serenity of the city. It would be years, however, before I had the opportunity to climb Kinnoul Hill, which overlooked the city, once Scotland's capital, that honour now being claimed by Auld Reekie, Edinburgh the magnificent. Perth, city of fame and feudal restlessness, now tranquil and beautiful with its river Tay, a petticoat moat, skirting Kinnoul then snaking east to meet the Firth of Tay, affords me some of my most pleasurable reminiscences. But I saw nothing then. I came here with a purpose, which was not to admire the city with its treasured parks and lakes, not to go swimming in, or lazily go boating on, the Tay. I went there to enlist.

On arrival at the barracks, I was ushered into the presence of a short, fat man. He sat behind a scruffy looking desk with the usual telephone and two wire baskets marked 'in' and 'out'. A chair was placed opposite him, near to and facing the desk. Here was a man of authority. On his epaulettes he sported a crown, which I knew to signify the rank of major. 'Thank you, Orderly,' he said to the private who had presented me. 'Dismiss.' Following a smart salute and a half pirouette, the orderly marched out. The major smiled and patted his bulging abdomen in a spirit of esprit de corps, an expression I was to hear much about later. I recall wondering how much beer he had to consume each day to acquire his tub and egg-shaped, blue-veined, red tomato nose.

'At ease, my boy,' he said. I wasn't sure what he meant, but I assumed he meant me to make myself comfortable, so I sat on the chair opposite him. *HE* wasn't at ease. I could tell by the sudden disappearance of his smile and the swelling of his surface nasal veins. He said, 'I don't mean tae be unkind, but ye shouldna sit doon in front o' an officer.' 'Sorry,' I said, moving my chair to the side of his desk. A timid knock came at the door. The typist to take notes, I supposed. So far, I hadn't noticed any women about. 'Approach,' he called loudly. A private soldier built like a Clydesdale stallion advanced upon us with a tray upon which were placed a teapot, a cup and saucer, a spoon, sugar and milk and a small plate of digestive biscuits. The stallion placed the tray in front of me on the desk. This was exactly where he had placed the tray since the day it became one of his duties to place the tray. I didn't know it then, but I know now that if I had been sitting where he placed the tray, dangling my legs, he would have dumped the tray neatly in my lap. The stallion stood there like a tree looking at the wall two feet above the major's head. 'Thank you, Orderly. Dismiss.'

Exit Pegasus after the customary salute. I hadn't expected a red carpet, nevertheless I considered it most thoughtful of them to provide me with tea and biscuits. Boy, was I ready for it! There was only one cup and saucer so I assumed the major had already partaken of his cuppa. 'Would ye mind getting back frae the desk?' said the major in a strangled voice. I scraped my chair back about a foot. 'And stand up, if ye don't mind,' he croaked. I stood up. It was fortunate I hadn't reached for the goodies on the tray, for the major slid the whole caboodle on to his blotter. Pouring a cup of tea, he sipped it noisily, crunching a biscuit or two and dabbing his lips daintily with the napkin, ending the ritual by blowing his nose in it. As he slurped and munched, he threw me an occasional stare which reminded me of Oliver Hardy who, after a pratfall, glared at the camera. After finishing his ambrosia, he pointed across his desk. I looked but saw nothing unusual. 'Stand over there,' he grunted. He burped, a loud and full-bodied burp, then stared at me – for my reaction, I think. Maybe he had served time in Egypt, where, I believe, after feasting with a sheik, one's survival depended on how loud one burped. 'Now,' he wheezed, 'as I was about to – burp – this is your lucky – burp. First ye – burp over tae the medical. The doctor there'll burp ye tae see if ye are – burp for service. Then we'll sign ye up. Well, off ye – burp.' The time had come for me to tell him I didn't want to enlist in the Black Watch. I said, 'The Medical Corps is what I had in mind.' His tomato ripened in sudden and shattering disbelief. When he regained his composure he informed me, 'I jined as a private. Now I'm a major. See?' He tapped the crown on one of his epaulettes. I nodded.

'Congratulations. How long would it take for me to make major?'

His body seemed to swell. For a moment I was worried, but it was only the result of an unusually sudden inhalation.

'First ye get yer medical, then we'll discuss things like that.'

He dismissed me with an imperious wave and started shuffling through his out basket.

At the Medical Centre, another major made me jump about for several minutes while he played his chanter. Then he took my pulse and respiration. 'You're in good shape,' he said, and gave me a slip of paper to take back to the roly-poly major.

'Excuse me, Major, but I wanted to enlist in the Medical Corps.'

'Glad to hear it,' he answered, 'but you'll have to go to Edinburgh for that. Have you signed anything, yet?'

'No.'

'Good. Here's the address.' He scribbled an address on a piece of notepaper. I walked smartly back towards the roly-poly major's office. Passing the huge wrought iron gate, the entrance to the barracks, I noticed, on a small gate at the side, a sign 'OUT'. I wheeled right and made for the bus terminal.

On my arrival home, I was welcomed as if I had been away for years.

'What happened?' asked Dad.

'I have to go to Edinburgh if I want to enlist in the Medical Corps.'

'There's no hurry, is there?'

'I suppose not,' I answered. I was unaware that I was looking around the living room. 'No, I suppose not.'

'Why don't you get another dog?' Dad suggested.

'I'll never have another dog.'

Twice I had been home on vacation while I was employed at the hospital. On the first one, after a year's absence, Nell had leapt at me and bitten my hand in sheer joy, drawing blood. She had made sounds like a baby crying. I had rough-tumbled with her until she had had me pinned to the floor with her great shaggy paws as if to say, 'I've got you. Now, try to get away.' When she had got through with me, it had been necessary to have a shower. She was rewarded with many walks and swims. Granta was able to come with us to the beach, which was only two blocks away from his home. Next year had been much the same, but Nell followed me everywhere, worried, I think, in case I should suddenly disappear again.

Five months previously, Dad had written to say that Nell had been hit by a motor vehicle and had been killed instantly. She had seemed lost and careless after my second disappearance. At thirteen she was also getting old and a little wobbly as well as deaf. Poor Nell, she simply walked out on to the thoroughfare at the wrong moment.

Well, now I had no dog, no motor bike and no job. All of these things accounted for my sometimes surly attitude. I didn't want *another* dog. Besides, if I enlisted I would not be allowed to keep a dog. I felt bitter about many things and hated myself for it.

Two days after I had been to Perth, Dad said, 'Do you remember Jimmy Morris?'

'Yes, I remember him. He bought a motor bike shortly after I bought the Bradbury. A Coventry Eagle.'

'That's right,' answered Dad. 'Jimmy's father works beside me. He told me that Jimmy is going to England. He landed a good job there.'

'Good luck to him. Nice chap, Jimmy. Have you any idea . . .?'

'I certainly have,' said Dad, cutting me off. 'He is going by bus and taking everything with him - except his bike.'

I felt my heart pounding. Jimmy had taken good care of his bike. Dad said quietly, 'We still have the money you sent us from the hospital. We didn't need it. You can have it back if it will help.'

'How much does he want for it?' I asked excitedly.

'I believe he wants fifteen pounds. If you would like . . .'

I didn't wait for Dad to finish.

Another Interview

'I can manage fine. But thanks, anyway. See you later.'

Jimmy lived only two streets away, and I ran all the way to his place. Play it cool, I thought. I knocked. No answer. I knocked louder. Seconds later Jimmy opened the door. 'Hello, Ralph.'

'Hello, Jimmy. Thought I'd come round and wish you luck in your new job.'

'You didn't have to run,' said Jimmy, grinning.

'Run?'

'Yes. I was packing upstairs and I saw you through the window. I'm not going for another three days.'

'Yes, well, I didn't want to miss you.'

'Of course. I'm asking fifteen pounds.'

The charade was over. 'Have you had any offers, Jimmy?'

'Some,' answered Jimmy.

'Would you consider twelve pounds?'

'It's worth fifteen. It's worth more like twenty.'

'I'm out of work.'

'I'm sorry about that, Ralph, but . . .'

'Fourteen?'

'I've had an offer of fourteen, but I'd rather you had it for fourteen than Bob Carter.'

'Then it's a deal?'

'Deal.' We shook hands on it.

'Can I see it?' I queried.

'Come on.' We went to his back yard where he had a toolshed. There was the Coventry Eagle gleaming like new. The rubber was good and it looked as if it had just come out of a showroom.

'I don't have the money with me, Jimmy. It's at home, but I want the bike.'

'Look, Ralph, take the bike home with you and come back with the money. If you change your mind, bring it back and I'll let Bob Carter have it.'

The little two-stroke purred like a sweet natured kitten, and I couldn't get back fast enough with the money. Bob Carter was there looking

angry as a boil. He glared at me when I arrived.
'You could have waited,' he shouted at Jimmy. 'I would have given you fifteen, dammit.' I counted out fourteen pounds.
'Sorry about that Bob, but Ralph has his money ready.'
'So have I,' Carter yelled, producing a bundle of pound notes.
I held out the money to Jimmy. Carter counted out sixteen pounds.
'O.K. Sixteen bloody pounds,' he shouted.
'How much have you got there, Bob? You know this bike is worth twenty.'
'I don't have twenty. Eighteen is all I have.'
'Have you got anything lined up yet, Ralph? A job, I mean.'
'Eighteen, then,' yelled Carter.
'No, I haven't, but maybe I'll join up.'
'Oh. What regiment?'
'The Medical Corps.'
'You can't keep a motor bike in the Army, can you?'
'I don't think so. I don't really know.'
'Well,' said Jimmy, taking my fourteen pounds and stuffing it into his trouser pocket, 'if you have to sell, you always know where to get eighteen for it.'
The words nearly stuck in my throat, but I squeezed them out. 'Jimmy, I want this bike, but if you would like to change your mind . . .'
'I took your money. The deal is closed.'
'Eighteen,' Bob Carter whimpered.
Jimmy gave him a withering glance, then disappeared into the house. Before he closed the door behind him, I called, 'Thanks, Jimmy, and good luck in your new job.'
'Good riding, Ralph,' he responded and closed the door.
Carter spat on the ground, then strode off, angry and frustrated. I had the bike. In the excitement, I had given no thought to the transfer licence. The window of the bedroom upstairs opened and Jimmy called, 'Hey, Ralph, don't forget this,' and he threw me the licence, which fluttered down into my waiting hands as if in joyful anticipation of good times in the new partnership. Jimmy and I waved to each other and

Another Interview

I was off.

On my way home, I waved pleasantly to Bob Carter as I came abreast of him. He glared at me as if I had done him a great injury and his lips formed in a silent obscenity which I prefer not to record.

To hell with him.

OEDIPUS WREAKS

I still had my driver's licence and I immediately got the transfer of the bike authorized.
'Are you happier now?' Dad asked.
'Was I unhappy? I know, I know. But I still have to find a job.'
'What nicer way do you have than to scoot around on your bike looking for something?' replied Dad. 'And, if you feel inclined, you can run me to my work depot, thus saving me a bus or tram fare.'
'On the pillion?'
'Certainly not. On the handlebars.'
'If that's your cup of tea. When do you want to start?'
'I have tickets until the end of the week. Beginning Monday. All right?'
The weather was beautifully sunny until a clap of thunder warned us of a downpour on Sunday evening. On Monday morning it stopped as suddenly as it started.
'What do you think, Dad,' I said hopefully. 'Would you like to chance it?'
'The sky is a bit moody but we can wear raincoats just in case.'
We had barely started when the sky opened up and another heavy downpour drenched the town, already clean and shining with a night of heavy rain.
'Hold tight,' I shouted. 'I'll take you to the bus stop anyway. It goes right to your depot, doesn't it?'
'Yes, but go easy, Son. The road is slippery.'
Streams of rain water rushed along the gutters into the half-clogged grids. We had almost reached the bus stop when a car driver, seeing no

one waiting, whizzed by without stopping. We were on a side street, so I had to stop anyway but if some other clown took chances like that there could be a nasty accident. No traffic was in sight, so I revved the engine and letting in the clutch slowly, I said, 'Don't worry. I can get you there in plenty of time.'

A large, dark figure stepped out almost in front of us. I jammed on the brakes and swerved in order not to collide with him. The bike skidded on the slippery road and suddenly we were sliding along the tarmac and into the gutter. We were soaked. I helped Dad to his feet, then turned towards the idiot, who just stood there making no effort to assist. Oedipus! Constable Oedipus! It had been eight years since I had seen him but he hadn't changed. The same petulant face and loose, pouty mouth.

'You dumb cluck!' I yelled. 'What's the idea of jumping out in front of us like that? Are you all right, Dad?'

'I'm all right. How about you?' I noticed his voice was shaky.

'I'm all right. Are you sure you're . . .?'

'Yes, yes. Fine.'

Oedipus had taken shelter in the shop door nearest him. Fortunately neither Dad nor I had any injuries, so I picked up the bike and it started right away.

'The bike seems all right. Jump on and I'll take you back for some dry clothing. I can still get you to work on time.'

I glared at Oedipus standing grinning in the doorway. He looked more like some bloody gargoyle than a local bobby. He was wagging a limp hand for us to come over to him. With the other hand he was fumbling under his oilskin cape. He drew forth a notepad and pencil. How many notebooks and pencils had he gone through in the last eight years?

He was still fanning the air with his other hand.

'What now?' I shouted.

'Here you. Both of yous. Come over 'ere.'

There was no way out. I parked the bike and we joined him in the doorway. 'All right,' he said, flexing his pencil arm. 'Your names?'

Why can't I remember Granta's admonition, and keep my big mouth shut? Instead, I said, 'Only you could be stupid enough to stand in front of a motor bike on a wet road.'

He ignored my remark but he had a venomous gleam in his eyes.

'I'm goin' to ask you once more, then I may 'ave to take you in.'

Dad gave him our names and address while I stood by, fuming in silence.

'What are we being charged with?' Dad asked politely.

'Faulty brakes, and ...'

'What the hell?' I yelled.

'... and dangerous driving.' Oedipus was scribbling.

'There's not a thing wrong with my brakes,' I shouted, 'and you know it.'

'Well, we'll let that go maybe. Dangerous driving.'

I was about to explode when Dad gripped my arm firmly. 'Let me do the talking,' he cautioned.

'But you can see the skid marks,' I roared.

'And obscuring the rear licence plate,' he mumbled as he wrote.

'That's a lie!' I yelled. 'You were in front of me.'

Oedipus ordered Dad to sit on the pillion. His coat was clear of the licence plate.

'However,' said the constable, 'I'm not goin' to charge you with that. Maybe you didn't do it intentional.'

I was so angry that if I had been alone with him, I would have given him my fist on his repulsive mug. Dad thanked him and promised we would be more careful in future.

'That's all right then,' answered Oedipus. Turning to me he muttered, 'You'll get these brakes seen to?' It seemed good judgement to agree, which I did. I was beginning to realize I had been pretty rough with my tongue when he said, 'You'll get a summons to appear.'

'BALLS!' I yelled, 'it was entirely your fault.'

Again he flexed his arm and scribbled in his notebook as he mumbled, 'B-A-L-L-S. Using foul ... and abusive ... language.'

Dad held up a disapproving hand. 'Enough,' he said, boring me with a stern, paternal eye.

Oedipus walked away. Turning abruptly and looking at Dad he said, 'Are you all right, Sir?' Without waiting for an answer, he mumbled, 'Good . . . I'm glad nobody got hurt.' Then he disappeared.

We rode home, where we quickly changed into dry clothes. After being assured that, with the exception of a few minor bruises, neither of us was hurt, Mum said, 'I'll make a nice pot of tea.'

Mum was a firm upholder of the time-worn belief that a pot of tea would cure whatever ails you.

'No time for that, Mum,' Dad said. 'Ralph will tell you all about it when he gets back. At least, he'll tell you his side of it. I'll tell you mine when I finish work.'

I thought it was a pretty hypercritical statement to make, but I realized later that I should have kept my mouth shut. The purr of the engine, coupled with my black mood, didn't induce conversation, so we rode to the Depot in silence.

'That was a mistake, Ralph,' Dad said when he dismounted. 'You were extremely rude.'

'Would it have made any difference? He's been waiting eight years for vengeance. Ever since that Oedipus embarrassment.'

Dad smiled and nodded. Then he left. I felt better. On the journey home I went to a garage to have the brakes tested – just in case.

'There's no' a thing wrang wi' yer brakes, laddie,' announced the mechanic after driving the bike around the block. 'Why dae ye want yer brakes examined for anyway?' I told him what had happened.

'Ooooo. What wis he like? Wis he a big, boney lookin' chap wi' a moustache an' liver lips?'

'That's a fair description,' I agreed.

'Aye, that wid be Eedipoos. He's mean. They say he wid stick his ain faither in jail if he had wan.'

'He's the only rotten apple in the barrel. What's his real name?'

'Eedipoos. That's what everybody ca's him onywey.'

I didn't tell the mechanic how he had acquired his moniker.

'Would you mind giving me a note to say that my brakes required no attention. The date and time are important.'

'Nae trouble.'

Armed with this devastating piece of artillery, I felt secure and I waited with confidence for the arrival of the summons.

'Cupar?' I groaned when I read the summons. 'That's twenty miles away. Why do I have to go to Cupar?' I griped.

'Because of your insulting remarks to an officer of the law, I suppose,' Dad answered.

'State your name and age,' droned a cold voice. I did. 'I swear to . . .'

'. . . so help me God,' I repeated.

Oedipus gave his version, reading from his notebook, after which I produced the mechanic's note. The judge examined it.

'This seems to be in order. You are also accused of dangerous driving.'

'I came to a full stop, Your Honour. When I drove into the crossroads, the constable jumped out in front of me.'

'Is that true, Constable?'

'Well, Your Honour, you could put it that way.'

'I have no intention of putting it that way or any way at all. Did you jump out in front of the driver?'

'I didn't actually *jump*, Your Honour.'

'The Court declines a lesson in semasiology. Did you jump, leap, or present yourself in front of the accused? Yes or no.'

'Ah, yes. Yes, Your Honour.' Things are looking good, I thought.

'Now,' he said glaring at me. 'You are accused of using an obscenity. Guilty or not guilty?'

'Your Honour . . . I live only two miles from a golf course. And they are going to erect a tennis court . . .' There was a rumble of laughter from the audience. Laughter in Court - in brackets - is how it was described in the local rag. 'Naturally, the expression came . . . naturally.'

'Naturally,' said the judge. More laughter in Court. The judge banged his gavel on the bench. 'I shall clear the Court if there is any more laughter. This is . . . a court of law . . . not a theatre.'

Looking at me again, he asked, 'Now, did you use that word?'

'What word, Your Honour?' There was a slight titter. They knew better than to laugh outright. I could have done without them. The judge looked a trifle annoyed. His face seemed to redden but it could have been a reaction to his clearing of the throat. His eyes bored clean through me to the back of my skull. 'What word? I'll tell you what word as delicately as I know how. It is a word which may be interpreted as . . . alluding to the . . . somewhat ovoid genitalia.' He raised his gavel, and he was not disappointed. There was a sudden typhoon of laughter from the gallery, so to speak. It was impossible for me not to join in the jubilation. Down came the gavel, bang, bang, bang, bang, bang. The judge didn't clear the court but he assured them that this was their last chance, which suggested to me that he was enjoying it all as much as the audience. Why not? The judge was the male lead.

'The fact is, Your Honour, my brakes were in perfect working order.'

'The Court is not questioning the sufficiency of your brakes, or the validity of the note which you supplied in your defence. I wish to know whether or not you used . . . that word.'

'Oh, you mean . . . well, Your Honour, if it comes right down to it . . .'

He banged his gavel with such force I expected to see splinters flying. What went wrong? I must have muffed it somewhere.

The judicial words cut the atmosphere like the voice of doom.

'In one, or in two words – Guilty or Not Guilty?'

I blurted out fast, loud and clear, 'Guilty, Your Honour.'

'Twenty-five shillings or seven days.'

I was stunned. An icicle in the shape of a hit man in the shape of a policeman took me by the arm and steered me to the door. Outside, he dumped me and closed the door. Another policeman was sitting at a small table, drumming his fingers on a strong box.

'Twenty-five bob,' he said, holding out his hand for the loot.

'How did you know it was twenty-five?' I inquired.

'This is twenty-five day.'

'I don't have it with me,' I said, which was quite true.

He was unperturbed. 'O.K. They'll collect later – Leven isn't it?'

'Yes.'

'Right. Off you go.'
I was thankful I didn't say what I was thinking that bright, unhappy day. Dad said I was lucky and that he would pay the fine.
'No . . . *Sir*. I'll go to jail first.'
'You'll do nothing of the kind, and you know it,' answered Dad.

For the next two weeks no one in our house mentioned it. Maybe if we didn't mention it, it would go away. No - such - luck.
One morning Mum answered a solid but not intimidating knock on the door. I was in the living room playing with Polly, our Amazonian parrot. Polly had been owned by a publican for over thirty years and he - or she - had a large and varied vocabulary. As I was taking Polly into another room, I heard a male voice which I didn't recognise. 'Good morning, ma'am. Young fellow in?'
Mum called, 'Ralph . . . it's for you.'
I knew instinctively it was the police. It wasn't Oedipus. I knew his voice.
I heard Mum say pleasantly, 'Isn't it a beautiful morning?'
'Yes. A little cool, but it's a lovely day,' said the visitor.
'Oh my! Won't you come in? I don't know where my manners have gone.'
'Thank you.' A large, uniformed figure looked in at the doorway of the living room as I appeared. He had a ruddy complexion and he was built like a wrestler. Not a bit like Oedipus. He didn't have that mean and shifty look. His eyes were candid and unwavering.
'Good morning, Ralph. I'm Sergeant Shoebotham.'
'Good morning, Sergeant,' I greeted him, trying to weigh him up.
'How's the bike running?'
'It's running well, and the brakes are as perfect as they have always been.' Ignoring my caustic remark, he answered, 'That's good. My youngest brother had a bike like yours. *He* was always particular about his brakes.'
So what, I thought. He's giving me the soft sell.
'As a matter of fact, he rode in the Tourist Trophy races in the Isle of

Man. They're pretty exciting. Ever been there?'
'Yes. I don't recognise the name. When was that?'
'Up to about seven years ago. He had a slight accident. Not serious, but he quit racing. Well, you know why I am here, Ralph.'
I didn't answer. He continued, 'I came to collect the fine.'
'Did you bring your handcuffs?'
'I always carry them. Would you like to try them on?'
'Look, Sergeant, I don't have twenty-five shillings to spare. I'm not working.'
'You could pay it in instalments.'
His face was so kindly and his quiet voice so persuasive that I was on the point of giving him maybe half of it. Mum broke in. 'That was a terrible storm we had a few weeks ago.'
'Yes, it was,' agreed the sergeant.
'But I think we're in for a nice spell of weather now, don't you?'
'I certainly hope so.'
'Would you like to sit down?'
A barely perceptible smile played around the sergeant's mouth. 'I have to run now. But I'll call back next week, if that is all right with you, Ma'am.'
'Oh, that'll be nice. I'll look forward to seeing you,' Mum gushed. 'I'll see you out.'
'Take care, Ralph,' he said, and he was gone.
When Mum returned to the living room she said, 'My, he's a nice man.'
'Yes, yes, but you didn't have to LOOK FORWARD to his next visit.'
'I hope Dad is in on his next visit. They would like each other, I'm sure. Don't you? Would you like a cup of tea?'
'No, thank you, Mum. I think I'll go for a spin on the bike.'
'Will you be back for lunch?'
'Oh, yes.'
'Be careful, then.'
I drove to the short, steep brae that started at the entrance to Spinkie Den, then on to the open road which rewarded the traveller with a

panoramic view of the peaceful rural countryside between Leven and Lundin Links. Lundin Links was peculiarly remote from the rest of the countryside. Although in no way inaccessible, it nestled in a dreamlike atmosphere between the highway and the golf links. Everyone who lived there seemed old or elderly. They all lived in large homes fronted by carefully manicured lawns. Trees, equally spaced, stood guard against the infiltration of unwelcome visitors such as litterers and, I suspect, motor cyclists. Rose bushes were in abundance in every garden and their perfume was an appropriate companion to the antiseptic properties. Signs here and there warned the careless itinerant to 'Keep off the Grass'. Tradesmen were invited to use the side door. All the men were thin and wore plus fours. All the women were thin and wore pairs of pruning shears in their delicate white hands. I turned right to get to the curly brae which led downhill to the golf course. Two golf bags in plus fours glared at me when I passed. Three pairs of pruning shears stopped snipping and pointed at me. I waved but got no response except the affectation of a still life. I must try again on my return trip. I sped downhill to the golf course where I could see the railway lines and occasional glimpses of the Mile Dyke. How many times had I ridden the train along these tracks? How often had I crossed the stile which was built into the Mile Dyke? How often had I ducked behind that same stone dyke in response to the cry of 'Fore'? This was a nostalgic interlude. I felt I was eavesdropping and therefore felt a sense of guilt. Was this my last visit to this island of my childhood wanderings? Not knowing why, I had to hurry. Lower Largo perhaps. Yes, that was it. I drove back the same route I had come. The three pruning shears were still there. This time I waved 'goodbye'. One brave soul with a sense of humour held her nose with one hand and waved me goodbye with the clippers. In minutes I was in Lower Largo. Thank goodness it was still there. The statue of Alexander Selkirk still stood guard over the cottage where he spent his early years. Parking the bike, I walked along the narrow street where Alex had walked and quarrelled with his brothers when they were children, and which had required him to 'compear' before the kirk sessions more than two hundred and fifty years ago. This was the home of working men whose hands were rough with salty labour, and whose clothing was coarse and meant to last for years. Just as I had been drawn to this hamlet, I hurried away. Hurrying from the past? My absorption with the past was so overwhelming that before I realized it, I was back in Leven. Skirting part of the town where streets of houses had mushroomed, all alike except for the names, I cruised into the polygonal area called The Shorehead. The shops were there, the grocer, the haberdasher, the bicycle shop. All still there. And the short, narrow wynd called Union Street, which connected the High Street and The Back street. 'I used to live here when I was six years old,' I murmured to myself. All I really recalled with any clarity was the time when my aeroplane, powered by an elastic band attached to the propeller, landed on the roof of our tiny house. The doctor at the corner, a tall and sympathetic man, retrieved it by simply reaching up and handing it to me. Mum used to whitewash that slab of slate at the door. My next stop was the drinking fountain near the river mouth. The heavy iron cup, anchored securely to the fountain by a massive iron chain, was not as weighty as it used to be. I drank the cool, clear water, then drove on to the jetty. This mighty deck of concrete jutting into the ocean on a labyrinth of piles, cross-spars and struts of reinforced concrete, encrusted with barnacles, was the home of a million mussels and whelks. Also a frequent resting place for wandering starfish that clung to the lowest beams, the jetty claimed a special corner in my youthful recollections.

Daydreaming of those magic years, I was looking down at the swelling water when I was aware of footsteps behind me. I wheeled around to see Alex Noel walking towards me. Alex was smiling like a newly elected politician. 'Don't do it, Ralph! Don't jump!' he cried, laughing. This was the first time I had actually heard Alex laughing.

'Well . . . Alex A. Noel!' I greeted him and we shook hands. His left hand remained in his trouser pocket. 'I might have known you would turn up at such a moment.'

'Really? What moment is that?'

'What brought you here?'

'I saw you drinking at the fountain and I followed you.'

'Ah. To talk me out of jumping?'

'Perish the thought. What do you take me for?'
'Let me guess. Santa Claus is not really dead?'
'No, no, no, no, no! I wondered . . . before you do it, may I have your bike?'
'You don't ride a bike.'
'I can learn, can't I?'
'Alex . . . you *can't* ride a bike.'
'And why not?'
'First, you would have to know how to get your hands out of your pockets.'
'Now, *that* is dirty pool.'
'It certainly is,' I answered, 'and you still haven't told me why you are roaming around the Shore Head.'
'I suspect it is for the same reason that brought you here.'
'Nostalgia?'
'M-hm. I am saying goodbye to the old haunts. I'm going abroad.'
'To study?'
'To study, and to practice – psychiatry. I may never see these landmarks again.' Alex looked at me intently. He was still a young man, but sometimes he gave the impression of a cartoonist's version of an absent-minded professor. 'You have a question, Ralph?'
'Two. First, why do people pick on me?'
'Everybody?'
'Don't be stupid, Alex. I'm not on your couch.' Alex grinned. 'Once in a while somebody wants to challenge me.'
'Then we can discount paranoia. What makes you think you are an isolated case?'
'Got ya! I didn't say I thought I was an isolated case. And I stopped beating my mother the day I was born. I heard, through diplomatic channels, that I kicked the hell out of her in the last few weeks of pregnancy.'
'That's interesting.'
'Interesting?'
'If nothing else. Interesting.'

Ralph

'You know, Alex, I could take great pleasure in tossing you into the drink, but I don't want to contaminate the polluted water.'

'That, too, is interesting. Who challenged you, and in what manner were you challenged?'

'Alex, you beef me off. You answer everything with a cryptic observation or with a question.'

'Do I?'

'See? You did it again.'

'Did I?'

We both laughed at the impasse. 'All right. Big Mike, the two jerks in the pit with the hot lamp, three other hyenas who might have murdered me but for the protection of a policeman.'

'I know about Big Mike. Tell me about the others.'

I told Alex briefly about them.

'That,' said Alex, 'is analogous to a prehistoric raid. Cave man stuff. It could happen again, but likely won't. They have found somebody else to pick on. What was the other question?'

I told him about Constable Oedipus and his mean ambush, which had brought nothing but misery with the resulting fine or jail term.

'That is different,' said Alex. 'It sounds more like a feud.'

'How do I stand? Can they put me in jail if I don't cough up the twenty-five bob? Or don't you know?'

Alex paused before answering. 'They can - but they won't.'

'Why not?'

'If you go to jail, two policeman are required to escort you to Calton Jail in Edinburgh. Up to six days sentence would mean local confinement. Seven days or more would mean incarceration in a prison. Edinburgh is the nearest prison.'

I didn't like the words 'prison', 'confinement' and 'incarceration' but I remained silent.

'When you have done your sentence of seven days,' Alex continued, 'you will be - depending on good behaviour, of course - you will be escorted by two police officers to the place whence you started. This would cost more than twenty-five shillings. Moreover, let me finish,' he said, as I indicated interruption. 'Moreover, it would mean the loss of the services of two police officers twice in one week.'

Not only did he look like an old professor, but he sounded like my mental picture of one. 'That's great news,' I cried. 'Then you advise me *not* to pay the fine?'

'I'm not advising you one way or the other. That's up to you.'

'But you said they won't put me in jail. Right?'

'I also said, "they can". My profession, Ralph, is psychiatry, not fortune telling.'

'All right Alex, let me put it this way. If you were in my position, would you pay the fine?'

'Your question is hypothetical and incapable of a definite answer.'

'For God's sake, talk English. In my shoes, would you or wouldn't you pay the fine?'

'Probably not.'

'Good,' I cried, 'you've answered my question.'

'Not at all,' said Alex, reaching even deeper into his pants pockets. 'You have answered your own question.'

'Alex . . . I have never met a more insufferable wretch in my life.'

'You will.'

'I'm going home for lunch. Would you like to join me?'

'Thank you, Ralph. Much as I would like to, I don't have the time. I have to stop and smell the roses - and the sea. I'm sure you understand.'

'Perfectly. Well, goodbye, Alex. And good luck in your travels.'

'Goodbye, Ralph. I hope you find a job to your liking.'

We shook hands warmly and he was gone. I think I was just as important in his nostalgic meanderings as he was in mine. That was the last time I saw Alex. We never corresponded, but I have seen his name in newspapers now and again. He travels a lot, mostly in Europe. He probably wouldn't know me if he tripped over me, but I would know him. He would have his hands deep in his trouser pockets and he would be searching for a lost threepenny bit. He hobnobs with presidents, prime ministers and kings. Besides these, he seems to know a lot of actors, male and female. I saw his picture in a magazine with some of them.

The last time I read about Sir Alex was when his name had been submitted by a committee for nomination as president of a psychoanalytical society.

I suppose Alex knew where *he* was going.

OEDIPUS WRECKS

As promised, Sergeant Shoebotham arrived one week after his initial visit. When I heard his voice, I rushed Polly - or Polyanthus to give the bird her full name - into another room. Polyanthus. The only flowery characteristic about her was her vocabulary, and that was something over which we had no command. The sailor who stuck her with that name must have been stoned when he baptized her. Polly was a law unto herself. After an inappropriate greeting, when one considers his mission, Mum ushered the sergeant in and asked him to have a seat. I wandered into the living room to meet him.

Very pleasantly he said, 'Good morning, Ralph.'

It certainly was a *good* morning, thanks to Alex, I thought. Did I have news for Sergeant Shoebotham?

'Good morning, Sergeant. Do have a seat.'

'I'm . . . already seated, thank you.'

'So you are.' We sat at the table playing at who will be the first to speak. Mum had just made our mid-morning cup of tea and the aroma of freshly baked scones permeated the whole house. The tension was pretty electric when Mum appeared with a tray containing a teapot and a plate of scones.

'You'll have a cuppa?' she said smiling at him, and without waiting for an answer she asked, 'I hope you like girdle scones.'

'Mrs. McCaa, I *LOVE* griddle scones.'

'We call it girdle up here,' Mum said. 'The English don't know any better - Oh! you're English aren't you?' she apologized, biting her nails.

'That's perfectly all right, I assure you. My grandmother was a Scot.'

'Everybody's grandmother was a Scot,' I added, feeling on top of the situation. Sergeant Shoebotham was a master at ignoring any comment that smacked of disdain or discourtesy.

'Thank you very much, dear lady,' he said, drooling as he reached for a scone. 'Well Ralph,' he said with an easy smile, 'How are you?'

'Fine, thank you . . . and yourself?'

'Just fine.'

Mum had disappeared into the kitchen and returned with a large plate of oatmeal scones. 'There. Oatmeal scones. Now eat up and tell me all about yourself.' The sergeant was about to sink his teeth into a warm oatmeal scone when Mum shouted 'Wait!' The sergeant's face was a study. I don't know what he expected, but I believe he would not have been surprised if Mum had wrung her hands in an agony of guilt and shouted, 'I can't let you do it, Officer. The oatmeal scones are laced with arsenic.' Mum rushed back into the kitchen while I cut one of the plain scones into two neat slabs. Mum returned with a jar and a spoon. 'Blackcurrant jam,' she announced. 'I made it yesterday.' He cut his scone and packed it with a spoonful of blackcurrant jam. Mum watched anxiously as he lifted the jam-packed scone to his eager mouth. He closed his eyes in ecstasy as he chewed. It may have been relief that he was still with the living, but I rather think it was a reaction to the succulent flavour of oatmeal scones and blackcurrant jam. They exchanged glances of mutual appreciation as he reached for another scone. Mum whispered, 'Excuse me for a moment,' and again disappeared once more into the kitchen. By the time she got back, he was devouring his fifth scone. Mum returned with a brown paper bag. 'I don't want to press you for more than you are able, but . . . (Press! He had eaten five already!) will you take a few home with you?'

I know what I would have liked to do with that paper bag. Creep up behind him, blow it up and burst it with a mighty bang in the palm of my hand.

'Next week when you come, I'll bake some treacle scones. I'll bake some white ones too, in case you don't like the treacle ones.'

I fidgeted in my chair as I thought, 'For God's sake, Mum, before you're through you'll have *Oedipus* sitting here eating *MY* scones.'

'Another one?'

'I've just about had all . . .'

'One for the road.'

The sergeant held his hands up in a mimicry of warding off some Machiavellian temptation as Mum held the plate under his nose.

'Oh, my goodness,' he groaned, and as Mum withdrew the plate he murmured, 'Well . . . maybe one more.' The one consoling thought about the whole charade was that this was going to cost him twenty-five shillings.

'Another cup,' Mum urged.

'Well, I ah . . .' Mum poured him another cup.

Ye gods, he was right at home! The sergeant cleared his throat.

'Ralph . . . you don't remember me, do you?'

'I remember you from last week. Next week I'll remember you even better from this week.'

'Of course. But do you remember me from about four years ago?'

'I can't say that I do.'

'You were on your way home from a dance.'

'Oh?' Better be cagey here. I knew from reading the newspapers all about police entrapment. He glanced at Mum with what seemed genuine affection. 'You know, dear lady, I would accept these scones in court as evidence of your innocence of *any* mischief, *any* day.'

I was staggered. His unctuous tactics were nothing short of awesome.

'Yes, *any* day,' he repeated.

'You would?' Mum gushed, smiling happily.

'I would indeed,' he assured her, reaching for yet another scone. 'Mrs. McCaa, you must be the greatest baker of scones in the country. No, in the whole world.'

Mum beamed with pleasure. 'I have my father to thank for that. He was a baker, you know. He retired a few years ago.'

'You certainly inherited his talents.'

I didn't like the way things were going. He was up to something. Buttering up this simple, small-town housewife before swinging the axe. I was beginning to dislike him as much as I hated Oedipus.

'Now, where was I?' he mumbled, reaching. 'Oh, yes. Four years ago. We ran into each other, or should I say *you* ran into *me*. Three louts were chasing you. It was dark, but we are trained to remember faces.'

I was almost paralysed with shame. 'That was you?' I stammered.

He swallowed and nodded.

'Maybe you saved my life that night. Did that fellow recover all right?'

'No body was found, so he must have survived.'

'Have another scone,' I said, holding out the plate.

'I've still got one.' He looked at his pocket watch. 'By golly, I have to go.' He rose and made towards the door.

'Goodbye, then. See you next week,' I said, shaking his hand.

The cheerful goodbyes were probably what jogged Polly's memory. She burst into song, which she did with imprudent passion.

'Ohhhh, a life on the ocean wave is better than going to sea. Ta rum ti tum ti tum, Ta rum ti tiddly Dee.'

Sergeant Shoebotham stopped in his stride, looking towards the voice. 'Who's that?'

I said, 'That's Polly. Our parrot.'

'Has she been drinking?'

'No no,' I said, laughing. 'That is something from her past.'

'Don't let her drive your motor bike. O.K.?' He left before I had a chance to pay part of the fine.

When he arrived the following week, I was in the garden. I had not had time to banish Polyanthus and when I had hosed off my hands and entered the house, Polly and the sergeant were eyeing each other with suspicion while Mum looked on adoringly. I made for the cage. 'I'll put her in the other room,' I said. Mum dashed into the kitchen.

'No no, leave her. I'd like to make her acquaintance.'

'Be it on your own head, Sergeant. Have a seat.'

'Thank you.' Mum appeared with a plateful of treacle scones. She didn't have to coax him. He already had one in his hand.

He smiled at Mum. 'I don't suppose you have a little . . .'

'Blackcurrant jam? I have something else. Gooseberry. But I suggest you try the treacle scones with butter – that is, margarine. Butter is a luxury we can't afford.'

'That sounds excellent.' He spread a scone with margarine.

'I have some white ones, too. I'll get them, and some gooseberry jam.' Mum left for the kitchen.

'Well, Polly, and how are you today?' he said, munching and eyeing Polly in her cage.

'Go to hell,' said Polly.

'All right, if that's your attitude.' He took his handcuffs from a pocket and plunked them on the table. They sounded like the clink of money.

'Same again, Joe,' ordered Polly.

'I surrender,' he said. 'What now?'

'Fill 'er up, Joe.'

The sergeant asked me, 'Is it all right to give her a piece?'

'No, she doesn't get these. Give her a walnut,' I answered, placing the goodies in front of him.

'There you are, Polly.' She took the walnut in one of her huge claws and started to devour it. Mum appeared with a pot of tea and was pouring just as Polly was finishing off the nut.

'Same again, Joe.'

'Can she have another?'

'Not at the moment, Sergeant. She'll just waste it.'

'And they're quite expensive. A luxury you might say,' Mum added.

'Sorry Polly. No more at the moment,' he said.

'Go to hell!'

'Is she always so . . . belligerent?' he asked.

'She's just warming up.'

'Have you found a job yet, Ralph?'

'Go to hell.'

'I assure you she didn't hear that in our house,' I laughed.

'Once more, Polly, and I'll place you under arrest,' he said, pointing an accusing finger at her.

'Oh, shaddup you noisy bugger.'

I grabbed the cage and was on my way out.

'Goodbye Polly,' called the sergeant.
'Go to hell.'
When I returned - alone - the sergeant asked, 'Where was she before you acquired her?'
'She was in the Black Bull Tavern for over thirty years. She outlived the proprietor, who got her from a sea going man whom Polly also outlived. He had her for forty years, we were told. We have had her for about five. That makes a total of seventy-five plus. She could be eighty or more.'
'Remarkable. Ralph . . . have you ever considered joining the Police Force?' From the other room, Polly was still telling us to 'Go to hell.'
'Would I be eligible - with a record?'
'You're not a criminal, for heaven's sake. The local constabulary usually enlists men from out of town, but the London - Metropolitan Forces would be happy to have you, I'm sure.'
Mum appeared with a plate of plain scones and a pot of jam.
'Ah! The scones I love. May I?'
'Go right ahead,' gurgled Mum. 'I'm going to give you a pot of jam and some white girdle scones to take home with you.'
'You are much too generous. Thank you kindly, Ma'am, I can't say "No".'
Mum returned to the kitchen.
'I have an application form here,' said Sergeant S., drawing an envelope from an inside pocket. 'Think about it. Then, if you decide to apply, fill out the form and drop - in triplicate - and drop it in at the station.'
'That's very good of you,' I said.
'There's only one drawback. It may be six or seven months before they take action. You would be at home down there, you know. There are quite a lot of Scots down there.'
'Do you mind if I think about it for a few days?'
'Of course not. Now I must be off. I have a lot of office work to do.'
Mum appeared miraculously with a bag of goodies, just in time to say goodbye.

Mum closed the door behind him and said, 'He *IS* nice, isn't he?'
'He certainly is,' I agreed.
'Are you going to send in the application?' I was astonished.
'Mum! You've been eavesdropping.'
'You know, Ralph,' said Mum, fixing me with the equivalent of the famous Giaconda smile, 'I don't believe he will ever ask you for that twenty-five shillings. How can he?' Her eyes were twinkling. I stared at her in utter disbelief. This gentle, naive soul, baker of plain, treacle and oatmeal scones, maker of gooseberry and blackcurrant jam; she who had suckled me, changed my diapers, led me by the hand to kindergarten. My own mother . . . a con artist!

I'M IN THE ARMY, NOW

Feeble in tolerance. Weak in trust. That is how Dad put it. And this is why. I had submitted the application to the Metropolitan Police Force some weeks previously. If they had asked me a few questions, pertinent or otherwise, like, 'Do you have flat feet? Do you eat brose for breakfast? Do you wince when someone with halitosis breathes in your face?' or 'Do you forget to do up your fly?' - anything, anything at all, I would have answered cheerfully. I would have thanked them, then dismissed the entire matter from my mind. In fact, the only communication I received was to inform me that they had received my application, followed by a few phrases like 'In due course', 'Pending further scrutiny', 'If successful'. Waiting was nerve-wracking. I could become an old-age pensioner by the time someone found my application in the out basket - or the wastepaper basket. I had reached a point where I would have welcomed a letter saying, 'Your application has been examined and was promptly dispatched to the incinerator, because you are at the bottom of a long, long list of worthwhile applicants.' With that attitude, am I really intolerant? Am I truly distrustful? Mum kept saying 'Be patient. The sergeant said it might be months before they want you, and he is such a nice man.' 'How do we know for sure he recommended me?' I asked Mum. 'Maybe it was just a trick to get at more of your girdle scones and wheedle twenty-five bob out of us.' Mum said I ought to be ashamed. After giving it some thought, I *was* ashamed. A man whose brother had ridden a Coventry Eagle in the T.T. races couldn't be that rotten! Dad chided us both. He said that Mum would trust anybody and that she was completely without guile. Little did he know his wife of twenty-two years! If Mum had lived six hundred years ago, there would still have been a King Edward the First but no Hammer of the Scots. She would have seduced King Edward with her girdle scones and sent him back across the border rejoicing with a brown paper bag and a jar of gooseberry jam. Dad's words were the same as Mum's, 'Be patient.' His tone was 'Shut up or ship out'.

The day arrived when I had to take action. After several weeks of being patient I decided to 'ship out'. Taking a train to Edinburgh, I arrived at the address given to me by the Medical Officer at Perth. Two men sat at a desk behind two mugs of steaming tea. One had three stripes on his arm, the other had two. The three-striper, whose posture and critical eye supported his superiority over the two-striper, fixed me with a look-what-the-cat-dragged-in stare. The two-striper was a dead ringer for Stan Laurel, even to the way he fumbled with the little bag of – whatever it was.

'And wot can we do for you, young fella?' asked three stripes.

'I would like to enlist,' I answered.

The lower half of his face smiled exultantly.

'You wanna enlist, eh? Just take a seat over there and we'll be with you anon.'

'Anon?'

'It means – in a moment.'

'Yes, I know what it means. It was just . . . unexpected.'

'Well, anon or not anon, just have a seat. We're 'avin' a coffee break.'

I sat. The only reading material I could find were two comic books. The two-striper peered into the paper bag, then he extracted two eccles cakes. He weighed them, one in each hand, then passed the lighter one in front of Sergeant Anon.

'Wot's that?' asked the sergeant.

'They're called eccles cakes, Sarge.'

Sgt. Anon looked at the corporal contemptuously. 'I know wot they are, Corporal. Wot I don't know is why I get the smallest one.'

'They're tuppence each,' mumbled the corporal, switching them over.

'That'll be sixpence I owe ya,' the sergeant barked. They began to eat. As far as they were concerned, I didn't exist. I had had an early breakfast

I'm In The Army, Now

and I began to feel hungry.

'So you wanna enlist, eh?' said Sgt. Anon between bites. 'First thing you gotta know is who's wot in the Army. This here's a corporal and I'm a sergeant. You don't call us Noncoms "Sir". That's for Officers, so don't call me "Sir".'

'I had no intention of calling you *"sir"*,' I replied.

He glared at me and growled, 'You wanna enlist, don't ya?'

'I thought that had been established the first minute I arrived. Look, Sergeant, I had an early breakfast, so, if you don't mind, I'll get something to eat. I'll be back later.'

He was immediately galvanized into action. The fleeting look of apprehension which crossed his face was replaced by a metallic smile. I had, at that moment, Sgt. Anon's rapt attention. The corporal wet his finger on his tongue and picked up some large crumbs from the sergeant's blotting mat. I would like to say that the sergeant smacked the corporal's knuckles, but I would be lying.

'Let's see,' said Anon, 'you're from ah . . .'

'Leven.'

'Leaving. Take that down, Corporal.' To me he said, 'Would you mind sitting over here at the desk? Mr . . . Leaving, isn't it?'

'McCaa, *McCaa*. I *live* in Leven. L.E.V.E.N.'

'My mistake. I apologize. Leven . . . that's in ah . . .'

'Fifeshire.'

'Of course. And you want to enlist . . . in the Black Watch, right?'

'Wrong. I want to enlist in the Medical Corps.'

The sergeant scratched his chin. He thought he was philosophizing. No doubt he was about to extol the wisdom of enlisting in the Black Watch in preference to the Medics.

At last he broke his silence. 'Oh dear. This *is* unfortunate.'

'What is unfortunate?' I urged.

'The R.A.M.C. is not taking any recruits at the moment. What sort of work do you do?'

'At the moment, none. I am out of work,' I said.

He beamed and spread his hands in a gesture of 'all your troubles are over'. To the corporal he said with a voice of finality which he obviously regarded as irrevocable, 'The Black Watch'.

Turning to me he ordered, 'Now, just put your signature here, then while the corporal fills it in, you can tell me more about yourself.'

'No. You see, I have had considerable experience in a hospital, and I would be more useful in the Medical Corps.'

His sour expression told me clearly of his disapproval.

'Tell me,' he urged, 'about your hospital experience.'

'I was in a mental hospital for three years.'

They froze, then looked at each other in uneasy apprehension.

'As an attendant,' I added.

They relaxed. I saw that because Anon sat back and picked his ear. The corporal, in rank-aligned response, stuck a finger in his ear. They were so engrossed in these activities that it seemed time to go. This was an ordeal surpassed only by the only time I applied for unemployment insurance. I refer to a visit I made after being two weeks out of work. Never have I encountered a snootier or more idle group of beings than I did at the Unemployment Exchange. Maybe it was a sedentary occupational ritual, but they too were having tea. 'Take a seat,' I was told. After fidgeting for twenty minutes, a female string-bean beckoned me with her forefinger to approach. 'Fill in this form,' she said.

'Why the hell didn't you give me the form when I arrived? There's nobody else waiting. Are there any jobs available?'

She ignored my question. 'That table over there,' she said, discharging her trigger finger in the direction of the table in the centre of the room. They wanted to know everything I had done in the nature of employment. Like a fool, I wrote in my four years in the coal dungeons. I returned the completed application to the counter, but as no one paid any attention I sat down again. Fifteen minutes later, when they ran out of gossip, the group dispersed to rinse and dry their cups. The String-bean lifted my application and her eyebrows disappeared under her bang. She withdrew to her desk. About ten minutes later, she returned. The finger again. 'There's a good possibility for you to get something at Wellesley Colliery.'

'The pits are out,' I said simply.

I'm In The Army, Now

She brought the – whatever he was. He explained that I had to take whatever was available or . . . he extended his palms for my inspection.

'Or what?' I asked.

'Or we can't give you unemployment benefits.'

'You can stick them where the monkey stuck its nuts,' I growled, and I walked out. I have no intention of seeing the inside of one of these places again but if I ever do, and I am told to take a seat, I shall lift the best one I can see and take it home with me.

I have to be honest about the ear-pickers. It didn't last beyond thirty seconds. I had got up. 'I'll come back in a few weeks. Better still, give me your phone number and I'll call you.'

'You're on the phone?' the sergeant asked incredulously.

'No, but I can use a nearby phone kiosk.'

'Tell me, just out of curiosity, why don't you want to join the Black Watch?'

'I thought I had made that clear,' I answered.

He was almost poetic in his dramatic outpouring. 'There's glory in being a fighting man. The Black Watch have a grand tradition of . . .'

'I know all about "The Ladies from Hell",' I interrupted, 'I have done all the fighting I want to do.'

'Fighting?'

'Well . . . boxing.'

Anon elbowed his side-kick. 'Boxing!'

The corporal scribbled it down on the form.

'And, being a Scotchman, soccer.' Again the elbow. The corporal winced.

'I have seen a few games, but I don't play.'

'What else do you do? In the field of sports, I mean.'

'Nothing. Some swimming, but that is for pleasure only.'

Corpie didn't need nudging. He was scribbling and muttering, 'swimmer'. Enough was enough. I turned and made for the door.

'Halt!' It was Anon's voice. I turned at the door to look at him. 'I mean, hold on a minute.' His eyes registered some sort of a plea.

'What for?'

'Why don't you enlist in The Army Dental Corps? Capital T.'
'I'm not a dentist.'
'As an orderly. You could ask for a transfer to the R.A.M.C. later.'
This was more like it. They didn't want me to leave.
'When would I get a transfer?'
'Ah. Sit down please. Just sign the application and I'll be 'appy to answer all your questions.'
'Could I ask the questions first?'
His jaw tightened. 'What questions?'
'Do I have a guarantee that I shall get a transfer?'
'I can practically assure you that it is almost certain you might get a transfer.'
This man should be selling used cars. Yet, in my desire to end this aimless farce, I was weakening. He handed me a pen.
'Shouldn't you complete the form first?' I asked.
'That's a mere formality. Sign here,' he said, pointing to the appropriate space. I parked the pen.
'Just one more question. Do you mind?' His expression indicated clearly that he did mind. 'I just wanted to ask, what rank do I start with?' As I watched and waited, I appreciated - more than I did so many years ago - Miss MacTavish's directions to the King when he finally got the boot. 'Shock reaction, followed by a lengthy dramatic pause, then quiet response.' Sgt. Anon's recovery may have been a trifle too fast, but I wasn't surprised when he answered gently, 'You 'ave to join up as a private, then . . .'
'Then what?'
'You take it from there. It's up to you.'
'Fair enough.' Between the major at Perth, and these two clowns, it was obvious to me I would make major in six months. Wearily, he handed me the pen.
'May I read the form?' Anon elbowed the corporal and nodded.
'Boxing, swimming, soccer,' I read. 'Shouldn't that come out?'
'Like I said. A mere formality. We gotta put in something.'
'Maybe you should put in something like "With a view to transferring

I'm In The Army, Now

to the Medical Corps",' I responded. The corporal edged away from the elbow. He needn't have bothered. Anon nodded perfunctorily. 'Now, sign and you are on your way.'

'On my way? Where to?'

He looked dazed. 'Aldershot.'

'I've never been to Aldershot. What's it like?'

'You'll like it.'

'Why?'

For a few seconds, the sergeant buried his head in his hands. Then he looked at me. 'There is *everything* there.'

'Such as?'

Counting the items off on his fingers, he said, 'There's a swimming pool. There's a soccer field. There's a gymnasium. And there's pubs. Lots o' pubs.'

The form was filled out. It was overfilled. The pen was poised. 'I think I'll sign it now.'

Relief was written all over their faces.

I asked, 'When do I leave for Aldershot?'

'Right away. This afternoon.'

'I can't go this afternoon.'

'When . . . can . . . you go?' queried the sergeant.

'In three days.'

'How about tomorrow morning?'

'That's quite impossible. You see, I have to sell my motor bike. And I have to say goodbye to my family and friends. There are my parents, my grandfather and . . .'

'*Please*. Tell you wot. You sign up, then I'll make a phone call, see if it's all right.'

'What if it's not all right?' I asked.

His answer will show the mentality of these people and the ordeal I had been through. He screamed, 'For Gawd's sake, sign the bloody thing!' I dropped the pen on the desk. 'Perhaps I should come back when you have had a good rest.'

'No, no. No,' he groaned. 'Tell you wot. Sign up an' we can go, I mean, you can go the day after tomorrow.'

I was giving it some thought when he continued.

'In the evening. That gives you three days, and you'll arrive there about noon.' He should get that facial twitch seen to, I thought.

'Great,' I said. I signed. Smiles creased their faces.

'Right,' he said, handing me a ticket. 'This will get you a free ride from here to Aldershot.'

'What about the journey from Leven to Edinburgh?'

The smiles curdled. To the corporal he said in a weary voice, 'Give 'im a chit from . . . Leaving or wherever to Edinburgh.'

'Right, Sarge.' He wrote out a ticket.

'Do you have to make that phone call?' I asked.

'Wot phone call?'

'To see if it is all right for me to leave in three days time.'

'*We'll take a chance,*' the sergeant breathed.

'I didn't quite hear, Sergeant. Did you . . .'

'We'll take a chance,' he yelled.

'Yeah, we'll take a chance,' echoed the corporal.

'Yes, well, goodbye fellows. And take it easy. You can overdo it, you know. Get away from it for a while.' Neither of them replied. Outside, I took a deep breath of Edinburgh smog. I had never been through such a gruelling day in my life. Suddenly I had a longing for the calm and restfulness of the mental asylum. As luck would have it, I caught a train within half an hour. I had something to eat at the railway station. Have you ever eaten railway sandwiches?

Dad asked a lot of questions. Among them was, 'How much do they pay you?'

'Darn it,' I said, 'I forgot to ask.'

THE DEPOT

Had I been too rash? It was too late to think about that now. I took the local connection in time to catch the Edinburgh train for London, where I would change for Aldershot. I was sorely tempted to spend another day in Auld Reekie but I had promised. I visited the pet shop, working my way to Princes Street and - I give you my word, it was not intentional - I missed my connection. There was a later train in the late evening. It was a slower train. Feeling a sense of guilt, I boarded her and, to both your surprise and mine, I fell asleep almost immediately. I didn't get to Aldershot until late afternoon the next day, only to learn that I had to go to Crookham Camp, somewhere in the country. However, I was nearing my destination, the end of the rainbow, and my excitement grew. Posters beckoned me with the promise of a career. Dad's and Granta's apprehensions, as well as those of some others, were unfounded. My parents would be proud of me and I would prove to them I had made the right choice. The world was at peace. No war loomed ahead to spoil my dreams. I felt that I was a 'somebody'. I would meet a lot of pleasant men with whom I could form a lasting friendship. No more discord. No more challenges. No more fighting. There were, of course, the regrets: no more walks in the woods with Granta; no more Nell. That belonged to the past. I had to get on with the future. There were as happy, if not happier, times ahead. At the railway station in Aldershot there was a bus to take us to the R.A.M.C. Depot. By us, I mean the seven civilians who were on the train and were bound for the same destination as myself. None of them was communicative, so I asked, 'Any of you fellows Dental Corps?' A few negative nods were the only response I received. Like me, I suppose, they didn't quite know what they were getting into, and they were all younger than I and with less experience of the world at large.

The bus stopped at the entrance to the Depot and we piled out to report our arrival at the guardroom located at the entrance. After checking our names against a list, a corporal asked us, 'Do you want something to eat?' One or two muttered 'Yep' or 'Yeah'. 'I could enjoy a little snackaroo. Something light,' I said.

The corporal stared at me as if I had thumbed my nose at him with both hands.

'What's up?' I said. 'Did I say something wrong?'

'Not yet,' he replied. 'Follow me.'

He took us to the dining room, called a mess hall, where we were told to sit at one of the many tables. 'Hey,' he called to a man who was sweeping the floor, 'fetch eight stoos, on the double.' The sweeper dropped his broom faster than Moses dropped his staff when it turned into a snake. There must have been 'stoo' cooking, for there were eight plates of it on the table in minutes. I thought I might as well open up some conversation. After all, we were all strangers to one another. A shyness to converse was not unnatural.

Smiling at the corporal, I said, 'You're a corporal, I see.'

He inspected the two stripes on his sleeves and said with what seemed surprise, 'So I am'. Clearly an oddball, I thought. We all remained silent after that. The 'stoo' was followed by seven mugs of onion-flavoured tea. When we finished, the corporal ordered, 'This way.' We followed him to a hut where a large sergeant gave us a brief history of the Royal Army Medical Corps, mentioning what an honour it was for us to be part of such a distinguished Corps. 'How about the Dental Corps, Sergeant?' I asked. 'Yes, how about that?' he replied. He stressed the importance of Esprit de Corps, and how necessary it was to exercise this warmth of feeling ordained to pervade our illustrious family. Pride and devotion were mentioned. There was not a word about the Dental Corps. Of course, we don't think of dentists as the life of the party. All they do is inflict pain. I thought back to my first visit to the dentist, then I immediately switched my thoughts to something else. After all, one doesn't wish to relive such an experience. Do you? The sergeant droned on for another ten minutes, then he said, 'Any questions? Dismiss.' We were rushed outside without any appraisal of my Corps, but having been rushed outside, it seemed the wrong moment to bring up the question of a commission.

'Fall in!' shouted the corporal. We all stood like wet leeks.

I knew what he meant by 'fall in', but where? 'Never mind,' he said. 'Come this way.' We straggled behind him and were led to another large building where we were measured here and there for uniforms and a mountain of other stuff. There was the web equipment, the assemblage of which I mastered in only two years. A scruffy looking white belt made of leather, a swagger stick – that is a sort of giant chopstick, blankets, a brass thing with a slot up the middle for protecting clothing when you cleaned your buttons with your toothbrush. The handle of the toothbrush was used for 'boning' boots. In case you don't know what 'boning' is, boning is a daily exercise in self control. It involves applying boot polish to the footwear, then with rapid spitting and the application of friction, rubbing the boot with the toothbrush handle. As if by magic, a glass-like sheen appears on the leather. As time passed, we became so demanding of ourselves that this became not so much a chore as a triumph. The fact that we had to utilize both ends of the toothbrush may explain the necessity for the existence of The Army Dental Corps.

We were issued with a kitbag and a hat called a cheese-cutter, a handful of brass badges, blanco white and green, boot polish, puttees, and that was about it. 'Stuff the small things in your kitbag and follow me,' said the corporal. 'I'll show you where you will sleep for the next six months.' We got many of the small items in the kitbag, then followed him to a barrack room. On the way there we passed the . . . you know. 'This,' the corporal barked, 'is a warehouse. You will always deposit any excess baggage before going on drill parade. It is called a latrine. Don't splash or mess it up. You may be the one to clean it out.' My bladder was full so I asked if he would mind if I went inside. 'Hurry it up, then,' he said. I held out my load of equipment for him to hold, but he snarled, 'Drop it', pointing to the ground. All of us took this opportunity to relieve ourselves, then we staggered after him to the barrack room.

As far as I remember, there were nineteen beds, ten at one side and nine at the other. To the left of the door there was a small cubicle, partitioned to provide a private room for the N.C.O. or trained soldier responsible for our good behaviour, such as getting up in the morning. We were allotted a bed, after which the corporal left. The beds seemed to be about four feet by five. Maybe we were expected to sleep curled up like a dormant caterpillar. A florid looking man sitting on the bed next to mine said, 'Here, let me help you,' and he pulled out the lower half of the bed, which locked when fully extended. He then dumped the mattress, which was in sections, on the bed. This was more like it. A friendly face at last.

'Thanks,' I said. 'Have you been here long?'

'About a month.'

I sat on my bed and started to fill my pipe. My neighbour sat facing me. 'Say pal, mind if I have a bit of your tobacco to make a cigarette?'

'Of course not, but it's flake tobacco. You'll have to rub it,' I said.

He produced a folder of cigarette papers and rolled a fag while I lit my pipe. Exchanging friendly smiles with me, he removed about half of my tobacco from the pouch. Placing his booty carefully on a newspaper, he zipped the pouch and threw it back to me.

Throwing the pouch back on his bed I said, 'Put it back.'

Eyeing me speculatively, he made what turned out to be a pathetic misjudgment. 'Don't worry,' he said, grinning. 'I'll give it back to you on pay day.' Once more he threw the pouch back to me.

I said, very politely, 'Now look you – insult – you asked for enough to make a cigarette. You got it. Now, put the rest back.' I returned the pouch. He glanced behind him, wondering no doubt if he had an audience worth playing to. I noticed one man whose bed was directly across from Florid Face, watching with what seemed bored amusement. Florid Face weighed the pouch in one hand. 'You got plenty here,' he said, and he threw the pouch – not *to* me, but *at* me. I caught the pouch in mid-air, partly, I suppose because of my activities at the gym, partly by reflex action. Rising leisurely, I was reaching for the tobacco when Florid

Face jumped up and gave me a shove which landed me head-over-top on to my own bed. From there I slithered to the floor. A few snickers didn't make me feel any more amiable. Henry's voice came through from the past. 'Don't rush. Feint. Wait for an opening. Wham!'

O.K., Henry, I get the message. Taking it slowly around the bottom end of my bed, I concentrated on the tobacco. Florid Face towered above me, ready to delight the audience with another shove. Before he had time to repeat his comedy, I drove my right fist into his breakfast. With a loud yelp of pain he collapsed. The big man who had been watching with indolent amusement jumped up and walked cat-like towards us. My God, is he coming after me? Florid Face recovered quickly and he reached for his white leather belt which was lying on his bed. I backed away a few steps as he raised it above his head, but before he could bring it down the big man held his arm. This man was six feet three in height and looked even taller. With a jerk, he swung Florid Face on to his bed. Screaming revenge, he leapt up and swung his belt at the big man, catching him across the shoulder. The giant put his arms around Florid Face and squeezed. 'Holy mackerel!' I yelled, 'you'll kill him.'

'I didn't hear any bones cracking,' he answered. He wheeled his victim around facing me, his arms pinned behind his back.

'Would you like to finish him off?'

'Not while you're holding him,' I replied. He let his victim go and he fell on the floor, conscious but seemingly unwilling to renew the games. Everyone in the room was silent.

'Will he be all right?' I murmured.

'He'll survive. Don't forget your tobacco.'

With exaggerated casualness, I replaced the cause of all the trouble in my pouch. Poor bastard, he looked sort of lonely lying there. I zipped open my pouch and placed two slices of tobacco on his bed.

'I could do with a drink,' I said.

'All you can get this time of day is coffee or tea.'

'It's tea I want. Join me?'

'Sure.'

We wandered over to the canteen. 'My treat,' I said. 'I see by your badges that we are both in the same Corps.'

'Oh, are you in The Army Dental Corps, too?' I nodded.

'What's your name?'

'Ralph . . . McCaa.'

'Mine's Hort. Family name's Nelson.'

'Hort. That's an unusual name.'

'My name is Horatio. Horatio Nelson invites smart jokes, then I have to splinter a few bones.'

'I'll call you Hort. How long have you been here?'

'About ten days. How about some more tea? No, no, I'll get it.'

We both went to the counter. Hort paid.

'You know, Hort, I hate fighting. I didn't want to hit that idiot, but he asked for it. I hope there aren't any more like him.'

'There is one needs some training.'

'Yes? Who is that?'

'He wasn't there. He's the one who sleeps in the small room at the door.'

'A corporal?'

'A private . . . who thinks he's a field-marshal but acts like a hoodlum.'

'In what way?'

'From what I hear, he gets plastered every Friday evening. After lights out he comes in and tips the beds, one after the other, and nobody does anything to stop him.'

'Did it happen to you?'

'Yes. Last Friday. As I told you, I have been here ten days, so that the day after tomorrow will be a test.'

'You're telling me that you let him get away with it?'

'You said you don't like fighting. Neither do I, but when somebody pushes me, I get rough – I hurt people who force it on me. Hardy, his name is Hardy, got a warning. Next time, if there is a repetition, I promised to break him up into small pieces. Ralph . . . I like you.'

'So?'

'So, I will have to protect you.'

'Thanks Hort. I am indebted to you, but I don't think I need protection.'

'You don't know Hardy. Better stay close anyway. I'm a few years older than you, and I've had experience with his kind.'

'Do you mean here?'

'No I . . . better keep this to yourself . . . I was a policeman.'

'Didn't you like it?'

'Yes, I liked it all right, but . . . ah, never mind.'

'I'd like to know about it. You can trust me not to blab, whatever it is.'

Hort thought about it for some seconds. 'All right, I'll tell you. I was about ten years old. A guy in my class stuck me with the moniker of "Baby Face"! Well, that was all right as a kid, even if I didn't like it.'

'Is that so surprising, Hort, with the name of Nelson?'

'That wasn't entirely the reason. This kid said I was a double of the comedian, Harry Langdon. Do you remember him?'

'Sure I remember him. But I was only a nipper. You grew out of it?'

'I thought I had. Then this kid, no longer a kid, turned up.'

'Then you became Baby Face again?' Right enough he did have a chubby sort of baby face. Hort was in a talking mood.

'I told him to quit or I would clobber him.'

'So he quit?'

'After I clobbered him. Then he started to call me Harry.'

'That seemed a natural ahm . . . choice from Horatio to Harry.'

'I liked that even less than Baby Face. The name caught on.'

'So you told him . . . What happened?'

'I had to clobber four guys.'

'And that was the end of . . . it, of Harry?'

'No. They brought in reinforcements, ganged up on me.'

'So you got the hell out of it - fast.'

'No.' Hort looked around to make sure nobody was listening in. He was so serious that I began to wonder if I would be better off without his backing if I got into any more trouble. 'What did you do?'

'You won't repeat this to anyone, will you?' he whispered.

I didn't really want any of his gory secrets, but I would gradually dissociate myself from him, so I shook my head in agreement. 'No.'

'I tied them into a small bundle and threw them into the Thames. More came, and more. I tied them into bundles of ten and tossed them into the river. Soon they created a human log jam which became hazardous to shipping, so I had to stop.'

I was paralysed. I had been 'had'. Never in my life had I been so 'suckered'. I looked at Hort who drained his cup without a flicker of a smile. 'So don't ever call me Baby Face,' he said. 'And don't ever, ever, ever call me Harry.'

'I'll try to remember that, Hort. And don't you ever call me Ralpheeee.'

'Perish the thought,' he said. 'By the way, I think we're double parked. Drink up. I have to show you how to hang up your equipment. It needs practice.'

Baby Face, Harry, Horatio, Hort Nelson and I strolled back to the barrack room. Florid Face was sitting on his bed. He didn't look up. My thought was to offer him my hand and say 'No hard feelings, eh?' but before I had a chance to say anything, he rose and left. Hort watched him leave, his face expressionless. Florid gave him one quick glance and was gone. Maybe I should have a word with Hort about his unfriendly attitude. He was sitting comfortably on his bed when I decided to talk to him. This was a very private conversation, so we both spoke in undertones. I said, 'Hort - no offence you understand - but wouldn't it be a good idea to open conversation with whatever his name is?'

'Barton? Great idea. When he gets back I'll tell him I'm prepared to accept his apology. Sit down.'

'Shouldn't you, I mean to say, he got the worst of it, well, what I am getting at is . . .' I sat on his bed beside him.

'He slapped me with his belt, didn't he?' answered Hort.

My mind went back to being whacked across the ear with a strap at school. 'Yes, I know, but ah,' I was using my forefinger to emphasize what I was saying. 'But . . . forget it. You must have heard that violence begets violence.'

'That's true, Ralph. And sometimes violence is the only way to stop further violence. There are, of course, different kinds of violence.'

'Meaning what?' I asked.

'Take your encounter with Barton. You started out with verbal violence.'

'He started it. He aimed my tobacco pouch at my head.'

'By heaven, you're right. He *did* start it. Then he involved me.'

'But Hort, you weren't involved. You involved yourself. Didn't you?'

Hort gave me a withering look.

'Well – didn't you?' I said.

'No. I happened to be present, therefore I was involved.'

'Well,' I countered. 'I've made up my mind about you.'

'To what conclusion?'

'I see that I shall have to protect you.'

I detected a flicker of amusement in his expression.

'From yourself,' I added.

Hort Nelson's face creased into a beatific grin.

'Not bad,' he said.

For the next eight months or so, we were to become inseparable.

SCRUB, YOU SO-AND-SO!

'What's the big sigh for?' Hort asked.
'Oh, I was just thinking.'
'Good. That's a practice to be encouraged as much as possible. I knew a fellow policeman who . . .'
'Oh, shut up. Look, I joined up hoping to get away from fighting. I'm not two minutes in a barrack room when it happens.'
'It's a crying shame. If you can't escape fighting in the Army, where else can you go?'
'Would you like to know where you can go?'
'Between us we shouldn't have any more trouble.'
'Trouble?' I asked.
'Yes. With Barton, and any others who want to start something. If you glance towards the door,' Hort murmured, nodding in that direction, 'there's trouble.'
The figure in the doorway was five feet two or three in height, but he almost filled the width of the doorway.
'Is that . . .?'
'Hardy. A one-man demolition squad. You know, he visits each bed on Friday nights.'
'I remember reading about a fella named Hardy kissing another fella called Nelson. They were in the Navy though.'
'If he tries that, it'll be the kiss of death – for him.'
After surveying us from the doorway, Hardy came straight for us. He bulged his muscles and walked with a swagger. I recognised him immediately. He stopped in front of me and mumbled, 'A new one, eh?' Then he chortled, 'Hey, I know you. You used to go to the Palais.'

'I remember you at school,' I said.

'I didn't even *notice you* at school, if you catch my drift. But at the Palais . . . you were a real caper.'

'Well, that makes us even,' I answered. 'I didn't even notice *you* at the Palais, if you get *my* drift.'

His eyes glinted menacingly, then his face relaxed. 'Tell me, how did you make out with Betty whatsername?'

'I don't know anyone by the name of Whatsername.'

'You know who I mean. Did you see her home?'

'That is my business, and hers.'

'Stuck up bitch. She wouldn't let me take her home.'

'Is that so?' I answered.

'Yeah. That's so. And do you know why?'

'Probably she wasn't too fond of animals. Incidentally, I'm not interested in your problems.'

'I don't have no problems,' he growled. 'You got problems.'

'None I can't handle.'

'You want some?'

This game called for a series of one word answers beginning and ending with *no*. 'No.'

'Maybe you would rather dance, only we got no dance floor in the Depot.'

'No.'

'Course you could dance with me. Like you danced with that fella, you know, the boxer. Would you like to dance with me?'

'No.'

He was plainly becoming exasperated. 'No. Is that all you can say – no?'

'No.'

I could almost hear the wheels turning slowly in his sluggish brain, groping for some way to make me talk. He tried a new strategy. 'Hey, come on over to the canteen and I'll buy you a coffee.'

'No.'

'You don't like me, do you?'

'No.'

'Well, I don't like you either.' He glared at me for a moment, then he turned and walked briskly to his cubicle, slamming the door behind him. Hort rose and nodded for me to follow him. We went outside and walked out of earshot of anybody who might be listening.

'O.K. Ralph, let's have it. You've had trouble with Hardy?'

'I have never spoken to him in my life - until now.'

'But you knew him?' I nodded. 'You're marked for trouble with that creep.'

'Maybe he's marked for trouble with me,' I answered. Hort gave me a pitying look.

'What kind of trouble?' I inquired.

'Demolition.'

'Could you put it in words a little less final?'

'I told you about his antics every Friday, after lights out. I would bet that you are down for special treatment.'

'I'm all choked up. What sort of treatment?'

'Ralph, just for a moment, take this seriously. You made him look a fool.'

'He is a fool. He's an oaf.'

'Agreed. But a dangerous oaf. Tomorrow night, you will be his prize victim. I'll stand by in case you need help. I may have to crack a few ribs. If I am his victim, before you I mean, you can be ready, if necessary, only if necessary, to lend a hand.'

'O.K. Hort. I'll be ready. And I am taking it seriously. The way I see it is this. If I had shown any fear, he would have singled me out as his jester, to torment me as long as I am here. This way, we'll get it over and done with. Do you agree?'

Hort took such a long time to answer, I thought he was in complete disagreement. We were on the way back to the barrack room when he said, 'Yah, you're right.'

Friday came, lights out, we were all in bed except Private Hardy, who staggered in pickled, mumbling curses at everybody and everything. He slid into his room, so it seemed there would be no carnival tonight.

Hardy had stopped mouthing off. I turned over on my side and closed my eyes. Crash! I sat up in bed like a jack-in-the-box. There he was, standing laughing uproariously at the poor slob whose bed he had just separated in two. I refer to his victim as a poor slob because he didn't utter a word; not a sound. He just lay there until Hardy moved on. Number two got the same treatment, and reacted in much the same way. So I was to be next. It wasn't difficult to see in the darkness because of the moonlight which flooded the room. Hardy stood at the foot of my bed and waited. It was too dark to see his features, but I can imagine he was grinning in anticipation.

'Don't do it, Hardy,' I whispered.

'I wanna see you dance, you bugger,' he snarled in a low voice.

'I'm warning you, Hardy, if you do it I'll make you . . .' I got no further. Without warning, I was pinned down on the upper half of the bed with the lower half, upside down, on top of me. Hardy stood laughing at me trying to extricate myself. Now, after so many years, I can laugh too. Let's face it, I must have presented a comical spectacle. Releasing myself from the mess of tangled blankets and biscuits, I stood quietly by until Hardy's laughter subsided.

'Fun's over, Hardy,' I said. 'Make up my bed.' I didn't expect he would. By his renewed laughter, this must have been the funniest thing he had ever heard. I grasped him by the arm and jerked him towards the bed. His laughter turned to fury, and he lunged at me catching me unawares. I received a numbing blow on the shoulder. That was all I needed. I drove my left fist into his face, but it didn't seem to hurt him. He lunged at me again, but missed. Suddenly several of the men were out of their beds and rushing to the windows to warn us if anyone was coming. Hort hovered in the background, watching us closely but not interfering. We fought and slugged to the far end of the barrack room and back. He was a fairly easy target but he had no feeling. I couldn't hurt him. His aim seemed to be not to hit me, but to get his hands on me. I heard Hort's voice, 'Don't let him get a grip on you.'

I didn't really need Hort's warning. I saw what he was after. He couldn't hit me so he was trying to get a hold on me. In desperation, he

Scrub, You So - And - So!

lifted a fire bucket half full of sand and threw it at me. I saw it coming and dodged it with ease. Then, like an irate bull, he charged, running into a solid straight left. He sank slowly to the floor in utter surprise. With almost anyone else I would have given him my hand and found out if he had been hurt but Hardy was such an objectionable character, I had no such thoughts. I would have laughed at the sight of Hardy sitting on the floor, looking in bewilderment at the front tooth in his hand, but my hand hurt. He was dazed. My eyes had become accustomed to the dim light and I could discern the bewilderment on his face. I hoped he was in more pain than I was. One of my knuckles was swollen and unbearable to touch. When I looked at my bed up-ended and lying in a heap, my anger rose again. Hort was helping Hardy up.

'Gimme a hand here, Ralph. Let's get him to bed,' said Hort, looking at me.

'WHAT! Hold on,' I cried. 'I want him to make up my bed.'

Hardy, with the help of Hort, was staggering towards his room. I ran after them, but Hort caught my arm in a vice-like grip.

'That's enough, Ralph. You won the battle.'

Pulling my arm loose, I yelled, 'Like hell that's enough. He's going to make my bed.'

'If you make him remake your bed, you'll spend the next six months walking backwards. The foe is vanquished, the battle won.'

'A bloody philosopher. That's all I need.'

Hort threw Hardy on his bed and barred the entrance.

'I'll make your bed,' he said. I tried to rush past him but he pinned my arms against the wall.

'I said I'll make your bed. Cool down and think.'

I did think and in seconds I cut the fuse. Everyone was back, or getting back into their fleapits except the two who were re-making them.

The following Friday, Hardy came in half-canned as usual. He did his act, missing my bed, then down the other side, missing Hort. Grumblings filled the room, but that was their problem. I wore a splint for about ten days, but there was no fracture.

'Slipped on the steps,' I told the doc.

'You shouldn't have any more trouble with those steps again,' said the young lieutenant grinning.

Word gets around fast, I thought. Some three weeks passed without any trouble. Only the misery of blancoing, boning, polishing brass and drill parades was beginning to transform me into a kind of zombie.

One day, in the canteen, Hardy sat down at our table uninvited. This wasn't unusual except that there were other tables unoccupied, and we were not, by any stretch of the imagination, buddies. He placed his coffee on the table; then he said, 'Your coffee is nearly finished. I'm gonna buy you both a fresh one.' He beetled off to the counter. I said to Hort, 'Maybe I should put his coffee on another table.'

'Leave it, if you don't mind. Let me handle it.'

Hardy returned with two coffees and pushed them in front of us. Hort shoved his aside. I followed suit.

'Push off,' said Hort, quietly.

Hardy bristled. 'I'm trying to be friendly. What's the matter with you?'

Hort was as calm as ever. He said, 'I told you to push off. Now push off.'

'You think you own this place or something?'

Hort turned his head and looked at me. 'Did *you* understand what I said?'

'Perfectly.'

'Nothing obscure, indefinable, ah . . . ambiguous about it?'

'In nautical terms, it was perfectly clear. You told him to shove off.'

Hort turned again to Hardy, who was little short of having an apoplectic attack. 'I'm going to say it just once more. If you don't take my advice, I'll wrap your bed around your head tonight, after dark. Now, push off.' There was a dangerous look in Hort's eyes.

Hardy turned and strode off, but he wheeled about to retrieve the two cups of coffee, favouring us with a magnificent scowl. When he had gone I said to Hort, 'Weren't you a bit rough on him, Hort? What harm would it have done to accept his coffee? He was trying to make up for his lousy behaviour.'

'You're right, Ralph. We could have drunk the coffee and then told him to push off.'

'He needs a few more friends. It might change his whole outlook.'

'He hasn't got a friend in the whole bloody Depot, and he's not going to rake me in like a beginning to a garbage collection. If he cleans up his act, maybe my attitude towards him will change. If you want to make friends with him, go ahead, I don't mind, but don't try to drag me into his mental recession. Maybe you're right . . . maybe. Maybe I'm wrong . . . maybe not.'

I scratched the back of my neck, partly because I hadn't yet become used to the irritation caused by the rough collar of my tunic, and partly because it seemed the only answer I had at the time. Then suddenly I had the answer. 'Yeah, maybe you're right . . . maybe. Maybe I'm wrong . . . maybe not.' Hort rubbed his eyes with his fingers. Perhaps it didn't mean anything . . . Perhaps not. Perhaps it did . . . Perhaps.

That night, minutes after lights out, I called across to Hort. 'Are you awake, Hort?'

'Yes, I'm awake. What is it?'

'I've been thinking. You're right.'

'Thanks, Ralph. Goodnight.'

All was well. We were rid of Hardy. Barton kept out of our way. Peace reigned at last. I fell asleep wondering how I could have got into so much trouble in only one week, considering what a quiet and inoffensive person I was. Well, that's life, I suppose. I dozed off.

It happened the next morning on roll call parade. I was told to report to the gymnasium at nine a.m. that day. I told Hort about it.

'I suppose this was inevitable. I should have insisted those two clowns in Edinburgh remove the boxing, soccer and swimming entries before I signed it. Maybe I should have joined the French Foreign Legion.'

'Do you want to get into sports?' Hort inquired.

'No, no and no.'

'Then, be of good cheer. I have news for you, but . . . there is a catch.'

'Quick, quick. The news first.'

'You don't have to participate in sports. You do, however, have to practice physical exercises. King's Regs.'

'Then I can refuse to fight in the ring?'

'You don't refuse anything in the Army. You only decline.'

I was about to interrupt when Hort stopped me. 'Here is the catch. You must dress in whatever outfit is required to play or participate in any game.'

'Hah! That's no catch,' I cried.

'I haven't finished. Having dressed as ordered, if you decline to take part in a sport for which you are outfitted, you will probably spend a lot of time scrubbing floors, heaving coal, or something of that nature.'

'King's Regs?'

'Nauseating bully's Regs.'

'So the choice is – scrub a few floors for a few days, or spend the next seven years of my life right here, bashing or being bashed.'

'Simply put, yes. Now, if you are good at whatever it happens to be, you will become one of the chosen few to receive preferential treatment.'

'Hm. Preferential treatment.' It might not be so bad after all. 'I'm beginning to get interested. Could you expand, tell me what sort of preferential treatment I may expect?'

'Certainly. You'll be able to demand an extra sausage when sausages are served at breakfast. You'll be allowed to sweat off a few pounds at the gym while other poor beggars are sitting peeling potatoes or attending classes on map reading and English. And nobody will order you to remove your puttees to see that you are not wearing civilian socks. You can . . .'

'You can change the subject.'

I reported as ordered. A short, compact sgt.-major threw me some gym togs and gloves.

'Put these on,' he said. To another chap standing around he said, 'Tie his gloves.'

'Excuse me, Sir, but what is it I am supposed to do?'

'I want to see if you are any good with gloves.'

'I can tell you now, Sir. I'm hopeless with gloves.'

'I'll be the judge – O.K.? Let me be the judge.'

'Sir, I don't want to box, Sir.'

He feinted three or four swipes, stopping an inch from his target. I made my great mistake. I didn't flinch, knowing he wouldn't hit me unless I was defending myself.

'All right, soldier, box or I'll let you have a real one,' he said.

'If you hit me, Sir, I'll report you for assaulting me, Sir.'

He couldn't have been more astonished if I had broken his nose. He glared and spoke with great deliberation. 'Would you rather scrub floors?'

'If I have to, Sir.'

'You have to. Have no doubt, you have to. Follow me.'

We went to his office, a one-room hut which was spotless and tidier than any office I had ever seen. The S.M. said, 'Sit down.' We both sat on the only two chairs and he stared at me for a moment. 'You didn't dodge my gloves. This tells me you have boxed . . . Well?'

'That is in the past, Sir.' That was mistake number two. I should have said, 'Never had gloves on in my life, practice or match. In fact, I don't even know when Boxing-day is.'

'All in the past, eh? Veeeery good. Your History Sheet tells me that you have boxed, played soccer and that you are an accomplished swimmer. Before long, you will change your mind. That bucket over there, fill it with water. You will find soap and a scrubber in that cupboard. Make a good job of it.' Then he yelled, 'Get on your feet.'

Hort didn't tell me it was that easy. I scrub the floor and I'm off the hook. The floor was so clean, it was obvious I was not the first. The S.M. came back in about half an hour. 'Ready to fight?' he asked.

'No, Sir.'

'That floor is not clean. Scrub it.' He left.

The floor was so clean I threw some water over it and mopped it up. Very soon there appeared the sprightly S.M. 'Ready to box?' he asked.

'No, Sir.'

'Tomorrow, after you have scrubbed the floor, you will clean the windows, inside and out. Are you getting the idea?'

'Sir, I believe the idea is that as long as I decline to fight, my gym activities will be confined to scrubbing floors and polishing windows.'

He was obviously not pleased with my answer. Because I was dressed for the gymnasium exercises, I was in shorts and sprinting shoes. My knees were pretty raw, but not yet skinned. 'Dismiss,' he snarled.

For many days I scrubbed the floor and cleaned the windows unnecessarily. If the dum-dum only knew it, the more I scrubbed, the more determined I became not to box. A little coaxing might have changed my mind. I'll never know. My knees were now covered with two huge scabs, which were not painful but inclined to catch on my clothing.

It was on the fourth or fifth day of this routine – I don't remember exactly – that Hort looked closely at my scabby knees.

'Have you been wearing some protective material over your knees?' he asked.

'Certainly not.'

'Are you sure? All right, all right. I believe you,' said Hort, guarding himself as though he expected me to punch him. 'Now, if you can hold out until Friday, that's only the day after tomorrow, with luck we can hobble past the General Officer Commanding this neck o' the woods.'

'G.O.C.'s Inspection?'

'That's right. So guard those scabs as if they were the crown jewels.'

'You know, Hort, I get a sinking feeling in my gut when you start working out some elaborate scheme, especially where the G.O.C. is involved. Maybe we should just forget the whole thing.'

Hort looked so surprised and his reaction looked so genuine, that if I had not seen him in action before, I would have been completely taken in. But what a ham! He always overdid it. With his hands spread out in an attitude of supplication he uttered in a kind of croak, 'After all I've done for you. After all I've schemed, "Forget the whole thing"?'

'Right,' I yelled, 'Forget the whole thing. They're my knees. And they're my scabs.'

'Just make sure you keep them until Friday, Ralph. They are more precious than the . . .'

'The crown jewels?' I groaned. 'Yes, I know, I know.'

EF ITE, EF ITE, AH-HAUT

Like Caligula and several others, scrubbing floors and polishing glass was all bad. Drill parades, on the other hand, were not much better. In fact, drill was something I could hate with a white-hot loathing years after I no longer had to be a part of it.

I had not yet discovered a real taste for words, and while I spoke with a distinct Scottish accent, which, incidentally, has never quite abandoned me, I spoke no other language except English, my second language. Having grown up from childhood hearing and, to a great extent, speaking both languages, I did not consider myself a linguist.

Consider, then, my surprise when I discovered that on parade I was obliged to learn a third language. The first word I learned was 'A-teee-cha'. This meant we had to jerk ourselves smartly to attention. It was explained to us, in English, that attention meant we were to convulse to a position where our heels were touching and our toes pointing outward at an angle of approximately forty-five degrees. At first this was accomplished to numbers but these were later discarded. Following 'cha', was 'one'. 'One' meant that the left foot was rammed, with force, into the ground, as near as possible to the concentric point in relation to body balance, retaining an upright position. On the command 'doo', the right foot was raised and brought in close to the left tibia, then rammed into the ground with bone-shattering ferocity.

On the very first day, Private Paddy O'Mara, a heck of a nice fellow and very religious, brought his right foot down on 'doo', driving his heel into his left ankle, which would have eliminated the Army as a profession for anyone with prominent left ankles. Of course I didn't think about that until later, because O'Mara let go a howl that would have curdled the milk of any cow within half a mile.

'Oh God!' he screamed. 'Oh God in Heaven! My foot! My foot!'

It was difficult above the shrieks of O'Mara, to hear the corporal when he yelled, pointing, 'You and you, help him to the First Aid.' The two so ordered helped him to the Medical Station, his cries of anguish reverberating off the barrack-room walls all the way until he was indoors. He was hospitalised for a few days. Any thought I had of trying the same thing was instantly abandoned when I recalled his screams of supplication to his Creator. Actually, I place the blame squarely on Corporal Harburn, because when Paddy didn't get his heels close enough to be almost touching, Harburn yelled, 'Get yer heels together O'Mara. Yer meat stinks.' Paddy became flustered and was trying his best to please.

Before we were what could be called 'fluent', the 'Ateee-cha' was discarded in favour of 'Squaw-cha'. We then went on to 'Quiiik-mash, ef ite, ef ite, ef ite.' Everybody got that right away, almost. You'll be astonished at how many men didn't know their Ef from their Ite. The corporal's response made it perfectly clear, however, and the same mistake was never made again. 'Maaak tie' was easy, but then came a subtle change. 'Ef ite' became 'Ep eye' repeated until we were in swinging harmony. Believe me when I say that, after 'Ep eye, ep eye, ep eye, ep eye', there was, on my part anyway, a tantalizing urge to sing 'yippy eye o eye AAA'. If you are wondering whether I ever succumbed to the temptation, no. 'Fom-a-foe' was tricky, demanding concentration at first, but we soon got it. Now came the most musical command of all, 'Staaa-deezy' which followed 'Sta-dat-eee'. 'Staaa-deezy' was quieter and more distinct than other commands, except 'Dismiss'. In a way it resembled a railway engine delivering its last wheeze before coming to a stop at a station where only one little old lady waited to get on. I got the impression that the corporal had lost his enthusiasm, if not his interest, in the whole business. Musical? Well, the first syllable 'Staaa' was in 'C', an octave above middle C. 'Deezy' was more or less thrown in as two grace notes in 'F' or 'F sharp' below 'C'. Then came that emotionally comforting word, delivered in clear-cut English, 'Dismiss'.

That was as far as I got with drill when I was consigned to the

Ef Ite, Ef Ite, Ah - Haut

hardwood and glass caper. My scabby knees didn't hurt, but I had to be careful not to knock them against anything or to catch them on clothing. Hort had some scheme in mind, but he wouldn't elaborate except to say that it had something to do with the G.O.C.'s inspection. He was never happier than when he was planning or pulling off some plot which would make someone squirm with discomfort. There was never anything violent or brutal about his machinations, but one had to be careful not to become an embarrassed, even slightly injured, innocent.

On Thursday, the day before the G.O.C.'s visit, I was contemplating the pail, which was half full of water, wondering what would happen if I threw the pail through the closed window. Of course I would explain that I thought the window was open, and the pail slipped out of my hand. Who would buy that? Not me to be sure. At that moment, the spry little S.M. appeared, suddenly and silently as usual.

'Put these things away, get dressed, and report for Map Reading in one hour. First, get those knees attended to,' he barked.

'But, Sir, I haven't even started the . . .'

'Don't argue. And don't come back here until after the inspection.'

'Inspection, Sir? What inspection is that, Sir?'

'Never mind. Dismiss. You can attend all other classes.'

'I could come back in the evening, Sir. After supper.'

'Dismiss. Go on.'

Not only was he trying to get rid of me in a hurry, but he knew that I was provoking him into doing, or at least saying, something wrong. The time had come to slap him. For many days he had made my life miserable.

'Thank you, Sir. Oh, Sir?'

'What is it? Come on, I'm busy.'

'Yes Sir, I know you're busy, Sir. You are always busy, Sir.'

'McCaa, if you have something to say, say it, then leave.'

'Yes, Sir. Thank you, Sir. My barrack room is that way, Sir,' I said, pointing in several directions.

'What do you want me to do? Take your hand?'

'Oh no, Sir. On the way there I pass the latrine, Sir.'

I could almost hear his malice. He said nothing, just glared, unblinking into my eyes. They were the eyes of a pugilist. I had experienced some of that too, so I stared back at him.

'Will it be all right with you, Sir if, on the way I stop for a crap, Sir?'

For a moment I thought he was going to strike me, his eyes were so malignant. He was white with rage. If I could get him to punch me, just once, it would be worth it. He was too experienced for that though. I mimed the motion of dropping my pants and squatting slightly, at the same time passing one of my hands across the front of his eyes. No luck. His eyes faltered, and without another word he turned and left. There was no doubt in my mind that, after the inspection, I would be returned to the same routine. I wondered what Hort had in mind.

Hort wasn't in when I returned to the barrack room. Hardy was. He was in his cubicle, alone. The door was open and we glanced at each other when I passed. I sat on my bed contemplating the past several minutes. Hardy appeared and stood staring at me in silence. His design was clearly one of intimidation. What should I do? Should I say 'Hello Hardy'? I didn't know his first name. An opening like 'Hello Hardy' could be interpreted as an invitation to become more friendly. On the other hand it could be seen as a challenge. On the other hand it could be taken for capitulation or, on the other hand, it could be accepted as surrender. I had to make a quick decision. He took three or four steps towards me so I leapt to my feet and faced him, my legs apart and my hands hanging loosely by my sides. This was not the best stance to take on the chance there might be a scuffle but I hoped I gave the impression of the good guy facing a shootout with Wallace Beery, ready to draw two six-pieces and drill him full of lead. I wiggled my shoulders – a kind of warm up for the moment of truth. Apparently I did the right thing for Hardy turned about and left without a word. If Miss MacTavish could see me now!

I sat down again, thankful, I admit, that it had ended like this. A few minutes later Hort appeared with several other recruits.

'I'm glad you're here,' said Hort.

'Why?'
'I don't have to look for you.'
'Brilliant.'
'Well, we have just come off drill parade. Do you know what we have to do? Of course you don't. We have to get our bodies up to the soccer field and just stay out of sight. Before that, we had a session with the first aid instructor. What do you think we practised?'
'You fitted a Thomas splint on somebody's leg and asked a few dumb questions. Then you were shown the pressure points to arrest a haemorrhage, after which you asked a few more dumb questions.'
'Ralph,' exclaimed Hort with mock astonishment, 'you're clairvoyant. All right. What's bothering you?'
'If you really want to know, you're bothering me. You ramble on about drill parades and first aid, and you're not interested in what's happening at my end.'
Hort became secretive and looked around him at the innocent young men who were all minding their own business. His act was lousy, overdone beyond credibility.
'Follow me,' he whispered, nodding towards the door. I followed him outside and we walked towards the coal-yard where it was private. Sometimes, when we passed the enclosure where the coal was dumped, we could catch a glimpse of one or two poor slobs heaving the coal to the back of the enclosure. Nobody was there today.
'O.K. Hort,' I said, talking through one side of my mouth, 'we're alone. Now we can talk. Here's my suggestion. You go in waving your sub-machine gun. You fire off a few rounds into the ceiling, then wave it at the customers. You tell them to lie flat on the floor, face down. I come in and instruct the tellers to fill up the pillowcase with tens and pound notes. The car is left running for a quick getaway. I leave first, get into the car and . . .'
'Hold it. We'd never get away with it. I should know. I'm an ex-policeman, remember? We'll have to have a driver, one with experience.'
'Now listen, and listen good. We get Lefty Hooligan. He's da best.'
That was one of the only things I hated about Hort. He was able to

expand this burlesque. Remember, I mentioned he was a real ham? Well, he also was talking through one side of his mouth.

'That's very good, Hort. Very good,' I said, applauding sarcastically. 'Now, tell me why we are here.'

'In the Army Dental Corps? Or in the coal-yard?'

'Both if you like, but first, in the coal-yard.'

'Ah, that brings us back to the first aid lecture. I had a few questions to be sure. First, I asked what procedure I should pursue if someone were incapacitated by a physical injury.'

'In English, you mean if he got hurt?'

'Exactly!'

'Then why didn't you say so?'

'For two reasons, Ralph. First, that is the language of the three-tailed bashaw. Second, your victim, sorry, your respondent is concentrating on your verbiage and misses the point of your question.'

'I think I may have missed the point of why I got involved with you at all.' Hort paid no attention to my protestation.

'"Proceed with the injured party to the nearest First Aid Station",' he replied. 'See what I mean? He had tripped and fallen headlong into my idiom. This is tantamount to hypnotic stimulus to become part of the action, as it were.'

'Indubitably,' I answered, glassy eyed.

'You see, Ralph. Now you're doing it.'

'Truly your motivation has been successfully rewarded,' I grinned clownishly. 'Now, Horatio Baby Face Nelson, tell me, just what in hell has all this to do with the cloak-and-dagger meeting in a bloody coal yard?'

'Right. My next question was, "What about some unusual condition or situation like, oh, injury, say bleeding on . . . say . . . G.O.C.'s Inspection?" For a moment he looked perplexed. I thought I had him. Exasperated, he said, "If a man, male or female, needs att . . . any person, male or female requires medical attention at any time, you see to it that he gets it . . . or she. Any time." And don't you ever call me Horatio or Baby Face again or I'll clobber you.'

'Then you can basket me over to the First Aid Station.'

'Now, let me see your scabby knees. Good. I have good news. The great man's Inspection is today, not tomorrow as originally arranged.' Now I understood the Gym Instructor's urgency to get me out of the way. I told Hort what had happened.

'Couldn't be better,' Hort exclaimed. 'Now, you just stay out of sight until I come for you.'

'Out of sight? Where do I go to be out of sight?'

'Where everyone can see you, of course. Maybe you should come with me somewhere around the stadium. Limp a little. Put on a bit of an act.'

'Right. Say, did I tell you about my debut as an actor, when I played the part of a sorry knave?'

'Several times. This time I want you to be the sorriest knave in the entire history of sorry knaves.'

'All right, Hort. The bottom line. When?'

'I don't know yet at what hour exactly. But it will be exactly when the general is viewing the gym parade.' Hort was grinning like a pussy full of cream.

We wandered around the soccer field despite the fact that there was nothing happening there. However, from that location we had a good view of any activities, usual or unusual, from our vantage point. Hort tapped me on the shoulder and pointed imperiously to a small knot of people moving in a dignified clump towards the latrine.

'Look yonder, scabby knave. Observe the brass, moving with stately gait, bestir your loins.' Hort had never looked happier. I was on the point of backing out, but Hort was so sure of himself and so persuasive that it was difficult not to go along with his schemes.

'Hort, do you mind if I ask a question?'

'Speak quietly my friend, the ears have walls.'

'Hort, you'll probably lie about it, but when you talk like that, has anyone ever thrown up in your face?'

'You wouldn't dare,' Hort answered. 'If you do, I'll call the whole thing off.'

Here was my chance. If I could have thrown up at that moment, I would have. Hort wasted no time coaching me in what to do as we threaded our way between the barrack rooms to the place and the moment where I would give the greatest performance of my life, no make-up, no costume.

At the right moment, which was when the G.O.C. was inspecting a carefully chosen group of the healthiest looking recruits available, I removed a portion of the scab from my kneecaps and covered the rest with blood which was trickling down my legs. I bleed copiously but my blood congeals quickly, and there was no pain in this simple operation. Hanging on to Hort, one arm around his neck, I was half carried, half dragged past the G.O.C. on the way to the First Aid Station. For some seconds, except for Hort and me, the scene was a post-impressionist still life. Suddenly, a voice called out, 'Halt!' Hort stiffened smartly to attention and saluted. I slumped in a heap on the ground.

'Somebody help him. You,' commanded the general, whereupon somebody, I don't remember who, assisted Hort to get me back into a position resembling a question mark. My sorry posture was not an intentional plot. Questions were inevitable. Hort whispered in my ear as I was being resurrected, 'Don't overdo it. This isn't a Command Performance.'

'This'll teach him to hurl pseudo-Shakespeares at me.'

'What is the matter with that man?' inquired the G.O.C.

'He is bleeding, Sir. Profusely, Sir.'

'Anyone can see that he is bleeding. *How* did it happen?'

'I'd rather not say, Sir,' Hort said. 'I mean, I have only his word for it, Sir.' If I hadn't had speedy coagulation in my blood composition, I would probably have bled to death. It seemed more important to get to the bottom of how it had happened than applying medical aid.

The general was almost apoplectic. 'I demand to know how this man got into such a frightful condition,' he barked.

Hort, the louse, upstaged me again. Wiping a dry tear from his eyes with his middle finger he pointed at the Sergeant-Major. All eyes turned on him, so I was able to steal a glimpse of this little tyrant looking very

Ef Ite, Ef Ite, Ah - Haut

uncomfortable. The G.O.C. turned to his Aide.
'Get to the bottom of this and report to me as soon as possible.'
With a jerk of his arm, he indicated that Hort and his assistant should get me away at once. Never again was I told to scrub floors or to clean windows. And that was how Hort and I became regular coal heavers.

SOCCER

One day, after a load of coal had been dumped carefully against the remains of the last load, I said to Hort, 'Tell me again, Hort.' His quizzical expression indicated that he wasn't sure what he was required to tell. I threw a malignant glance at the new load of coal. 'Tell me again, so that I can wallow in your words and appreciate more the tranquil but exhilarating life into which I have been thrust.'

Hort turned his innocent face towards me, then aimed his baby-blue eyes skywards as if searching for a starting point.

'You mean about the kickback I gave the lorry driver?' he asked with an ingenuous grin.

'No, no. No. I mean about the cushy time the Dentals have in comparison to the Medics.'

'Oh, that? You must realize, Ralph, we are among aliens. But don't think of them all as monsters. Take Sgt. Smith, for instance.'

'No. Take Sgt. Bartle for instance, and I don't have to tell you where to take him.'

A word or two about these two sergeants. Bartle was rotten. Clean through from his peel to his marrow, he was rotten. He was almost one of a kind. For no earthly reason apparent to us, he had it in for Hort and me. Eventually we found out there *was* an earthly reason. He was a close pal of the Phys. Ed. Sgt.-Major, our wounded but, I am unhappy to say, not mortally, louse. Bartle frequently took drill practise. Hort was luckier than I because of his height. He was always at one end of the line-up, whereas I was always number three or four from the end. Having missed a good number of drill practices, it wasn't difficult for Bartle to complicate his commands enough to confuse me. My apparent unworthiness to hold the rank of private in the British Army was what spawned a certain Company Officer's Inspection one day. But there was also Sgt. Smith, military in his bearing, a disciplinarian, strict but fair – no shining armour, no white charger – but unafraid to voice his opinions. Sgt. Smith never yelled at recruits. If a recruit bungled some simple command or was inattentive, he wiggled his forefinger and the poor sucker on whom his gaze anchored doubled over to hear some whispered malediction which served both parties. There were no witnesses to Sgt. Smith's imprecations and the victim's face was saved. It happened to me twice, and after drill parade a couple of chaps who were in the squad asked me what Smith had said. I explained that he was congratulating me but didn't want to hurt anybody's feelings by shouting it out. Nobody bothered to ask me about it the second time. Where Bartle's progress reports were concerned, mine were all negative, hence the inspection by the Company Officer where I was the main course. In fact I was the only turkey on the menu about to be chewed up into a pâté, if I read Bartle's clock correctly. The Company Officer scowled throughout the whole banquet. Sgt. Smith seemed bored and uninterested in the whole business. No question, what I needed was a white knight who would put Bartle to the sword and the Company Officer to flight. After a lot of poking with his cane and nudging at equipment which Bartle turned over or inside out, depending on the nature of the item, Sgt. Smith, who was responsible for my military orderliness, stepped forward and asked, 'Is everything all right, Sir?'

'Hmmm. Yes, Sergeant. It . . . seems to be . . . so far.'

'If I may offer my confirmation, Sir, this man's equipment is, and *always* is the most orderly in the barrack-room, Sir. His bedding, equipment and clothing not only seems all right, it *is* all right, Sir.'

My white knight! The Company Officer's face looked so brittle that if he had yawned I'm sure it would have splintered. Without twitching a facial muscle, he turned his glassy stare on Sgt. Smith. He didn't have only a stiff upper lip, he had a stiff lower lip; all his facial muscles were stiff. His posture was stiff, his arms were stiff, and when he departed his walk was stiff. In my mind's eye, I pictured him at weekends folding himself up into a convenient carrying size and carting himself off by one of his ears.

'Perhaps you will be good enough to tell me precisely what that means, Sergeant?'

'It means, Sir, that Private McCaa's behaviour and military competence are exemplary, Sir.'

'Are you challenging my opinion, Sergeant?'

'On the contrary, Sir. I am corroborating your opinion, Sir.'

Pretty good, I thought. Sgt. Smith ought to be one of us, not one of them. The Company Officer gave him a hasty but perplexed glance, then departed, followed by Bartle. Sgt. Smith skewered me with a contemptuous glance, then barked, 'Get this pigsty cleaned up, McCaa.' Then he marched smartly after the other two. This was very unfair. The C.O. and Bartle created the pigsty. I hadn't realized it immediately, but they had hardly left the barrack-room when I saw that Sgt. Smith's remark was a piece of hocus-pocus. You might call it flattery in forked tongue.

Coal heaving wasn't so bad as it might have been. After Hort started giving the trucker his kickback, he carefully dumped the bulk of his cargo up against the existing mound of coal, leaving a trickle for us to shovel back from the entrance. He was, on occasion, so anxious to please us that if we were not present at the time of delivery, we would have to heave some back near the entrance in order to be able to heave it back again. You see, one of us could scratch away at the coal where he could be seen and where he could see anyone coming, such as a corporal devoid of fraternal sympathy or anyone who might be a stranger to the compensations of human enterprise. The other of us could sit out of sight and read, or write home for money. He could even indulge himself in a short nap. We took no chances of being caught. Whenever anyone came near, even dog-collared officers were not excluded, a small shovelful of coal, aimed in the direction of the sleeping partner, galvanized him into feverish activity.

It was while we were discussing the knaveries and merits of Sergeants Bartle and Smith that Corporal Harburn appeared. We knew he had a mission because he strode towards us in steps of thirty inches at a speed somewhere between 120 and 130 steps per minute. The corporal didn't mince words: 'McCaa, report to the gymnasium, where you will be given suitable clothing into which you will change into, then you will report unto the soccer field.' As I said, he didn't mince words. His grammar was a hybrid but his words unambiguous. This was a blow not just below the belt but right to the groin. Before I had time to recover enough to reply, Corporal Harburn was gone, 30/120. Why me?

'Now, what do I do?' 'You have two choices,' answered Hort. 'You can play soccer to the best of your ability. Or . . . you can kick the ball in the wrong direction. Or . . . you can pass the ball to one of the opposing team. Or . . . you can catch the ball and run. Or . . . you can alternate these manoeuvres. You have two choices. It's up to you.'

'Two choices?'

'Mine, or the one you are about to come up with.'

The soccer field was in perfect playing condition. That's what one of the players told me. I didn't know personally.

'What position are you playing?' asked a stringy looking fellow.

'Who? Me?'

'Do you see anyone else behind you?'

I glanced behind me. 'Ah . . . look . . .' I said, 'I have never played soccer.' His eyes were so piercing that they startled me into another quick glance behind me. There was still no one there.

'What position do you prefer?'

'More or less standing upright, I suppose.' I must have given him the right answer for, without hesitation, he growled, 'Keep goal'. Was it my fault that I went to the wrong goal posts, where a grinning, barrel-shaped youth was leaning against one of the uprights?

'Nice day,' I said, patting the goalpost with one hand. Stringy pointed a stubby finger towards the other end of the field, grinning even wider. 'It's at the other end.'

Stringy – he was the captain I found out later – yelled in a stentorian bawl, 'the other end is there. C'mon McCaa, double up.'

After only a few weeks in the Depot, it is remarkable how an individual, no matter what his temperament, will respond to vocal injunctions. Instantly, speedily, I ran. Retrospectively, I believe that if some sportive youth riding a bicycle up Cock-ma-lane, whose voice had just broken, had barked a command, nine hundred-and-ninety-nine-thousand, nine-hundred-and-ninety-nine out of a million recruits, after two months training, would have leapt into action.

I had just enough time to lean nonchalantly against the goalpost when the whistle shrieked for the game to begin. To my consternation, a human buffalo was stampeding towards me, pussy-footing a hard leather ball among his feet. I rushed to the centre of the goal-mouth in sorry time to catch the leather right in the stomach. All three of us landed in the back of the net in a heap. Three of the players grabbed the buffalo and hugged him back onto the field. Another one grabbed the ball and booted it into outer space. I lay for some seconds, unnoticed by the world. I think it is obvious why a sensitive person like myself should not be interested in the game of soccer. Scarcely had I time to straighten my stockings and remove some of the dirt from my face and clothing, when I saw him, the same, the same absurdity bearing down upon me again. Someone tried to intercept him, but I was not in a frame of mind to take chances. No Pavlova, no Nijinsky, no prime minister ever executed a swifter, more spirited pirouette than I. Landing against the net at one side, I pressed myself, safely I thought, behind one of the upright barricades smiling. I didn't know what happened. Hort told me when I regained consciousness at the First Aid Station. The post wasn't embedded in the earth as firmly as it might have been and the shattering power with which the football hit the post was transferred to me. It gave me the only nosebleed I had had since I had been clobbered by one of the members of the Gym Club years before. Although unaware of how it had happened, I remember screaming at the buffalo, 'You did that dewibewatewy!' Then I passed out. Never again was I ordered to play soccer or to box, which is not meant to indicate that life was now all beer and skittles.

WHERE GOETH THOU

Bartle was still as rotten, Sgt. Smith still as decent, the Gym S.M. still as ugly, Hardy still as uglier, Hort still as protective and I was still not unhappy about Hort's protectiveness. I soon caught up with the others in English, Map Reading, First Aid, etc. Hort and I went out more at weekends to one of our favourite watering places in Farnborough. Every Friday - payday - we took off early enough to be among the first customers to rush in as soon as the local opened. We never got drunk. How could we on ten shillings a week? I made no-interest loans to a few of the other recruits during the week. Never more than a shilling though. If they didn't pay it back on pay day, it was never repeated. I don't think I was out more than a couple of bob.

Life in Crookham Camp was beginning to be a bit of a drag. Probably that was because Bartle and the Gym S.M. had found new victims for their type of sadism. However, it was none of my business to find out. Change was in the wind. We knew it although there was nothing we could finger. Then, one day, there it was on the bulletin board. We were to be granted ten days' leave, after which - Ah-ha! - after which we would learn where we would be posted to. Our - at least my - jubilation curdled on the spot. I knew Siberia was out of the question, but where? Would I be sent to a dental centre somewhere in Bonnie Scotland? Or would I be sentenced to serve time in some isolated region, God knew where? My reaction to the first moments of speculation was a chilling alarm which, upon deeper conjecture, turned to abject terror, groundless perhaps - perhaps. Names like Khartoum, Khyber Pass and other remote places beginning with K loomed in my mind. There was Kirkcaldy and Kinghorn, of course, but I was unaware of any troops being billeted there. All the joy of going home for ten days evaporated with the spectre of what might follow.

In a matter of seconds I realized how foolish my thoughts were and I forced myself into a 'wait-and-see' frame of mind. One anxiety could lead to another and I could end up in a state of acute paranoia. As it was, with the exception of Hort, I had never got to know anyone really well over the past six months. When we were not on drill parade, attending lectures on map reading, brushing up our English or writing some other examination papers, or in my case, scrubbing floors already more antiseptic than the decks of any operating surgery, I was polishing brass, blancoing equipment or boning army boots with spit and polish which we burnished with the handle of our toothbrushes. Whenever we had the chance, Hort and I got out of the Depot as fast as we could. We spent our last Friday at the pub in Farnborough, some miles from the Depot. Some of the others, yesterday recruits, today trained soldiers, were there. They looked no different to me than they did yesterday, despite the fact that none of them knew where they were going after their ten days' leave. After a couple of glasses of ale we started singing. Before you could say 'What are you having?', we were raising the rafters with our singing and joking but there was no destructiveness, just high spirits and vociferations des-criptive of the feelings we had for the Depot and its staff, bless 'em all.

It must have been getting close to 'Gentlemen, please' when I tapped Hort on the shoulder in order to have his undivided attention. 'Shuppose,' I said, with as much dignity as I could muster, 'Shuppose they keep us in the Depot. Ever thought about that, eh?'

'Bilge,' Hort answered philosophically. 'I'm going to Dartmouth.'

'Maybe they'll shend me to Dartmoush and shend you to Invernesh or Persh.' 'That's possible,' answered Hort, 'I've never been abroad.'

'Neither have I. I don't shuppose you play the bagpipsh?'

'No.'

'And you don't have a kilt.'

'I'd look like hell in a kilt.'

'You're right. With a Devonshire akshent you'd look like hell in a kilt, heh heh heh.'

'If you can find your mouth, drink up,' said Hort. 'It's nearly closing time. And you might as well know it, your act stinks. C'mon.'

'Jealousy, Horatio. My act was very convincing. Just trying to ward off the depression that'll settle on us as soon as we leave the pub.' On the walk back to the Camp we didn't talk much. That is probably why I remember so distinctly Hort saying, 'Are you aware, Ralph, that after we leave this place, we may never see each other again?'

'Sure we'll meet again. When you get your annual leave, you can spend part of the time at where I am stationed, then I'll come to where you are stationed. At different times, of course.'

'You bet,' said Hort.

Although I had consumed only six half pints of draft ale, and the night air had cleared my air passages, the rest of the journey back to Crookham Camp was relatively silent. It had come as a pleasant surprise that there would be no more drill parades or barrack-room inspections before we embarked on our ten days's freedom. We were told this by Corporal Hubble, who glared at us menacingly. No one cheered but there was a barely audible sigh in the ranks. Hort and I, like so many others, sat moping about, just waiting for time to pass. We were to go on ten days' leave not knowing where we were being sent afterwards. Maybe they were afraid that only half of us would come back if we knew. This was a farewell act of sadism. What else could it be? On Saturday afternoon Hort said, 'How about going down to Aldershot? Could be our last visit.'

'I think I had better save the few bob I have for tobacco,' I answered.

'That bad, eh?'

'No. But it's a long time to next payday.'

Our pay was two shillings a day, but four bob was kept back each week for incidentals. Incidentals were, for instance, socks which had been darned so often that there was little of the original toggery left, cap and epaulette badges lost or mislaid, which is the more delicate way of saying, 'some so-and-so pilfered them'. Well, soon we would be bound for integration among humanity. And we would be rich. Our pay would be two shillings and ninepence a day. What wealth! The baker and the butcher had paid five shillings a week. The coal mine had paid fourteen shillings a week, less unemployment and union dues. The Isle of Man had paid five pounds a month; twenty-five shillings a week. Hmm. Two and ninepence a day isn't that good after all. However, bad as it was, the past was no hell.

I heard a faraway voice – Hort's. 'Tell you what. We'll bum a ride and go to the theatre.'

I was stricken by a lightning attack of nostalgia. It seemed like a lifetime since my acting debut with Sgt.-Major MacTavish. I was not unhappy to forget that, but there were the sweet memories of Dorothy with her peaches-and-cream complexion and gurgling voice. Dorothy was married now and had two children. We didn't see her any more. But these memories belonged to the past; to my youth, gone, gone forever, just fading memories in the annals of my tender years. Here I was, now twenty-one and a half years old and . . .

'Ralph! Where the hell are you?' Hort's face showed concern.

'Oh, I was just thinking of – you know – the past.'

'It must have been pretty untidy,' Hort grunted. 'At one point you looked like you had walked into the women's washroom. At another point you looked like you had just left.'

'Oh, clam up will you. All right, we'll go to Aldershot. When does this show finish?'

'Eleven o'clock.'

'Eleven?' I yelled, 'Forget it!'

'We're finished here. What can they do to us?'

'I'll tell you what they can do to us. They can throw us in the slammer for a couple of weeks. There are a couple of sods just waiting to get us, especially me. Forget it, Hort.'

'Maybe you're right. What do you want to do?'

'Anything. As long as it doesn't contradict Standing Orders.'

'C'mon, I'll buy you a hot chocolate.' We went to the NAAFI, where we made a cup of hot chocolate last for more than an hour. We talked about the spiteful, and in our opinions, sadistic few who had exercised their miserable tyranny under the protection of that abused and misinterpreted word discipline. 'There were some decent buggers among them too, Hort.'

'Name one.'

'Smithy, Sgt. Smith.'

'Name two.'

'What about the educational sergeant?'

'Name three.'

'He was human. Remember the time when he told us an egg couldn't be *nearly* round? Anybody can see at a glance that an egg isn't round, or *nearly* round. Right? Either it is round or it isn't round. Right?'

'Right,' answered Hort with unquestionable conviction, 'a hen's egg is NOT round. It isn't even nearly round. A turtle's egg is a different story. It couldn't be rounder, could it?'

'No Horatio, it couldn't be rounder. And compensating for your inability to grasp the fact that nothing can be rounder than something else, nor can something be *nearly* round, because round is an absolute, also, in compensation for your disability in the attic, you have been equipped with a great physique.'

'Thank you, Ralph. And may I say, with a feeling of gratitude, although you would never be confused with Mr. Universe, you have the intellectual ability to say the wrong thing at almost any time.'

Then Hort honked. He didn't laugh like most persons, he honked through his nasal passage near the back of his throat, on short, sharp inhalations. Eyeing him with the cold stare which he deserved, I said, 'Hort, would you be awfully put out if I annihilated you?'

'Mind if I sleep on it?'

'Take your time,' I answered. 'And while we are on the subject of English, do you remember when the Ed. Sarge. asked us if anybody in the class had matriculated?'

'Yeah. And Dopey Greenwell said – honk honk – only when I was very young. Honk honk.'

'And his mother wouldn't let him drink liquids after six o'clock,' I screamed through my laughter.

Ralph

'And Greenwell never matriculated since,' Hort howled between honks. Maybe it was the purplish red colour of Hort's face, maybe it was the recollection of Greenwell's attempt at being learned, perhaps both, but my involuntary howl of mirth brought the buzz of voices round us to a sudden halt.

'Then,' Hort boomed, 'when the Sarge asked him to explain to the class how he arrived at his interpretation of the word "matriculation" for peeing the bed, he said - honk honk - he said it was from the Latin "matricula". Mat for matress - honk honk - and tricula for trickle - honk honk honk.'

Hort's honking, aided by my uncontrollable laughter, claimed the attention of everyone in the canteen. Then somebody yelled, 'Go on, get it off your chest before the postings go up.' We were immediately jerked back into line with the miserable uncertainty of the future.

I was studying the expressions on the bewildered faces of those around us when young Larkins burst in yelling, 'Postings are up! Postings are up!' If Larkins had suddenly appeared brandishing a submachine gun, yelling 'Don't nobody move', the response for a quick count of eight would have been no different. Everything, chairs, cutlery, humans, ashtrays, everything was a still life. Then, with a cacophonous yell from some forty voices, there was a human stampede to the door. Hort grabbed me by the wrist as I leapt to my feet. 'Cool it, cool it, Ralph, unless you want to be trampled to a dirty mark on the floor.' I sat down again and we were alone.

I burst out with, 'I thought we were not going to know until after we got back from leave.'

'Relax,' said Hort. 'Frankly I'm in a mood not to give a damn where I go. Wherever it is, we'll be away from here. No more Depot. No Aldershot. No reveille. Comforting, isn't it?'

'Yes, it is. Still, I'd like to know where . . . No, you're right. No more Crookham Camp. No more parades. Say, Hort, I wonder what it's like in a dental centre? What do we have to do?'

'Nothing.'

'Nothing?'

'You wear a white gown and try to look intelligent.'

'There must be more to it than that.'

'That's all I ever saw them do when I was in the infantry,' Hort assured me with an indulgent shrug.

'In the infantry? No. Forget it.'

'Look ah . . . you stay here if you want to, but I have to have a look at the postings.' Hort drained his cup of chocolate, then we both leapt from our chairs and made for the door and the Orderly Room.

'Will you get a load of that,' said Hort as we approached the mob. Blokes in khaki, milling about like bees round a queen, generated an ominous buzz. As we got closer the buzz converted into whoops, mutterings, curses and, in some cases, silent and staggering dismay.

'You wait here,' said Hort. 'I'll fight my way through.'

'I can fight my way in,' I yelled above the din.

'Getting in is the easy part,' he shouted, pushing me aside. 'It's getting out that's dangerous.' He elbowed his way through the coagulation of humanity milling about the bulletin board with no effort as his brawny arms swept bodies aside to left and right. I had no trouble keeping him in sight because of his height. He seemed to be transfixed beside the board for more time than was necessary. When he turned away and I saw his features, a grim expression clouded the usually benign face. He looked shaken.

'Well, c'mon, let's have it,' I burst out impatiently. It seemed ages before he answered. His voice was far away. 'Military Hospital, Aldershot.' His voice was that of a broken man. It wasn't Hort's at all. 'Oh, Hort, I'm so bloody sorry. Really I am. What can I say Maybe you can . . . naw, I don't know what to say. I feel awful. Did you manage to get a look at my ah . . .?'

'The same.'

I was stunned; paralysed. Where my blood went I don't know. I felt drained. 'WHAT?' I roared when I regained near-rationality. I clawed my way through the mess of khaki-clad humanity. There it was. Pte. R. McCaa . . . Military Hospital, Aldershot. There must be a mistake. I was near the entrance to the Orderly Room, so I knocked. I heard a voice from inside. 'It's open.'

I opened the door and entered. The Orderly Sergeant was sitting at the desk fondling a mug of tea and reading a book which lay on it, reading as though there was nothing the matter. This, of course, was an habitual adjunct with all NCOs in the Imperial Army in similar circumstances. He was the sergeant who had conducted our classes in English. I stood to attention.

He looked up after marking his book with a ruler. 'Yes, what do you want?'

'Sergeant, I think there must be some mistake . . . on the sheets . . . pinned up . . . on the board . . . outside.' He stared at me. 'Why the hell doesn't he say something, anything?' I thought. After a generous sip of tea, he moved a copy of the obnoxious sheet from the out tray and placed it in front of him.

'Name?'

I told him my name, which he knew as well as I. He examined the sheet.

'Ah, yes. Your name seems to be spelled all right. Capital M, small c, capital C, small aa, McCaa.'

'No, Sergeant. It's the destination. Aldershot Military Hospital.'

'I see.' He examined the sheet again, then, looking me in the eye with a bland expression, he said, 'That seems to be spelled all right, too.'

'The sonova . . . he's enjoying himself,' I thought.

'I should be going to a dental centre, Sergeant.'

'So you should, and so you are, in Aldershot.'

'Aldershot?'

'Aldershot. Until you are trained.'

'Trained?'

'Trained.' He took another sip of tea. Wetting his whistle for the next round no doubt. 'Private McCaa, do you know anything about casting models and making bite-blocks?'

'No, Sergeant.'

'How about the sterilization of surgical instruments?'

'Well . . . no.'

'Mixing amalgams, handling drugs, recording dental charts and recording daily treatment of patients, preparing monthly and annual reports for signature?'

'I'm afraid not, Sergeant.'

'Then, perhaps, you will be good enough to tell me what you think you would be doing in a dental centre. Wearing a white gown and trying to look intelligent?'

'I'm not sure. I mean, I don't know.'

'Then I shall enlighten you. You will be billeted at the Hospital. You will spend most of your time in a dental centre where there are two officers. You will like them. Now and again, you will spend a few hours in the Dental Laboratory. There, you will meet the Regimental Sergeant-Major. You will not like him any more than he will like you. Not that he will dislike you personally. Rather, he will consider you a nuisance, an untidy and unnecessary appendage to his establishment, which seems never to be uncluttered. By the way, I know that Private Nelson and you are palsy walsy. That is why I sent both of you to the same station.'

'YOU sent us?' I gasped.

'Who did you expect would do it? A field-marshal? Dismiss.'

He was reaching for his mug so I thought it would be a splendid idea to vanish, which I did. On the way out, the sergeant said, 'McCaa, it is only for three months.'

OLD FRIENDS

Everyone – that is everyone except Hort and I – was in the grip of a kind of fever. Not everyone was altogether jubilant, but at least they did know where they were bound after their leave. Hort and I knew also, but we were still not out of the jungle. Well, it was only for three months. We had all got our ten days' leave, after which I was to be an inmate of the Hospital in Aldershot. I wrote home immediately to tell the good news, leaving out the bad. I went home dressed to kill, figuratively speaking. I didn't want to kill even Sgt. Bartle. Maybe the little Gym Sgt.-Major, maybe not. I'd like to think about that. I arrived home in uniform of course, creased trousers – we slept on them – puttees, cheese-cap at a rakish angle, not forgetting our little swagger cane. The welcome when I arrived home was explosive. You'd think I had been away six years instead of six months. Mum, Dad, Margaret my sister, and my two brothers hadn't aged very much. Actually, after twenty-four hours at home, they seemed not to have aged at all. All right, it was only six months, but I had become a man. No longer was I the gawky teenager who had joined up for seven years. I was now a self-assured young man, ready to mix amalgams and sterilize dental forceps to the death in defence of my country. Mum had baked all four, plain white, white with currants, oatmeal and treacle scones, as well as a dumpling, which was usually reserved for Christmas. Dad still listened a great deal to his music, which didn't sound half as bad as it had six months ago. Polly was still as mean as ever. She remembered me clearly and greeted me with the loud piercing command that I descend to the nether regions. A walnut fixed her though; after that she was very friendly.

After the hugs, handshakes, kisses and congratulations, I looked around. Somebody was missing. 'Where's Granta?' The expressions changed from smiles to concern. 'What is it? He's all right, isn't he?'

'He's fine,' replied Mum. 'He is in the Kircaldy Hospital for a few days.'

'But you wrote to say he had retired and was in great health. Is it serious, not his heart or something?'

'No no, nothing like that.'

'Then, for any sake, tell me, what is it?'

'He fell.'

'Oh, no! He should know to lift his feet on rough ground. I've warned him several times.'

'Out of a tree,' Mum murmured.

'What's that?' I yelled.

'He fell out of a tree.'

'What the hell! - sorry, what was he doing in a tree?'

Dad put his arm on my shoulder. 'He was looking for *you*, Son.'

'Up a tree! UP A TREE!' I shouted. 'Is his mind . . . what did he say? Did he think *I* was up a tree?' Mum took over again.

'He called "Ralph. Tell Ralph. I have to tell Ralph." Then he passed out.'

'My God, where was this tree? Were you with him?'

'No,' answered Mum, 'we were in the garden. We saw him starting to climb the tree over at the burn. We called to him not to do it. He paid no attention and I ran over to try to stop him.'

'But you were too late?'

'Yes, I'm afraid so. He slipped and hit the ground with a thud. That's when he called, "Ralph. I have to tell Ralph." Then he passed out.'

'Look, Mum, Dad, I have to go and see him. Did he break any bones?'

'No, but he has a few bruises. He'll be all right. There's no need to rush down there right away.'

'Oh, yes there is,' I cried, and rushed out without more ado.

The tramcars were still running and they were quite frequent, so I didn't have long to wait.

Walking, the nearest tram stop was about half a mile from the hospital; running it was nearer a mile. I plumped for half-and-half. On arrival at the hospital, out of breath, the nurse I met as soon as I entered said, looking appropriately serious, 'She is still hanging on, but you had better go right in.'

'She? But it's Mr. Young I came to see.'

For a fleeting moment she looked embarrassed, then her expression was replaced with the cutest dimples I have ever seen on any face.

'Oh, him,' she said, denting her dimples even more by grinning with lips glued together in a tight cupid's bow. 'So, you're the victim,' she gurgled. 'The old devil. Sorry you're so disappointed.'

'I didn't say that,' I blurted. 'The old devil's right. I hope he didn't embarrass you with some offensive remarks about your dimples?'

'No more embarrassing than your remarks about my dimples,' she smiled. 'He had been given a sedative and was unconscious when he was admitted. He noticed as soon as he opened his eyes.'

'Noticed what?'

'My dimples. He said he would have mentioned it before he regained consciousness, but he didn't want to make a blind date.'

'You're kidding? He tried to date you?'

'Not at all. He tried to date you and me. Don't blush. I have already done it for both of us.'

'May I see him now?'

'This way.'

'Ralph,' he shouted. 'What kept you? Sorry I wasn't at home to meet you.' He was about to get out of bed but Dimples, Miss Ali Morton, swiftly pushed him back again. 'You watch that young lady, my boy. She's strong.'

'So I notice. How are you?'

'I'll bet she can climb a tree faster than you or me.'

'Which leads me to ask what you were doing up a tree at your age.'

'I found a mavis' nest with three eggs. I'll show it to you before you go back.'

'Correction,' I growled. 'You'll *point* to it before I go back.'

'Now,' he said, grinning like one of Ovenstone's cream cookies, 'I'm going to test your power of observation and you have only three guesses. I'll give you a clue by telling you that it is not her real name. Three guesses.' He extended an arm indicating that the object of the conundrum was no other than Dimples.

'Dimples?'

'Dang, boy! I wanted to say it.' His grin was fading as his eyelids slowly closed. He was asleep. Dimples pulled the bedclothes up to his neck and we left the ward.

'Where do you live - Kircaldy?'

'No,' she grinned. 'Leven, about two blocks from your Mum and Dad. In fact, I know your Dad.'

I must have looked startled, but her smile put me at ease.

'You're not a secret sister of mine or something like that, I hope?'

'Nothing like that.'

'When is your next day off duty?'

'Tomorrow.'

She loved walking, or hiking, I should say, so we enjoyed a couple of long walks round familiar roads and lanes, lanes and paths lightly trodden by humanity. Shakespeare might have said somewhere: 'What glorious wealth youth does not comprehend.' Maybe he did. However, I am ignorant of it.

During my leave I wandered alone a lot, recapturing, I suppose, the flavour of my boyhood past, sometimes bitter, sometimes sweet, certainly all too short. Taydon Cottage on South Street where Granta used to live when Granny was alive. Buchlyvie Terrace tenements facing the Rabbit Row where I kept the pigeons, and where the lilac tree which blossomed babies grew and flourished next to our 'residence'. Yes, and the washhouse which nobody seemed to use except small boys, who dived in there for a quick draw on a fag end which they had found nearby. The blacksmith beside the cinema. We called it the smiddy. I and other boys used to search for cogs which had been removed from horses' shoes and replaced with new ones. Gourley's, Cormie, Robinson at the Shorehead. Tom and I were friends, though not really close friends. We were in the same class at school for some years. Union Street too where we stayed when we flitted from Aberhill. Dr. Johnstone's home and practice was, and may still have been then, located at the corner of Union and High Streets at the Shorehead. Dr. Johnstone wasn't our family doctor. I met him only once. I was a little over five years of age, and possessed an aeroplane, which was made airborne by winding the propeller, to which was attached a rubber band hooked on to some part at the tail end, thus (I hope I am not boring you) thus providing tension. The plane was then launched by throwing it skyward and, at the same time, releasing the propeller. On the occasion in question, my airplane landed on the roof of our cottage near the eaves. I started bawling. A tall man approached from the Shorehead end of Union Street. At five years of age I didn't know much English, and presumably he said something like, 'You poor little fellow. What's the matter? Did you fall?' On the other hand, he may have said, 'Struth, I don't believe I have ever seen such a homely child. Bloody noisy, too.' This tall man was Dr. Johnstone, so I shall presume that, being a doctor, he was compassionate, oozing the first mentioned response to my bawling. I'm sure I covered all the vowels and the diphthongs in the English language. I may have created some new ones. Anyway, I bawled and pointed to the roof. Miss MacTavish, had she been there, would have been proud of me. Dr. Johnstone reached up and, without effort, recovered my aeroplane. I stopped bawling.

How can I remember all this? I don't. I do, however, remember the incident. The neighbours were peering out of their windows, just as they do today, one or two of them actually coming outside to assist, or perhaps just to listen and observe. They gave me a blow-by-blow account of the drama when I was old enough to relive and appreciate it.

I wandered over the links, lingered at the salmon bothy, stroked the mile dyke fondly and searched for a lost golf ball. There was no one near to whom I could present the trophy, so I slipped it into a pocket and forgot all about it. I wonder where it is now? Spinkie Den was a bonus. With only a side glance at the swimming pool where, when I was a tadpole, I had been dumped by some youths older and bigger than I, establishing the realization that I could swim, I stopped at the rustic bridge to watch the baggy minnins hiding in the shadows. It brought to

Ralph

mind a time when Granta showed me how to guddle. Granta was superb at guddling. Today he would be known as a superguddler. If guddling were an Olympic event, Granta would have brought home the gold. To observe him in the art was like watching poetry in motion. Leaning precariously over a ledge of turf-covered overhang above a quiet pool, he would, ever so slowly, ever so gently, feel for a trout lurking between a boulder and the bank in a quiet basin of water. There was nothing clumsy, nothing hurried about the manoeuvre. 'Don't grab,' Granta cautioned me. 'Tickle him until he begins to smile. Then, when he is in a blissful trance, with a quick motion, lock him in a warm but firm embrace and hurl him into the air and on to the bank.'

'How do I tell when he's smiling?' I queried. Granta pursed his lips and looked me straight in the eye. 'That,' he said quietly, 'is something that comes with experience. And experience is something that comes with practice. And practice is something that comes with determination.'

'I have a lot of homework. It's not easy to get in a whole lot of practice.' He fixed me with his crinkly-eyed, thoughtful stare. 'Yes, boy. The three Rs. They're more important. They come first.' Granta was now unable to do all the wonderful things he used to do with me, his accomplice, when I was a child. He now went for short walks and used a cane. A tear trickled down my cheek as I laughed aloud, all alone on the rustic bridge. The old goat! Climbing a tree, for heavens sake!

Travelling along Windygates Road, I was delighted to see the Monkey Puzzle tree was still standing guard at the corner of Cock-Ma-Lane and Windygates. I ambled down Cock-Ma-Lane and over the railway crossing, passing the close where I had encountered the policeman who saved my life. The High Street brought back many memories. Oh yes, that's where Mr. Cutt, the Asst. Schoolmaster and his wife lived. I used to deliver morning rolls there when I worked as message boy with Ovenstones the baker, and where I became suddenly wealthy when Mrs. Cutt gave me half a crown one Christmas. It may not seem a lot now but I earned five shillings a week, and half a crown bought an awful lot of penny-worth-o'-broken-biscuits at Wm. Lows the grocer on High Street, or a hapny-worth-o'-spilt-fruit at Aiken's. I wondered if Mr. Douglas was still in his butcher's shop, and if he would remember me. Gourley, m-hm, where I bought the *Exchange and Mart*. I can see Ovenstone's from here. I wondered whether Nessie Williamson and Margaret Mortimer were still there. I used to walk Margaret home to Leven Vale when it was dark sometimes. I got a welcome thrupenny bit.

I can't see it from here, but it is just over there - The Greig Institute. We used to play at dabbie against the surrounding wall opposite Buchlyvie Terrace. There was a special stone in the wall where we held our Lucky Charm cigarette cards, which we then released to let them flutter to the ground, hoping they would land on another card, winning all that had been dropped. Tom Robertson was better than anyone else. He nearly always won. I'll have a drink at the fountain at the Shorehead from one of its iron cups which are chained to it. The Bawbee Brig. I had better cross the Bawbee Brig. Who knows, I may never cross it again.

Halfway across the Brig I stopped to look over the stone wall. Good heavens! Did I actually snail along that ledge on the outside of the wall? I must have been about twelve when Jock Kinnaird and I stopped one day to peer over the wall at the river below. We noticed a thin tube of - something. We just had to know what it was lying innocently on that ledge. Jock volunteered that I should go. Creeping along the narrow ridge, trying not to look down at the black water below, I began to wish that I had never started on my perilous journey. The water looked awfully far away down there, and awfully fast. Not until then did it occur to me that I might fall and find myself swimming for the bank. And the rocks that lined the river's edge in a jagged decoration could mean sudden death. In truth, I don't remember thinking of death at all, but that a fall on to these rocks would hurt, and probably leave a tear in my clothing as well as a tear in my eye at the thought of the withering reception I would get if I damaged my clothes. Would I do it again? Perish the thought. Reaching the prize, I carefully grabbed for it and threw it over the wall to Jock. We could make neither head nor tail of it. 'Maybe it's toffee,' suggested Jock. 'You could taste it.' 'On the other hand,' I countered, '*You* could taste it. I took the risk of getting it. Let's find out what it is first.'

I showed it to Dad who, without hesitation, recognised it to be a stick of dynamite. 'Where did you get it?' he asked bluntly. His tone indicated that any location would meet with disapproval, so I answered truthfully but without unasked-for explication. 'The Bawbee Brig.' Happily the answer was good enough. 'Very careless of somebody. Very careless, indeed,' Dad mumbled. 'Leave it with me. I'll get rid of it.'

I thought I ought to see Methil Docks again. Climbing the foot brae to Aberhill, I passed the Tramcar Depot and travelled down the road to Methil, past Small, the shoe store. We were well acquainted with the Smalls when I was a child of five, but since moving to Leven the families seemed to have lost touch. Walking the breakwater at the docks where I had fished for mackerel with great success, I left the docks by way of the entrance instead of walking along the railway lines towards the Shorehead and climbing the fence near Somerville's as I had so often done in earlier years. Them days is gawn.

I was about a week home on leave when Sergeant Shoebotham knocked on the door. Mum answered it. I heard a friendly voice say, 'Good afternoon. Ma'am.' 'Glory be! Sergeant Shoebotham. I thought you must have been sent to another station.' 'No, I'm still here. I'd like a word with Ralph. Is he in?' I approached the door as he entered. 'Hello Sergeant, I greeted him. 'Did you remember this was the day Mum baked scones or is it just a coincidence?'

'It's a well remembered coincidence,' he laughed, waving an envelope. 'Here it is. You sit an examination under my supervision. Then if, I mean when, you pass the exam, I'll give you a ticket to go by rail to London where you will be interviewed. I see no problems. Something wrong?'

'I'm afraid there is, Sergeant. Please sit down.' He sat. 'I'm in the Army, seven years. It's six months since I left.'

His disappointment was obvious. 'Well, it has been a long time coming,' he said with a shrug. 'What a pity. I know you would have been a good bobby.' I thanked him. 'Well, the day isn't a total loss,' I said cheerfully. 'I'm sure you can smell the scones. What do you think, Mum? Shall we fill him up with scones? Then when you are in the mood, show me how to arrest Polly.' 'Why not?' he growled. 'I have my handcuffs with me,' and he plunked them on the table with a clatter. Polly, silent until now, spoke up. 'Fill 'em up, Joe.' Grinning, Sgt. S. asked Mum, 'is there a walnut available for that bird before he or she resorts to bad language?' Polly burst into one of her multi-keyed sea shanties. There was no arrest that day. Mum produced a walnut. I brought in Polly and we all had a scone or two with Mum's delicious blackcurrant jam, except Polyanthus, of course. She preferred her favourite walnut.

The ten days' leave passed all too quickly, and once more there were goodbyes with wishes that I would eventually be posted to Edinburgh or Perth. Granta and I had two short and enjoyable walks. He was getting frail, so I pretended I wasn't in condition to take too much walking. I think he twigged my moonshine but he never let on. On the train back to Aldershot, I finished a novel which I had bought six months ago. In addition, I bought a Scots magazine and a couple of weeklies. They helped to take my mind off the thought of spending three months in Aldershot.

ALDERSHOT

'You will proceed to the Military Hospital, Aldershot, without delay, where you will report to the N.C.O. on duty in the Orderly Room. On arrival, you will be assigned to your quarters and given instruction regarding discipline. Your duties will be detailed tomorrow morning. Diiiiismiiiis.'

With these words we were emptied out of the Camp into military limbo. Outside the Barracks, when I was satisfied no one with stripes on his arms would see me, I thumbed my nose at Crookham Camp and hastened towards the bus stop. Hort was in a silent mood.

'Forget it, Hort. They'll come after you, and they'll find you.'

'In Tibet?' I thought about it for a few seconds. 'Count me out,' I said. There were only the two of us of The Army Dental Corps. There were, however, several others of the R.A.M.C. We might have been from another planet. THEY were Medics, WE were Dentals. They kept together in a heterogeneous cluster. Hort and I stood apart. It didn't occur to me at the time, but I suppose we too were a cluster; a cluster of two. This sort of thing didn't bother Hort. Nothing much bothered Hort. All in all, the Medics were not really unfriendly. We were soon to find that the discipline at Aldershot was not at all rigorous. Despite the more flexible rules, breaches of which could not be officially condoned, nearly everyone was too occupied covering up their own infractions to be bothered with anyone else's misdemeanours. We soon learned the ropes and knew how far we could go without encouraging attention. Of course, there's one in every barrel. There were two here, Corporal Sludge and Private Swill. These names, as you will already have guessed, are not their real names. Nor do I intend to tell you. This happened long ago and they may have had families, God forbid, who resembled them in nature. Corporal Sludge was a sort of gross Caliban – no, that is an unfair comparison. He was an unpardonable septic tank, fit only for cannon fodder. The heaviest cross one had to bear was to have to sit near him at meals. At first, Hort and I were puzzled why there were always empty spaces about him. It was not unusual for some unfortunate soul sitting opposite or next to Sludge suddenly to see an empty seat and cry, 'Hi there, I've been looking for you,' and take off with his plate and cutlery. One day at lunch he sat opposite me at the same table. Surreptitiously, I inspected the soles of my boots. It wasn't that. Then, right in my face he said, 'Phew, that soup's hot.' It caught me just as I was inhaling. I nodded and rushed outside in desperation to suck fresh oxygen into my lungs. Being in the Dental Corps was bad enough, but to flee when Sludge was about to favour me with conversation which was not without a generous measure of his halitosis established two strikes against me. Let me recant my remark about his being good only for cannon fodder. He would have made devastating ammunition against an enemy, more deadly than mustard gas or any other form of chemical warfare of that time. Swill was something else. He resembled a sorry knave. Not the sorry knave envisioned by Miss MacTavish. He had a constant nose drip, and he had seemingly never heard of that masterpiece of wardrobe accessories, the handkerchief. He was the only companion Sludge had at meals, and that wasn't constant. Considering the disposition of Sludge's breath and the traffic jam in Swill's nostrils, it doesn't need a psychologist to explain why Private Peebles, a rather sensitive little chap, barely managed to dodge Swill's drip as they passed one day. In a rare and emotional outburst Peebles hissed at Swill, 'I wish you'd trip over your drip.'

Sotto voce, I pointed out to Peebles that while I admired his skill in unrehearsed rhyme, he could hardly trip over it. He might, of course, slip on it. He was unappreciative. Glaring at me, he told me to get lost. Lousy Medics! Swill was Sludge's snitch. He was King Snitch himself. One night, after closing time, we decided to have a casual walk before returning to quarters. The night air was warm and the sky was clear so why not? We crept in quietly and, we thought, without detection. The following morning, however, on roll call parade, we were told to report to the Orderly Sergeant. Hort and I went to the Orderly Room as ordered. We were marched in to face the sergeant on duty and – who else? – Corporal Sludge.

'Now then,' said the sergeant, 'it has been reported that you came in last night after lights out. Corporal, what time did these two men come in?'

'Eleven-thirty approximately, Sergeant.'

'Eleven-thirty approximately. I see. By the way, where were you, approximately, when you saw them?'

'I didn't actually see them, Sergeant. It was reported to me.'

The sergeant nodded his head in complete comprehension. Turning his eyes on us he said, 'Well, that looks bad for you two.' I thought I saw a sly smile of satisfaction on Sludge's face.

'Tell me, Corporal, in that you were not there when these two miscreants, I mean accused men, reported in, who told you about it?' Now it was our turn to smile, but we dared not.

'I'd rather not say, Sergeant.'

'Of course not, Corporal. That would be hearsay.'

Hort's belly rumbled, and it was all I could do to keep a straight face.

'It would be much better to bring the witness here. Stand easy, you two.' We stood easy. I didn't feel easy.

The Sludge left. The sergeant called out, 'Leave the door open, Corporal.' We stood there, fidgeting but silent as the sergeant sipped at a mug of coffee and shuffled some sheets of paper around. In about four to five minutes, Sludge and Swill appeared. 'Ah! why am I NOT surprised?' He motioned to the corporal to bring us to attention, then he regarded us sternly. 'Now then, did you two come in after lights out last night? Approximate time, twenty-three thirty?'

'We went to a show, Sergeant,' I answered.

'Did you enjoy it?'

'On the whole it wasn't bad, Sergeant.'

'What about you, Nelson?'

'I found it very edifying, Sergeant,' Hort answered, 'especially the

Fairy Queen.'

The sergeant stared at Hort in what can only be described as astonishment and disbelief. 'I'm giving you this warning, you two. If you appear before me again, I'll have you up before the Company Officer. Dismiss! And let me add,' he growled, 'your taste is all in your mouth.'

We about turned and beat it through the open door. As we retreated, we heard the sergeant say, 'Close the door, Corporal. I want a word with you.'

Outside, we started to laugh. 'The Fairy Queen. He must have seen that show,' I said.

'Yes, I saw him there the same night we went.'

'The sarge is right you know. That show was a bit grubby,' I said.

'You did a lot of laughing,' answered Hort. It was true. The entire house did a lot of laughing – and hooting – and barracking. Many of the women must have been dredged out of late retirement. One singer, I swear, was in her nineties. Every one of the performers was shop-worn. One dancer capered around the stage on shanks that would never have passed an army medical. One man did a piece from Wuthering Heights. He strutted about the stage bellowing and threatening non-existent victims of abuse. He wore riding breeches and boots with tops reaching to his knees, whacking the boots with his riding crop too often. At one point he whacked too high and with a small yelp, he winced. The audience were in sympathy because there was a prolonged 'Oooooooo'. For their compassionate demonstration they received a baleful glare from Heathcliff. The Fairy Queen was a short, fat man in a tutu. He carried a wand. His introduction was, as he tippy-toed in:

> 'I am your fairy queen
> Of whom you are so fond.
> Tell me, I pray you, tell me,
> Where shall I put my wand?'

In one collective, unharmonious roar, six hundred khaki-clad voices gave him an immediate and colourful answer. The poor little man on stage looked utterly dejected as he revelled in the response, after which he treated his audience to a deck of off-colour jokes. That was our only visit to the theatre, so we had nothing better or worse with which to compare the show.

We spent some of our time at the Dental Laboratory, where a group of Dental Corps N.C.O.s and private soldiers were employed making dentures. We were taught how to cast models from impressions. Also, we learned how to make wax bite-blocks, which the dental officers in the surgeries fitted in the patient's mouths and had them bite on after softening the wax over a flame of methylated spirits. All this seemed to come easy to me and I enjoyed it. The rest of our on-duty time was spent in a Dental Centre, where we learned how to mix the various amalgams and porcelain fillings, and how to fill out a Dental Chart, one of which every soldier had. We had to sterilize dental instruments between patients and make ready for the next victim. There was a lot more to learn, such as knowing King's Regulations and Medical Regs, especially Medical Regs. I shall not bore you with details however. There were two officers working in the Dental Centre to which I was sent, Major Craig and Captain O'Connor.

Major Craig was an ascetic looking man, but with a sense of humour. He was a thorough gentleman – more accurately, I should say, he was thoroughly gentlemanly. He always ended a request with 'please'.

'Amalgam for two fillings, please.' 'Two, sir?' 'Please.'

He was an excellent teacher and never complained about my staring into the mouths of patients to see what was going on. My over-curious attitude paid off beautifully. 'Probe, please.' 'Mitchell's Trimmer, please.' Before long, I knew what he wanted and he only had to hold out his hand for an instrument and I almost invariably knew which one to give him. I have to admit there were times when I would have liked to slap a sausage or a live frog into his open palm, but I curbed the urge. Anyway, I never had a sausage or a frog in the surgery. Captain O'Connor was an athletic man, friendly and talkative. He trained the water polo team in Aldershot. 'I bet you're a good swimmer,' he said one day. Taking a chance that he had never seen my medical History Sheet I said, 'If I were

dumped into a pool, I think I'd make it to the surface sir.' Another question he asked me was, 'Do you drink, McCaa?' 'Do you mean . . .?' 'That's right,' he answered. His tone suggested disapproval, so I said, 'No Sir. Well, maybe an occasional beer, Sir.'
'That's good, young fella,' he said. 'Stick to the non-alcoholic drinks and you'll be all right. I niver drink anything but draft meself.' 'Please' was not part of his vocabulary, but he was never nasty. He simply said, 'Let's have some copper amalgam for a couple o' cavities. One big un and one small un.' At first I expected him to end by saying, 'Then aim for the net, man! Shoot, shoot!' But, as I said, 'please' was not in his vocabulary. In fact, with the exception of Major Craig, 'please' was not part of any military vocabulary. I realise it would be more than a little odd if, under fire for instance, it were considered expedient to observe the niceties of verbal communication. Imagine – just for the hell of it – shells exploding all around you, bombs exploding everywhere, and bullets whizzing past your ears. The lieutenant, cool as an eskimo pie, stubs his cigarette in the palm of his hand and says, 'I say, chaps, I implore you, please, drop your wounded and seek cover. It's only a suggestion but there's a – what is it called – a foxhole I believe. Silly name, but there it is. Make a dash for it please, and . . .' By the time he got it all out we'd all be blown to hell. Perhaps I exaggerate a little but you know what I am getting at.

We had just one other adventure with the Snitch. It was three days later when we came in late again. In the dim light we could see movement in the Snitch's bed. We went to bed in the darkness, then Hort started to scrape something, which I learned later was a spoon, on the iron of his bed. 'Do you hear something, Hort?'

'Yep,' Hort growled.

'What is it?'

'I'm sharpening my jack-knife.'

'At this time of night! What on earth do you . . . can't it wait till . . .'

'No, it can't wait. Now is the time, the solemn, predetermined, wretched hour.'

'Oh, Hort, Hort! You can't! You mustn't! What is it the hour for?'

'I am going to cut off his cookies.' Again, Hort resumed his scraping, the spoon scraping back and forth along the iron of his bed.

'And serve them on a skillet!' Hort rumbled.

'Will you repeat that,' I mumbled.

'And yours too if you so desire it,' snarled Hort.

'No no. Why should you have all the fun?'

'Grab him and hold him in your special grip my trusty friend.'

'No no! Not that!'

Even my long departed Airedale bitch would have known it was a prank. A few snickers trickled from various fleapits. Hort and I stole like two cat burglars emitting two fiendish yowls as we exited, worthy of anything attributed to the genius of Alfred Hitchcock. With screams of panic, stricken Snitch leapt out of his bed and hightailed it outside. Hort and I dived back into bed. In a nearby sack, a sepulchral voice murmured, in gratuitous praise, 'My compliments to the chef.' Titters were instantly killed when the lights suddenly went up and the night sergeant appeared, followed by the gesticulating and screaming Snitch.

'Nelson and McCaa! Nelson has a knife!' screamed Snitch.

'All right, McCaa. And Nelson, you too. Get up. Both of you.'

I shaded my eyes against the harsh glare of the electric light bulbs. Hort was so sleepy that he found it hard to keep his balance as he groped his way in the journey around his bed, collapsing again in sleep. I could have killed him. He out-acted me again. What a ham!

'Nelson,' grunted the sergeant, 'I am aware of your shenanigans so cut out the carnival. Did you threaten him with a knife?'

Nelson was horrified at the idea and he visibly shuddered at the thought. Do you see what I mean? He upstaged me once more.

'I'll talk to him in the morning.' A search of his bed was abandoned and the sergeant ordered the Snitch to sleep in a hospital bed.

'Oh, Sarge,' I said, 'that man has nightmares. Didn't you know?'

Again, he searched Hort's bed and found no knife – or spoon. Hort was wide awake by now. 'Sergeant, I'm going to make a charge, tomorrow. Look at my bed. Now I have to make it all over. And it'll be cold.'

'Yeah,' I said. 'Mine, too. And me, too. I'll make a complaint.'

The sergeant glared at us and said, 'You do that. You'll have plenty of opportunity. Be at the Orderly Room at 8 am tomorrow. You are under open arrest.'

'Can I go to bed now?' Hort murmured.

The sergeant didn't answer. To the Snitch he said, 'You come with me. You will sleep in the Hospital tonight.' They both left and we were again in darkness. 'That was a master performance,' said a sepulchral voice from the dark. 'My compliments to the chef,' said another. A few titters accompanied these remarks. In a strong and pseudo-threat suggestive voice, Hort depth-charged the words, 'Anybody gonna snitch?' The only answer was a few artificial snores.

The next morning we were on the verandah at the Orderly Room wondering if we would get the axe. The R.S.M. came out smiling. 'Good morning, gentlemen. You go inside,' he said to me. I went inside. I have to tell you, this Regimental Sergeant-Major was like nobody of that rank I would have envisioned in my most phantasmagorical illusions. He had an almost cherubic face with a moustache which, in plain English, translates into 'fatherly'. I had met him in passing a couple of times when I said, 'Good morning, Sir.' 'Good morning,' he had responded, 'Ah, McCaa, isn't it?' 'Yes Sir.' The second time we met, he addressed me as Ralph. I told Hort about it. Hort asked me if he was sober. Anyway, he detained Hort for about three minutes, then he opened the door and called, 'McCaa'. I went on to the verandah and saw Hort marching away. 'Hort told me all about it,' he said. 'Now, Ralph, let me have your version.'

He was smiling. Maybe his smile was too benign to be believable. Maybe it was the word 'version'. Maybe both.

'You look uncomfortable, Ralph. Don't hold back. Just . . . in your own words.' I tried to separate his smile from the expression in his eyes. Yes, it was there. Blue steel. Cold, blue, calculating steel. 'Yes, sir. Well, sir, Private, Aha . . .'

'Snitch?' he said, grinning even more.

'Sir? Sir, he reads a lot. Soft covers. I'd rather not continue, Sir.'

'By all means do, Ralph. In your own words.'

'Yes, Sir. You know the books. Monsters and evil beings from outer space. The one he's reading now has a cover with a spider who has the face of a horrible human being. The spider has a dagger in his claw. The girl is clutched in his other claws, and . . .'

The R.S.M.'s eyes had become horizontal slits. 'Is that a fact, McCaa?'

I was not unaware of danger, but I was just getting warmed up to my 'version'.

'*DISMISS!*'

'I think, Sir, he must have had one of his nightmares, Sir.'

'I said DISMISS! BEAT IT!'

I beat it, fast. The Snitch was confined for observation for the next four days. Somebody up there must have believed me.

INVERNESS

Eureka! At last! It wasn't what I had hoped for, Edinburgh or Perth, but I was going to Bonnie Scotland. Inverness. The Cameron Highlanders' Depot. I was excited. I had never been to Inverness. I wondered if there was really a monster in Loch Ness. Do you know what I think it is? Nah. I could be dead wrong. Yet my guess is as good as many others. There are so many theories as to what it is and how it got there, they can't all be right. Do you know what I think? I think the authors of some of these weird theories came up the Clyde on a bike. I have my own ideas what it is and how it got there, but you probably wouldn't believe me, so forget it. The Camerons' Depot is situated on the fringe of the city. It sits quiescently on a hill, its left arm hugging the golf course and its right elbow resting comfortably on the distillery. I can neither corroborate nor deny the quality of pride or shame with which some of the natives may have been possessed, depending on their fraternal affiliations regarding the following. However, I understand, from a very reliable source, there is in Inverness more whisky than fresh water. True or false, such an idea should be nipped in the bud before some dipsomaniacal dictator invades our beautiful Highlands in the name of 'protector'. That is what I thought then. Now I don't worry about it. The U.S. wouldn't stand for it. I don't want to get into a harangue about foreign policy however, so let's change the subject. I arrived in the afternoon to find no one in the Dental Centre, which was located in part of the Medical Centre. There was, however, an orderly with the Medics lying around. I asked him if I could see the Dental Surgery. 'Sure,' he said, 'it's open.' I dumped my kitbag on the bed, which was an exact replica of the one I had had in Aldershot, then wandered into the Dental Surgery.

It looked clean – clean enough, but untidy. Change was imminent. I am not a fusspot but I do not like to see any loose ends lying around. My predecessor as dental orderly had left the day before I arrived and the dental officer had obviously finished a job and just walked away from it. I cleaned and sterilized any dental instruments which were lying about, putting them away in the glass cupboards provided for that purpose. It was supper time, so I sallied forth to the mess hall, where I was met by a sergeant who wanted to know 'who the hell I was'. I told him who the hell I was and was instructed to sit at the end of 'that table over there'. An inquiring glance around me told me that there was a corporal or lance-corporal at the end of each table, which accommodated a total of ten infantrymen. It took me no more than another three meals to be in a position to collect my meals at the cookhouse and take them to the Medical Centre, where nobody would hear our complimentary remarks about the food.

The major was an easy-going officer and good at his job as a dental surgeon. He was, however, seemingly unaware of the undercurrents to which his ship was subject. For example, he didn't know, or didn't let on that he knew, that the orderly, in this case I, was at the helm. It was a good many weeks before he became entirely house-broken. Once that idea took root, the rest became plain sailing. After all, it was I who did everything in the dental centre – except the dentistry of course. It was I who wrote letters between H.Q. and us. It was I who ordered drugs and other requirements as necessary, prepared weekly, monthly and annual reports, arranged an adequate amount of dental work without overdoing it, balancing one day, one week, against another. Me, I ran the whole shebang. All the major did was dentistry and putting his signature to anything I placed before him. I suppose he was just as necessary as I was to the smooth continuance of the Dental Centre.

It took time, but I believe he became aware that I did everything – everything except, as I have already mentioned, dentistry.

We used to visit Fort George to supply treatment to the Seaforth Highlanders. This required that I take the train from Inverness to Campbelltown, a little village about one and a half miles from the Fort.

Inverness

I caught the train – I think it was about seven thirty am – returning to Inverness in the late afternoon. Sometimes, after cleaning up the surgery, I had to run like the devil to catch the train. Three times I would have missed it had not the engine driver been looking back for late passengers. Then he would slow down to a near halt until I caught up. One day he was quite far on his way from Campbelltown when, waving frantically and out of breath, I realised I had missed the train. Collapsing on to the bench outside the ticket office, I was in a state of gloom. I had never seen an automobile pass ever. I could still hear the engine, now out of sight. Chug chug chug chugchugchug ... I could hardly believe it. This engine driver – this sensitive, compassionate, great-hearted man, this (why not) *angelic* engine driver was coming back for me! The engine chugged into the station, a head popped out of the engine cabin and a voice yelled, 'Don't just stand there, you bloody idiot. Get in before you miss it again.' I waved to him, giving him a quick salaam, and got on fast. After that, I made sure I was waiting at the station in good time. (Oh, scrub the word 'angelic'.)

I became acquainted with a man about my own age, also a lance-corporal, in the Service Corps. Arthur Chapman, like myself, was something of a loner, so we started to kick around together. We went swimming in the ocean just below the Depot. One day I bought an old row-boat for half a crown. We had fun with it for a short time. One day it disintegrated before our eyes and we had to swim for shore. This happened over half a century ago, but if anyone wants the location of the wreck, I can pretty well pinpoint it.

One day when I had been about a year in Inverness, I was cleaning up the bloodstains in the spittoon when I received an unwelcome visit from a belligerent sergeant by the name of Harcourt, whose younger sister I had met at a dance and with whom I had had several dates. Despite, or because of (I shall never know), my association with his sister, his attitude was distinctly cold. Today, it was frozen. Of course, in the British Army 'at that point in time', as any practical politician would put it, an intermixture of lance-corporal and sergeant would not produce a convivial cocktail. In fact it wouldn't make even a shabby shandy. Even if both were indisputably the owners of a B.A., consociation between two different ranks was a no-no. It may have changed by now. What I am pointing out is that the big, big freeze may not have had anything to do with his sister and me. I was soon to know. Normally, if we happened to pass each other, and if no one was near, he would respond to my smile with a twitch of his mouth which, translated into English, could be a smile returned. Today there wasn't a chich of a twitch. He glared at me with two unblinking lasers and growled in lethal accusation, 'Corporal McCaa.' Against the advice of Miss MacTavish many years ago, and up to this moment I swear it was involuntary, I registered that unforgivable mechanical gesture of shock. I grabbed at my chest where lay that organ so often lauded and maligned in plays and novels. Sergeant Harcourt mistook the gesture to mean 'Me?'

'I don't see anyone else here. Do you?' I knew I had been alone until his arrival, but I looked behind me anyway. I nodded agreement. Unable to account for his warlike attitude, I continued wiping away at the spittoon, never taking my eyes off him. 'Does my sister know about your disgusting behaviour?' he snarled. I pointed weakly at the spittoon. 'This? It's part of my job.'

'Don't get smart with me! My sister's a nice girl. I suppose you think this Mabel is a nice girl too. And more generous!'

'I don't know anybody called Mabel. Who's Mabel?'

'Who's Mabel?' he mimicked. 'The pregnant party. That's who Mabel is.'

I was speechless as the implication seeped into my brain. There followed what Miss MacTavish would have described as 'a pregnant pause'. I would describe it simply as 'shock'. Sergeant Harcourt clicked his heels to attention, like George Sanders when he was about to slap somebody across the chops with his glove and demand satisfaction for something or other from the poor slob.

'Be on identification parade today at thirteen hundred hours.'

'Now, hold on there, Sarge. I'm not going on any identification parade.'

Sgt.: Corporal, be there – or else. That's an order.

Inverness

I: What do you mean, 'or else'?

Sgt.: My sister is a nice, clean girl, that's what.

I: I think Eileen is a nice, clean girl whether I go on this identification parade or not.

Sgt.: (Clenching his fists.) Don't you get smart with me, you two-faced sonova... brother, what a packet you've turned out to be. I should bash your face in for this!

A wave of anger swept over me. 'Would right now be a good time? Let's go out the back and I'll jerk that lousy tongue out of your mouth and pull it through between your ears.'

'Corporal,' he sneered, 'don't say you didn't ask for it. Be at the gym at three o'clock. And bring your own stretcher. That's another order.'

'I'll be at the gym, but I won't be on this parade.'

'You're under open arrest. Insubordination.' Unseen by the sergeant, who had his back to the door, the major appeared.

Major: Good afternoon, gentlemen. Problems?

Sgt.: Sir. Yes, Sir. No, Sir. That is, yes and no, Sir.

Major: No, don't go, Sergeant. What's the corporal been up to now?

I: Sir, I don't like the inference that...

Major: Quiet, or I may deflect to the opposition. Sergeant?

Sgt.: I would rather have the corporal tell you, Sir.

Major: But I'm asking you. You know how self-effacing corporals can be.

Sgt.: Yes, Sir. Well, Corporal McCaa is required to appear on an identification parade and he refuses to participate, Sir. It means he refuses to...

Major: I gathered that is what you meant, Sergeant.

Sgt.: Thank you, Sir. This constitutes insubordination, Sir. King's Regulations, paragraph 426, sub-paragraph C and D, as amended by Army Council Instructions, paragraph 281, Sir.

Major: Good heavens! That doesn't go with an operating gown. (To corporal) Is that blood on it?

I: It isn't cold perspiration, Sir.

Major: Ah, yes. You plead innocence. Only the guilty break out in a cold sweat. There, Sergeant.

I: I didn't do anything, Sir.

Major: Then unquestionably you are guilty. Anyone in the British Army must always be doing something. Thinking is excepted, of course. Right, Sergeant?

Sgt.: Right, Sir.

Major: So is standing at attention forever. Stand at ease.

Sgt.: Thank you, Sir. (Sergeant stands at ease.)

Major: (To me) Elucidate.

I: I don't know *anything* about this ... thing.

Major: *Thing!* Go warm up on a medical manual or two, Corporal. And Sergeant, stand easy. You make me feel uncomfortable. (Sergeant stands easy) That's better. Let's have it, Sergeant.

Sgt.: Sir ... the corporal has been accused by a party of the opposite sex, Sir.

Major: Really? Well, let's forget Army Regulations for the moment and get down to the meat of the ... I refer, of course, to the subject, not the object.

Sgt.: Sir?

Major: Continue, Sergeant.

Sgt.: Yes, sir. A female by the name of Mabel, Sir. She is with child.

Major: Ah ha. What you are trying to tell me is that she is pregnant?

Sgt.: Yes, Sir. And Corporal McCaa ah ... did it, Sir.

Major: Did it! Are you saying he is the author?

Sgt.: Sir?

Major: The father?

Sgt.: That is what she claims, Sir. Corporal McCaa, The Army Dental Corps. The identification parade is in exactly ... (Looking at the time on his watch) in about one minute, Sir.

Major: (Grinning at me) What's she like, Corporal?

I: I don't know, Sir, but if she is to your taste, she is all yours.

Major: That, of course, is insolence. Right Sergeant?

Sgt.: Yes Sir. King's Regulations, paragraph 299 ...

Major: That'll be all right. Later.
(A Sergeant of the Cameron Highlanders has come in. He stands at attention, awaiting permission to speak.)
Major: Corporal. Do . . . you . . . know . . . this . . . Mabel?
I: No Sir.
Major: Then you can have no qualms at being on this parade.
I: I have no qualms. It's the principle of the thing.
Major: To hell with your principles. I believe you, but you have to realize that . . . that . . . that . . . (To sgt. who has just arrived) Oh, what is it, Sergeant?
Sgt. 2: Sir, I just wanted to tell Sergeant Harcourt and Corporal McCaa and yourself, Sir, the pregnant party came up a little early and the identification parade is over.
Major: I see . . . Did she . . . get her man?
Sgt. 2: Yes sir. Corporal McCaa, The Army Dental Corps. She pointed *them* out, Sir.
Major: Continue, Sergeant.
Sgt. 2: They were Corporal Kerr and Corporal Johnson, Sir.
Major: That's nice. Twin fathers.
Sgt. 2: Yes, Sir. But not identical, Sir.
Major: A discriminating observation, Sergeant.
Sgt. 2: I thought so too, Sir. I was a stand-up comic before I enlisted. I could show you one of my routines, Sir.
Major: I'll take a rain check. Thank you both. You may leave. (Sgts. whip to attention, salute, about turn and leave.) Do me a favour, McCaa and, at three o'clock, knock the H out of Harcourt.

The meeting at the gymnasium didn't materialize. Sergeant Harcourt didn't turn up either. I wasn't unhappy about it. Living in Inverness was, in some ways, pretty bland. Two events, however, come to mind. One was when I bought a bike, a secondhand, or it could have been a tenth- or twelfth-hand, vehicle. I was tired of walking the same old route into Inverness and back. It was monotonous. Besides that, I had a notion to see a little of the surrounding terrain, so I bought a bike. It was rather bare, but it was inexpensive, monetarily anyway. It was devoid of brakes other than the back-pedal system which, I was assured, I would master within minutes. As with my very first bike, when I was a tadpole, I thought all I had to do was to throw my leg over the saddle and away we would go. Beside the guardhouse, to the right, there is an entrance leading to a beautifully curved tarmac driveway designed for motor vehicles. On foot, we used the narrow brae on the opposite side of the guardhouse. This saved a couple of furlongs, walk if one was bound for Inverness. Now I had a bike, and it was all downhill on this driveway. The invitation was irresistible. And on this drive there was a curve, E-I-E-I-O. And on this curve there was a car, E-I-E-I-O. I was sailing down this 'made exclusively for me' blacktop when I jammed my foot down on the ascending pedal. The bike shrieked in agony and froze. I continued on my journey, landing face down on the rotten, black, unsympathetic brae. The car had stopped just as abruptly as I. I was so shaken that I could manage only to turn and lean on one elbow. One of the occupants in the car rolled down the window and called, 'It's all right. We can get around you.' They continued their journey with a stiff upper lip.

Regaining an upright posture to the accompaniment of a loud 'Ouch!' and a few obscenities, directed mainly at the occupants of the disappearing car, I inspected my hands. They were not raw, but if the wounds were joined together there would be about four square inches of skin missing. A drop of blood dripped from my nose, but there were no bones broken. The bike lay there, laughing silently. I threw it in the bushes to be retrieved later. Then I walked back through the gates with my arms in the air in an effort to retard the flow of blood. Two privates, curious to know what the trouble was, joined me, one at either side as I made my way to the Medical Centre. If it had been wartime, I would have looked like a POW in civvies. I sold the bike back to its former owner for half the price I paid. One day I borrowed an ordinary bike and rode it to Fort George and back. Once was enough. When I arrived at the Fort I thought I needed a hot drink. I was in civilian clothes, so for a minute I stood at the cookhouse door, wondering how I could make myself welcome. It was a Saturday afternoon. If you have ever invaded a cookhouse, except to peel spuds or clean out dirty pans, I give you warning. Don't. On this occasion I was confronted by a corporal. He glared at me malevolently. I glared back. 'Where's the cook sergeant?' It worked. He probably thought I was a young subaltern. He thumbed toward the bowels of the cauldron. He was in white and had three stripes pinned to his sleeves. I tried to look arrogant, but not too offensive. 'Sergeant?'

'Who are *you*?'

For a moment I wilted, but I recovered quickly. 'How are you feeling?'

He wasn't going to be conned – easily. 'Who *are* you, and who let you in here?'

'The corporal, that one,' I said pointing.

'What do you want?' he rasped.

'Nothing. I'm simply asking if you are feeling better now.'

'What the hell is this! You get your grub the same as everyone else. The same time as everybody else. Now, get out of my cookhouse.'

'All right, Sergeant. That's O.K. with me.' I turned about and walked off, looking back to sneer: 'It's your loss.'

Now, sergeants are like people. For that matter, so are corporals. So are staff-sergeants and warrant officers. They *like to know*, especially if it is to their benefit. I should know. I've held all of these ranks. I didn't get far when a gruff voice – his – growled, 'Hold on there. What's your game?' See what I mean?

'No game,' I answered.

'C'mere.' I sauntered back with affected nonchalance.

'I don't know you. If you're not after grub, what is it you want?'

'I told you. Nothing. I'm just asking if you are feeling better.'

'I'm just fine.' He stared at me coldly waiting for my response.

'Well, that's great. Glad you managed to shake it off.'

'Oh, that bloody cold. That was bloody weeks ago.'

'Good, good. Five minutes would ensure you never catch another one.'

'What are you bloody talking about?'

'Have you looked at your teeth in the mirror, Sergeant? Really looked?'

'I never had no trouble with my teeth. You see anythin' wrong with them?'

'If you're happy with brown teeth – harbouring germs.' I shrugged. There was a mirror not far from where we stood. He dashed over to it and grinned at his teeth. 'Is that bad?'

'Germs. You're damn right that's bad. If you'd like to drop over to the Dental Centre, I'll get rid of them in five minutes.'

He now played hard to get. Scratching his neck he grunted, 'Trouble is . . . when?'

'Right now, if you can spare the time. But don't tell everybody. I don't want the whole regiment lining up for one of my specials. Now that I'm here, I wouldn't mind a splash of tea. Nothing to eat.'

His stentorian voice shattered the near silence. 'SMITTY . . . look after this guy. And look after him good.' Smitty was the corporal I had first met in the cookhouse.

'Thanks, Sergeant. Can you make it now?'

'Yeah. You get your tea first.' He was in command again. I quenched my thirst with well creamed tea, then held up my finger to indicate I had finished. A curt nod of understanding and he followed me to the Dental Centre. On the way over I said, 'I'm Lance-Corporal McCaa.' 'What the hell kind of a name is that?' he grumbled. In truth, until that moment, I hadn't given it a thought. At the risk of losing what ground I had gained, I asked, 'What's your name, Sergeant?' I think he suspected what was coming.

'Jones. Herb Jones.'

'What the hell kind of a name is that?' I responded.

His dead-pan wrapping cracked into a broad and somewhat fiendish grin. With a thump on the shoulder he growled, 'Hey, you're all right.' Five minutes with the polishing brush and a gob of pumice powder on the dental drill had his teeth sparkling like engagement rings. And that was how I was able to walk into the cookhouse at any time and help myself to whatever took my fancy.

The transfer! That was something else. Not earth-shaking but to me, more final regarding my future, more causal to my enslavement to a pair of pensive but so humorous eyes.

One day we received a circular from Edinburgh. It contained a request for applications by any orderly in the Command to exchange stations with a corporal in the Dental Centre at Edinburgh. The invitation was alluring. The bait irresistible. Immediately I leapt to the typewriter and made my application, placing the invite together with my reply neatly on the major's desk. When he came in, I observed his reaction surreptitiously. He read both letters, following his action with a long silence. I don't believe it would have made any difference what he said or did, but he certainly chose the wrong attitude. Without looking at me he said in a whisper, 'In future, Corporal, you will kindly consult with me before replying to any matters of this nature.' Then he crumpled the reply into a ball and threw it in the wastepaper basket. Maybe he was right. Maybe he wasn't. I will admit I am not the easiest person to manoeuvre, but I don't think I am the most contentious beggar alive either. I resented his words. I resented his action even more. I responded to this effect: 'Sir, I think you are correct in saying that I should have spoken to you about it before I typed a reply. I think, also, that throwing the reply in the waste basket was uncalled for.' I could see his neck redden, then he turned in his chair to face me. 'You're right, Corporal, and I apologise. I was taken by surprise.' Then he grinned and our eyes met. 'Let's forget the whole thing, eh? I've got accustomed to you, dammit.'

Somehow I couldn't drum up a smile in return. His grin vanished and we stared at each other for a few seconds. This was a pause more pregnant that the bird who identified the twin fathers responsible for her condition. Under official conditions I believe it may have qualified for a place in the Guinness Book of Records. The silence was broken by the major. 'Very well, Corporal, retype it and I'll sign it.'

'Thank you, Sir.'

A few days later there was a telephone call from Edinburgh. I had been chosen from five applications. This I found out later. Auld Reekie, here I come! A letter was in the mail confirming the transfer. When the

major appeared, I tried to soften the blow by trying to look 'not too happy' about it. Perhaps I overdid it for he said, 'You can still turn it down if you want to.'
'It's done, Sir.'
Auld Reekie!!!

AULD REEKIE

If you have to ask where Auld Reekie is, then your geographical education is woefully barren. I arrived at Edinburgh's Waverly Station in the early afternoon. It didn't look very reekie to me. It looked beautiful. This was so different from the daily excursions I enjoyed as a child with my parents, when they could afford them. I looked up at the Castle in wonderment, wonderment that I would actually be living there. My eyes devoured the Gardens on Princes Street and the magnificent monument erected to Sir Walter Scott, designed by George Kemp in the Gothic style. It is a tragedy that Kemp died before its completion. It was a fairly long walk uphill to the Castle, especially when I was laden with a heavy kitbag and a suitcase and wearing the hot, heavy and clumsy khaki uniform. My excitement at just being there, however, made the climb to the Castle seem short and untiring. On the esplanade I stopped to gawk over part of the city like a tourist. The small door in the heavy, studded gate was open, so I walked right in. The guardroom was on the left, so I reported my arrival.

'Oh yes,' said a sergeant, examining a ledger on the desk, 'we're expecting you. Report to the Dental Centre.'

'Where is it?' I asked.

'Go up the hill and ask somebody to point.'

I wandered up the hill and stopped a private soldier who was rushing somewhere. He pointed. 'Somewhere down there,' he answered and rushed off again. A large stone building confronted me. I entered and wandered about on three floors. When I was about to give up, a corporal holding his jaw came towards me. It looked promising.

'Where's the Dental Centre?'

Still holding his jaw, he grinned, fiendishly I thought, and pointed. He then beetled off at a dizzying speed. I can only deduce that he thought I was a patient arriving for treatment. A small sign with the name *Dental Centre* on it and an arrow pointing told me I had found it. I knocked on a door marked *Surgery*. A full corporal, whose name, as I was later to learn, was Clarke Nobby or Knobby Clarke, opened the door and pointed, indicating the room next door. I began to wonder if anyone here spoke English. As he was closing the door, I jammed my foot in it like a vacuum cleaner salesman. 'Hold it. I'm going to work here.'

'Ah. You're whatsisname from Inverness. Come in.'

Captain J.M. Cowie greeted me with apparent pleasure. 'Make yourself at home.' Major Pearson, after finishing what he was doing, said, 'Glad to meet you. You'll find a gown hanging on the door. Mix me some amalgam. Three fillings.' Lance-corporals don't argue with majors, not during the first meeting anyway, so I donned the gown and mixed. When the day's work ended and the officers had gone, I asked Knobby about sleeping quarters plus other pertinent information. He didn't seem to know anything about anything, and as he lived outside the barracks – he was married – he had to rush for his tramcar. I found a sergeant who led me to a barrack-room with twelve beds. 'Take that one,' he said, pointing to an unoccupied bed. He then disappeared. In his favour I should point out that his pointing routine was the most professional I had encountered so far. What did I expect? A red carpet? I dumped my luggage on the floor and pulled out the bed. I thought I recognised the squeak of metal on metal, but examination proved inconclusive. They're exactly the same throughout the British Army. Only the squeaks are different. The biscuits, too, were the same: hard and stuffed with last week's bread pudding. I was tired, so I lay down and fell asleep. About an hour later, awakened by verbal explosions consisting mainly of derogatory epithets, I sat up with something akin to alarm. It was, however, a friendly eruption, the reaction to having been dealt an unwanted card in a game of blackjack. 'Wanna come in?' someone shouted.

'Not today, if you don't mind.'
'You play though, don't you?'
'Occasionally. You're allowed to gamble then?' I asked.
'We take turns at keeping watch outside.' I was flattered. Already I was a trusted member of the syndicate and they didn't even know my name. 'Where's the canteen?' I asked.
'One floor up and turn to your right. Better hurry though, it closes in ten minutes for about two hours.' I hurried up to the NAAFI where I gulped down a carton of milk. Then I asked for a cup of tea. It was lousy tea, but it was hot. I was happy. Why happy with lousy tea? I don't know, but I was. 'Stop griping,' I said to myself. 'I'm not griping,' I answered back. Another cup of tea. Might as well get used to it. The serving woman opened the door and said, 'I want you fellows out of here in two minutes.' They began to drift out in ones and pairs. 'You can finish your tea,' she said. She closed the door on the last customer except me.
'You're new here?' she said.
'Yes. I arrived a couple of hours ago.'
She was fully twice my age, so I didn't suspect that I was about to be propositioned. 'You don't have to hurry,' she smiled.
'Thanks. This tea is pretty hot, but you probably want to rest.'
'I'm pretty hot too. I'll lock the back door.'
I must have coloured for she said, after locking the back door, 'You're blushing. Don't tell me that you are one of the - uninitiated!'
'Uninitiated? Is there a club?'
'Do you like my legs?' she smiled, lifting her skirt almost to her navel. 'They're a good match,' I blurted. I fled.
If you are disappointed, I apologise. I guess I 'blew it'. I didn't go to the canteen for two days, and when I did I invited Knobby for a coffee. It was a week before I ventured out of my citadel despite the urge to see the city. It seemed that I should first get acquainted with my surroundings inside, especially the routine in the Dental Centre. Knobby thought it would be a good idea if I looked after the paperwork, ledgers, dental charts, letters, weekly and monthly reports and so on. 'Good training,' he said. The cleaning up was, of course, my responsibility also. One day I

said to Knobby, 'You quite happy with the way I am doing the clerical work?'
'You're coming along just great.'
'Then I'll leave the cleaning up for you. Okay?'
'I have to catch my tram. Besides, that's your job, ain't it?'
I agreed. 'The clerical work is yours. Right?' He looked trapped.
'My tram.'
'They almost tailgate, Knobby. The choice is yours.' He chose to clean up. With a little patience, I improved his knowledge of sterilization and care of dental instruments.

Just after this nice arrangement, I decided it was time to see the world. I decided that on this first excursion I would go by myself. We were allowed civilian clothes, so donning my plus fours, which was the style at that time whether or not one played golf, I meandered down to the guardhouse and reported that I was going out. The sergeant nodded and I turned to leave.

'Hey, Mac. Take one.' I looked down at the cardboard box, then back at the sergeant. 'I ah - don't believe I shall need one, Sarge.'

He scowled at me. 'Take one or dribble back in there.'

I selected one and departed. On the esplanade I stopped, looking left and right. Nobody was in sight. Peering over the wall I dropped it. The condom fluttered down to Johnson Terrace, missing the rocky precipice on its joyless pre-nuptial flight, to land at the feet of a young man who happened to be passing. Pocketing the goods, he grinned up at me and rewarded me with a 'Thanks, Buddy' salute. Waste not want not.

I roamed Princes Street, window gazing, returning along the Gardens pathway, then over to North Bridge as far as Patrick Thomson Ltd. No. I'll leave the Canongate for another day. Back on Princes Street I bought a coffee and a fried-egg sandwich from a street vendor near the Art Gallery. It was getting late and I was tiring so I walked leisurely up the Mound to the Castle. The great studded gate was closed. So was the small door. I knocked, then I pushed on the door. It was locked. Now, what? A voice shouted, 'Halt! Who goes there?' I knocked harder. The voice repeated, 'Halt! Who goes there?' Somebody was having fun with me.

Auld Reekie

Banging on the door, I yelled, 'Open up, will you. I want in.' Some twenty seconds later a sergeant appeared. 'Castle's closed to visitors. Oh, it's you. Doncha know ya gotta give the password?'

'I didn't know . . .' WHAM! I was on the point of stepping in when the gate was slammed in my face. I banged again. Sergeant Scowl appeared again. 'I don't know the password, Sergeant.' He must have thought I had impaired hearing. 'MILI-TARY TAC-TICS, COR-POR-AL. "FRIEND!" We don't wanna admit the enemy, do we? Yell it out loud and clear – "FRIEND!"' Again the door was slammed. The voice, after another knock, 'Halt! Who goes there?'

'Friend!' I yelled at the top of my voice.

The gate opened and a private, armed with rifle and fixed bayonet, shouted even louder than I: 'PASS FRIEND'. This was unbelievable. With my broad Scottish accent I wondered if it would work across the border. Maybe I would be skewered. Another thought occurred to me on my way up the hill. I couldn't get in without the proper tactics. I couldn't get out without the prophylaxis. Next time I was able to face both demands with a straight face.

Despite the fact that he was a Medic and I was Dental, Tommy O. and I took a liking to each other right away. He wasn't anything like Hort, you understand, he was not over-rationed with grey matter, he was small in stature, he was not endowed with an abundance of 'sense of humour' and, come to think of it, I now wonder why I ever bothered with him at all. Pardon me if this seems egotistic; it is not meant to be. Tommy O. was just friendly and undemanding, by which I mean he was not forever trying to scrounge money or tobacco from me like so many others, nor did I ever try to milk him. We paid our own way always.

AMOUR! AMOUR!

One day Tommy said, 'I'm going to the Marine Gardens this Friday. Ambrose and his Orchestra. Singer: The lovely Evelyn Dahl. And is she a doll!' Tommy shook a floppy right hand in front of his chest and contorted his face into simulated agony as if he had blistered his fingers on a hot stove. This was Tommy's version of ecstasy. 'I had planned on going home to Boreland this weekend,' I said. 'Some other time.' Tommy recoiled as if struck across the face. 'Maybe you didn't hear right. AMBROSE. AM-BROSE!' Tommy's theatricals were not extravagant in subtlety, they were purely mechanical but, in their own way, entertaining. He waved his hand in front of my eyes. 'There won't be another time with Ambrose.' Actually it didn't take much persuading to change my mind. I knew who Ambrose was; one of the best dance orchestras going. My mind had drifted back to the Palais de Dance in the Kirkcaldy Arcade. It seemed so long ago. *So* long ago, in my youth when nothing mattered but the way my hair was parted, the polish on my motor bike and the shine on my patent leather shoes, bayonet-shaped and wretchedly painful. And Betty Blue-Dress, what was her name? Oh, yes, Martha, Martha Noble. Now here I was, twenty-three years old, nearing middle age, practically over the hill one might say. Tommy's voice broke the spell. 'Ralph, where the hell are you?'

'I'm right here, Dodo. Is there something wrong with your eyes?'

'Well, what is it? Are you coming with me on Friday, or not?'

'Of course I'm coming. I've never danced to an orchestra like AMBROSE.'

'Say, Ralph, this girl, oh man, she's, she's . . .!'

'Now wait a minute. If you are taking a girl, you don't want me around.'

'No, you see, she is going with another girl, so I'm meeting her there. I don't want to get stuck with both of them.'

'So I get stuck with some dog. No thanks.'

'Ralph, you don't even have to dance with her. What do you say?'

The thought of dancing to Ambrose's orchestra was too much to turn down. 'All right, Tommy, but no obligations. Right? Deal?'

Tommy heaved a massive sigh and lay down on his bed to daydream of Friday, AM-BROSE, Evelyn Dahl and his girlfriend.

The Marine gardens, as the name implies, was located on the waterfront. The wash of passing small craft lapped against the piles of the boardwalk skirting the side of the building facing the ocean. Weather permitting, one could walk outside and smell the sea of the Firth of Forth, which rose and fell with the flow and ebb of the tides. The building itself was the size of a sports arena. This allowed lots of space around the dancing area. There were special nights for Old Tyme Dancing as well as modern ballroom dancing. We arrived fairly early and Tommy soon found his lady-friend and her companion. Tommy had barely introduced us when a suave English male voice behind me purred, 'May I have the pleasure of this dance?' My not unattractive blind date didn't answer but just drifted off with the smooth intruder. I wasn't unhappy about it. On the contrary, I was, without reasoning, relieved. 'Will you excuse me?' I said to Tommy and his companion, and I vamoosed. It had been so long since I had danced. Four years at least. 'Maybe I have forgotten how. Maybe I shouldn't have come. Maybe I'm talking drivel.' THERE SHE WAS! The laughing eyes. As soon as our eyes met, she dropped her gaze. It was too late – for her. I saw something in her eyes. Unfortunately, it was too late for me also. Some clown asked her to dance just as I was approaching her. I was jealous. Maybe I should see a shrink. Jealous! Of someone I hadn't even met! Maybe I should see a shrink. I already said that. Never mind. All I had to do was get over there before anyone else asked her to dance. The orchestra struck up with a tango. My favourite dance. Racing over to where she stood, I was just in time to see another oaf stumble off with her. After what seemed like half an hour, I saw them doddering past where I had been standing. She was peering about her. Looking for me, I wondered? I hoped. Maybe I had better get over there for the next time they pass. Maybe our eyes will meet again, and then ... and then the music stopped and I was again across the dance hall from where she and her two female companions were standing. Unseen by my quarry, I sneaked quickly round the fringe of the dancing area. The orchestra blared the opening bars of a quickstep and I was at her elbow. 'May I have this dance?' Her eyes looked up in surprised merriment. She nodded, and we were on the floor in a trice. We talked throughout the entire dance. Gee! She was easy to talk with. We covered the weather, always a non-controversial subject, comparing it with that of the South of England. The top of her head just came up to my chin. From there we discussed the superior service tramcars provided over buses. She had nice hair, too. We then got around to the heavier stuff like entertainments, the Zoo, the Museum, the Art Gallery, stuff like that, when, to my mortification, the band stopped playing and I was obliged to disengage my arm from her waist – about twenty-six I'd say, no corset.

'Thank you very much,' she said.

'It's my pleasure,' I replied. And she was gone. I took up a position where I could watch her, and spring across the floor before anyone else could get to her. It was with something of a shock that I found that while I was watching her, her two companions were staring at me. The tall one, whose name was Nibby I found out later, wasn't staring. She was glaring. I quickly averted my gaze. When I plucked up enough courage to dart a quick glance at them, the tall one was talking to Irene (that is her name, nice name, eh?) and jabbing a forefinger at her. I was prostrate. Irene looked across at me and a faint smile crossed her eyes. Faint, yes, but significant. If Irene had been around in Leonardo's time, Mrs. Giaconda would have been dumped. NOW! The orchestra struck up the opening bars to the waltz. 'Remember.' I was halfway across the floor when the same lout took her arm. She hadn't seen me coming. Retracing my steps, trying not to bump into the mass of humanity which was surging on to the floor, I watched for them coming. 'Hi, stranger.' It was Tommy and his lady. 'Hi, Tommy.' There they were. His mouth was flapping like a ventriloquist's dummy while my madonna was trying gallantly to keep from under his feet. She glanced over at me. Her tortured eyes - well pleading eyes - sought - there is no other word for it - succour. Well, here goes. I had to give her succour from that sucker. I tapped him on the shoulder. 'Excuse me.' I whisked her away leaving him nattering something or other. 'Will you marry me? I mean, would you like a soft drink? Or an ice cream cone?'

She burst out laughing. 'I would like to sit down. My toes are mashed.'

We sat near the refreshment counter, 'Thank you for rescuing me.'

'Thank you for being rescued,' I answered. 'What'll you have?'

'First, let me tell my friends why I am here.' She rose to leave. 'But,' she pleaded, 'let's keep our betrothal a secret - from everybody.'

She was back in about two minutes. 'What'll you have? Sorry, they don't serve alcoholic beverages.'

'I don't drink alcoholic beverages.'

'Orangeade, or root beer, or . . .?'

'Ice cream, please. And stop staring at me. It's embarrassing.'

I bought two ice cream cones. 'Where do you live? Or would you prefer to cover the weather forecast?' That delicious smile again.

'If you promise not to propose, we can talk about anything you like.'

'It's a deal.' Irene lived in Stockbridge, sometimes known as Stockeree. She worked in the Royal Blind Asylum, which she liked. I told her that I lived in a castle but that I had no white steed. We exchanged lots of information about each other that evening. Did I escort her home? Part way. She had to change tramcars on Princes Street. That was where, she insisted, we part company.

'That'll be fine with me,' I said. 'What about Sunday? You don't work on Sunday I hope?'

'No, but I am going on holiday on Monday. I shall be tied up all Sunday, packing and seeing some of my friends.'

'How long will you be away?'

'For two weeks. I arrive back about six, Saturday evening.'

I was speechless for a moment. 'Two?... Weeks?'

'Yes.'
'That's ridiculous.'
'Why?'
'Because.'
'Because what?'
'Because I am going on two weeks leave the day you arrive back. That means we can't meet again for a whole month.'
'We'll probably meet again at the Marine Gardens.'
'It's not that. I was going to ask you to look after little Jock while I am on leave.' Her eyes registered alarm. 'Jock? Your . . . son?'
'Well, not exactly. I assure you he has a delightful nature. He loves people. His table manners are impeccable. Or should I say peckable. He'll take the very bite out of your mouth if you let him.'
'A dog?' She gulped.
'A budgie.' Maybe it was relief. Maybe hysteria or madness. She exploded into a gale of boisterous, bubbling, rippling, riotous laughter. When at last she gained control of herself, she gurgled, 'I can hardly wait. I have never had a pet bird in the house.'
'That's great,' I enthused. 'Now, here is the bad news. He likes to be free all the time.'
Her face clouded. 'Perhaps he would be lonely when I am at work.'
'Yes, that's possible,' I said, 'but don't worry about it. there is no way I can deliver him. You see, I will be boarding the train shortly after you arrive home. Unless . . .'
'Yes, yes, go on!'
'Unless I hand him over to you at the station. He will be in his cage, of course.'
Her eyes had the look of a woman who, just as the switch was about to be turned, heard the fateful words, 'Hold it! This woman has been pardoned!'
And that was the precise moment I knew I had her where I wanted her. She was at my mercy. Well, she was at Jock's mercy. Same thing, right? Before we reached Princes Street, I had pinned her down to a date on Sunday, the day I finished my leave. 'Shall I call for you at your

home?' I asked.

'It would be better if we met somewhere on Princes Street,' she answered.

'O.K., the post office?'

That would be fine, she thought, and it was time to change trams. On the way up to the Castle I was miserable. Two weeks before I would see her again... briefly. Then two more weeks after I had handed over Jock. Tommy arrived back in barracks a little after me. It was too late to talk. Next morning, at breakfast, we sat together. I was still feeling miserable. Tommy came straight to the point. His point. 'How'd you make out last night, Ralph?' There were times when Tommy had the charm of a hopechestful of scorpions.

'Now, look, runt,' I snarled in a low voice, 'I don't "make out" as you so delightfully put it, with anybody.'

'No luck, eh?' was Tommy's smug reply.

This was one of the moments when I had to ask myself why, why did I ever get mixed up with such a louse.

'The subject is closed,' I snarled, this time in a louder voice.

'Ralph, I met a chick a few days ago. She has a pal who is unreal. I'll fix something up for this weekend.'

'No thanks. I have my girl.' I told him briefly what had happened.

'Forget her,' was his curt reply. He was really beginning to anger me.

'Listen, maggot, and listen carefully. I've fallen for this girl. You are not capable of understanding this, but that's the girl I am going to marry.'

Tommy missed his mouth and the meat loaf splattered down his tunic and on to his plate.

'You're crazy! You didn't tell her that, did you?'

'Of course not. Well, once, in fun.' Tommy's recovery was instant.

'Great. Forget her. This girl I was telling you about...'

'Tommy, I'm serious. Dammit, man, I'm serious!'

'Ralph, you don't know anything about her. Where does she live?'

'Where does she live? Here, of course. A place called Stockbridge. I think that's what she said. Stockbridge.' I was beginning to sweat.

'Stockbridge? Does she have an address in . . .? What's her name?'
'Irene.'
'Irene what?'
'I didn't ask her. I don't know.'
Tommy did a slow burn. 'How . . . how could you get into a mess like this in only one meeting? When are you going to see her again?'
'In two weeks from now. When she returns from her holiday in Aberdeen.'
Tommy held his forehead in the palm of his right hand. Anyone who didn't know him would have thought he was in the most agonizing pain.
'I suppose it slipped your mind that you are going on leave in two weeks. No, let me guess,' he said as I was about to blast him. 'You will wave to each other as she gets off her train and you get on yours?'
'I don't need any of your sarcasm, so shut up, you worm.'
'Does she know where you live? Does she know you're in the Army?'
'Sort of,' I replied, trying to control my rising rage. 'I told her I lived in a castle.'
'And what did she say?'
'She said, "Have you got a . . ." Oh, hell! No, I said, "But I haven't got a white steed."'
'A . . . white . . . what?'
'A steed. A horse. You know, like the knights of old. You know?'
Tommy looked hurt and frustrated. 'No, I don't know,' he muttered.
'You're an ignoramus, and I don't want to discuss my private business any further.'
Tommy rose noisily, 'O.K., I can take a hint. Just tell me one thing. When you get back after your two weeks leave, then what?'
'I told you I don't want to discuss . . .' I rose and glared at him. 'All right. I'm going to meet her on Princes Street. At the Post Office across from the Waverley steps.'
'THE POST OFFICE!' he screamed, 'RALPH, SHE'S A HOOKER!'

'You watch your mouth,' I yelled, grabbing Tommy by the tunic front. A runt in the Medics called Joey Martin had appeared beside us, attracted, no doubt, by the verbal outburst. 'She ain't a hooker, Tommy,' he said. 'She don't take money. She does it for anything in pants, but she don't charge nothin'.' I could feel my nostrils twitching when I turned to glare at him. His grin vanished slowly. 'You're talkin' about Lovie in the canteen, right?'

'Beat it, maggot,' I snarled. He shrugged and scuttled out of sight. Zombie-like, Tommy also wandered off. I was a near wreck.

For two days before she was to arrive back, I hung around or near the Post Office. There was no sign of her - of course. It was a relief all the same, and blast Tommy anyway for saying what he had said. I didn't know any hookers, so I couldn't compare. Maybe I was simple-minded about women. I started to mix amalgam for ten fillings instead of the two called for. The day before she was to return, the day before I was to hand over my precious budgie at the Waverley Station, I wandered by the Post Office, ignoring the occasional invitational glances. I looked down Princes Street, glancing at the Scott Monument. Bloody monstrosity! Why anybody would build a thing that looked like a jagged parsnip sticking upside down out of the ground is more than I could understand. If she turned up at the P.O. I could pretend I didn't see her. But I would know for certain. If she wasn't on the train from Aberdeen, I would take Jock home with me to Boreland. I wandered back to barracks and prepared for my departure on Saturday evening. Anyway, who the hell wants to stay in Edinburgh?

It seemed that everybody's auntie stopped to show their nieces the pretty canary in the cage as I loitered about Waverley Station waiting for Irene's six o'clock train to arrive. It did arrive, right on time, and she was on it. Her eyes widened at the sight of the green budgie, alive and noisy. I had about an hour to spare, so I invited her to have a cup of tea and a cake to nibble. I was not merely relieved to see her - I was enraptured. I was wishing I had not promised to be on the seven something train to Kirkcaldy. In the excitement, I forgot to suggest that we meet somewhere other than the Post Office on my return from leave. After our light refreshment, I escorted her to her tramcar, carrying her fairly heavy suitcase with easy nonchalance. As we waited for a few minutes for the right car to come along, our eyes scanned Princes Street and the gardens that were so famous, admiring the graceful and impressive architecture of the magnificent monument to Sir Walter Scott which dominated the scene.

GRAVE MEMORABILIA

It was Sunday. We were going to take a tram to Portobello and go swimming that afternoon if the day was balmy. The day was balmy. I was barmy. How could I have forgotten to change the location where we were to meet? Anywhere but the P.O. would have been an improvement. I hovered near but not at the P.O., ready to pounce on Irene as soon as she appeared. I was early and unreasonably impatient. After all, it would be foolish for her to hang around - there - waiting for me to appear. At exactly 2 o'clock, as arranged, she alighted from her tramcar and made for our meeting place. I am not sure now, but I think I sprinted like a cheetah to intercept her, apologising for being late. We had a delicious swim, and I heard all about her holiday in Aberdeen. She knew her city well and on other dates we climbed King Arthur's Seat, rambled over its bogs, and picnicked on the banks of Saint Margaret's Loch. We roamed Colinton Dell, climbed the two hundred and eighty seven steps of the Scott Monument for tuppence each. I patted Grayfriars Bobby's dear wee bum on Candlemaker Row. We visited the Royal Scottish Museum, the National Art Gallery, and we watched the Punch and Judy show on Princes Street in their collapsible theatre, which was a favourite watering stop for stray dogs. In Edinburgh it always rains on Saturday nights, and at various posts of advantage, such as in front of the Black Bull near the Theatre Royal, bedraggled vocalists, glued to the gutter, sing 'The Bonnie Wells o' Weary'. Some of the 'regulars' of Irish descent requested 'Danny Boy', I understand, but the only song I ever heard was 'The Bonnie Wells o' Weary'. It is almost impossible to look them in the eye and pass without giving them a penny, for which I received God's blessing, which the vocalist really meant as he checked pub doors, at the same time moistening his lips with his anticipative tongue. We went swimming in the sea at Portobello several times. On one of these occasions she was wearing a new dress which, she proudly told me, she had made herself. It was a pretty dress and demanded admiration, which I readily bestowed. On the beach there were no huts in which one could change, so Irene wore her swim suit under her dress. Normally, undressing was easy. Dressing after the swim was a different cup of tea. It was performed, usually with a mélange of contortions, under an improvised beach-cape. Her dress was, without question, attractive, but she had either forgotten, or thought it unnecessary, to insert a zipper at the waist. The combination of trying to remain concealed after removing the swim suit, and the fact that human skin soaked in sea water for the best part of an hour does not dry instantly, created a - how can I put it? - an imbroglio. This seemed like a splendid moment to mount my invisible white steed and rescue a maiden in distress, and while doing so, engage in a little exploration. My prospecting was not archaeological in nature, you understand, merely geographical and arctic. Her squeals of objection to my unauthorised research were distinctly polar, and attracted the attention of a number of sunbathers nearby whose expressions displayed more envy than distaste of my invidious safari. I was the victim of cool reinstatement for a while but the day was too nice to spoil because of the inspirational opportunities provided by chance and, I don't deny, inclination. One Sunday morning Irene said I was going to see something special. The morning was warm with a slight breeze. A blue sky mantled the city and church bells pealed a welcome to the faithful. Pigeons delighted in the sunny quietude of the morning following the evening rain. And so on and so forth.

We boarded a bus which took us to Cramond, a sleepy little village on the Forth just outside the city. There we bought two snowballs. These delicacies were slightly larger than a golfball. The outside shell was of chocolate dipped in shredded coconut. The inside was full of a very good substitute for whipped cream. My companion showed me how to bite a small hole in the chocolate globe and scoop out the cream with my tongue. She was the first human being I had met who possessed a prehensile tongue. As we devoured our snowballs, we mosied past the remnants of the ancient Roman Fort, arriving eventually at the River Almond, which had sneaked its way in from the Firth of Forth.

'What now?' I asked.

'We go to sea.'

'What does it cost?'

'Not much. My treat.'

I was fumbling in my pockets for the fare when she announced, 'You bought the snowballs. I'll tip the ferryman.'

We were ferried across the stream, about one hundred feet, in a rowboat managed by an Ancient who was tipped for his service. The river was calm, the trip uneventful. Then she announced: 'We are now standing on Lord Roseberry's estate.'

'Should we be here?'

'There is a pleasant walk along a path by the shore from here to South Queensferry. It is open to the public. I used to live here.'

'Do you mean - with his Nibs?'

'No no. About a mile from here, there is a stone cottage on the shore. I lived here between the ages of nine and fifteen.'

'With your parents?'

'With my grandmother and my sister. My parents were separated.'

'Were you happy?'

'Rapturously happy. Would you like to hear about the men in my life?'

'If you don't relapse into raptures about them, why not?'

With a roguish grin, she started to give me a history lesson.

'There was Mr. Scott, pipe major and custodian of Lord Roseberry's library at Barnbougle Castle. And there was Mr. John Laurie. He had a room at our cottage. John was Chief Forester of the estate. He played the big drum with the Salvation Army Band at South Queensferry. He was also a skilful virtuoso on the concertina and an exponent of Scottish songs. When he was in good voice, which was almost constantly, he sang to his own accompaniment. I had a reee-al crush on Mr. Laurie.'

'Fascinating. What did he look like?'

'Tall, slim, handsome in his way. He had a bald pate with a white fringe from ear to ear and a Santa Claus beard.'

'I'll kill 'im.'

'I fear it is too late for that. Mr. Laurie passed away over a year ago. I can still hear him singing to his concertina accompaniment.'

'I'm sorry,' I said. 'Was he very old?' Irene nodded with some sadness. 'His repertoire consisted of, among others, "Rovin' Rantin' Robin", "Annie Laurie", "Jock o' Hazeldean", "The Barrin' o' Oor Door", "Mary of Argyle" and "The Weedie's Whisky O" which he sang with dramatic gusto. It goes like this:'

Without warning she burst into song.

> For it's up yon hill an' tak a gill
> A gill o' the Weedie's whisky O.
> The Weedie swears it'll mak ye queer,
> It'll mak ye queer an' frisky O.
> Wi' the very first drap, ma heels turn up,
> Wi' the drinkin' o' the Weedie's whisky O.

It sounded a little out of kilter but meeting her interrogative eyes, I pronounced it superb. I was rewarded with a quizzical stare. 'And delicate,' I added, dodging a right hook. She continued, 'Lord Roseberry apparently found it irresistible for, at the Christmas Party which he arranged for his employees every year at Dalmeny House, he always requested John's rendition of "The Weedie's Whisky O".'

She was just warming up, for she continued: 'Old John frequently visited a sweetie shop in South Queensferry - Confectionery. Prop M. Brown (pronounced Broon in these parts). From Maggie Brown he bought a quarter pound of "boilings" which were tumbled into a brown paper bag.' There is no record of his having bought anything more than the boilings. We had almost reached the cottage when Irene pointed to an area on the beach just above the high water line. She said, looking very grave, 'That's where the cemetery was.'

I immediately assumed my Sunday expression of remorse.

'That seems a precarious site for a cemetery,' I ventured.

She nodded bravely. 'My private cemetery,' she murmured, and turned her gaze skyward. She seemed in no doubt that the souls of the departed had all arrived safely in heaven.

'I erected little wooden crosses made of driftwood,' she continued, 'around which I hung daisy chains and cards of identification: John Seagull, Percy Pigeon, Peter Rabbit. If I thought they were girls, I called them Primrose, after the family name of Lord Roseberry.'

'If I am not being too nosey,' I asked, 'what did they die of?'

'I used to, when nobody was around, release the rabbits from Mr. Ewart's traps. Sometimes they were dead. The seagulls had oil on their feathers. In a storm, they couldn't fly to safety and they drowned.' Tears had welled up in her eyes at the memory of their wretched end. I gazed at the site, now smooth and almost forgotten. Without meaning any taint of ridicule, I felt that I should point out that while churches, pubs and parking lots, even the ruins of the old Roman Fort, withstood the ravages of time, they were made of stone, mortar and tarmac. Surely it was not surprising that the cemetery in the sand, marked with crosses of driftwood, daisy chains and boundaries of seashells – even the occupants of the graveyard – had been wiped out by the elements of nature in one of her unholy fits of rage. She nodded with sad comprehension. I gave her my hankie. Pointing to a rock on a sandbank nearby, she said, 'That's where the seal was lying.'

'Another tragedy?' I asked.

'I thought she was stranded.'

'How did you know it was a she?'

'She had great, soft, liquid eyes,' she responded.

I was floored. 'It was a she all right,' I said.

'I ran for Mr. Laurie. "Quick, quick!" I yelled, tugging at his arm. We both rushed out and looked at the seal. "Aha," cried Mr. Laurie, "I've always wanted a sealskin waistcoat." He stepped towards her, and I brushed past him to protect her. "You'll have to kill me first," I cried.'

'That was courage,' I said.

'She rolled down on to the sandbank and loped off into the water.'

'Without even a thank you for your majestic offer of self-sacrifice?'
'I think she must have known he was only kidding about the waistcoat.'
We passed the cottage. 'Aren't you going in?' I inquired.
She shook her head, rather wistfully, I thought. 'It would be an intrusion. I don't know who lives there now.'
'I understand.'
'I'll show you where Prime Minister Gladstone planted some trees. They are quite large now.'
'Was he the other man in your life?'
'I'm just coming to that,' she answered. 'Before you is Barnbougle Castle, once the home of Lord Register Primrose of Barnbougle Castle, now Lord Roseberry's Library.'
She was again beginning to sound like a tourist guide, so I intervened. 'The other man in your life?'
'Patience. Mr. Scott and his wife lived here. He wrote *The White Cockade*, among other things. On his retirement, he became custod . . . Yes. Well, I visited them frequently. One day, he showed me a dungeon where certain ahm . . . guests were incarcerated.'
'That's an ugly word.'
'Well, anyway, when the tide came in, the dungeon flooded, and the . . .'
'Guests?'
'Victims were drowned.'
'Have you any happy stories?' I asked.
'Yes. One day, I told Mrs. Scott that I had made apple turnovers at school. She insisted that I show her how to make them right away.'
'Did Mr. Scott survive?'
'You beast! They were a great success. Oh, one day I found a huge cairn in the woods. Over there,' she said, pointing. 'Mr. Scott, who was an historian, didn't know anything about it. I took him there, and he found out that it was the burial place of someone called Earl Carl. Do you want to see it?'
'Not really. By the way, I'm hungry.'

'Good! So am I. I'll take you to see Queen Margaret's Well.'

We came to a spring surrounded by a low cement wall. It was hidden behind weeds and shrubbery and it was hardly noticeable from the footpath. The water was cool and delicious. 'What was Queen Margaret doing in this wilderness, and who was Queen Margaret anyway?'

'Mr. Scott said she sailed from Fife and landed here. In flight possibly.'

'That so?' I said with waning curiosity. Having quenched our thirst, hunger was beginning to complain. 'Do you remember that delightful little cafe where we had a pot of tea and bridies?'

'Yes. Mr. Scott said that Queen Margaret married Malcolm Third, King of Scotland, that was Malcolm Canmore, whose frequent wars with England insured the independence of his kingdom ...'

'Good heavens! When did all this happen?'

'Oh a long time ago.'

'It must have been before Queen Victoria and all that, I must admit I'm a little hazy about some dates.'

'To the tune of maybe ten thousand years or so. In the days when knights were bold,' said she.

'Of course, when a king's longevity depended upon his fleetness of foot!'

'I feel that your thoughts are more on tea and bridies. Let's hurry.'

I ate two bridies. When I arrived back at the Castle, almost the first person I met was Tommy. 'Where have you been all day?'

'With my future wife. Where else?'

'Oh that again, I keep telling you. I'm telling you, it won't last.'

Last August 20th, we celebrated our fifty-second wedding anniversary. The same partner. With the laughing eyes.

Who me? Griping?

I'm not griping.